THE SPECIAL EDUCATOR
Stress and Survival

Barbara Rice DeShong

AN ASPEN PUBLICATION
Aspen Systems Corporation
Rockville, Maryland
London
1981

Library of Congress Cataloging in Publication Data

DeShong, Barbara Rice.
The special educator.

Includes bibliographies and index.
1. Teachers of handicapped children. I. Title.
LC4019.D46   371.9   81-1743
ISBN: 0-89443-358-X   AACR2

Library of Congress Catalog Card Number: 81-1743
ISBN: 0-89443-358-X

Printed in the United States of America

1 2 3 4 5

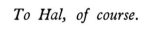

To Hal, of course.

Table of Contents

Preface

WHY A BOOK ON STRESS FOR SPECIAL EDUCATORS?

Because weekends, holidays, and summers are not enough. Because security and a sense of performing a needed service are not enough. Because working with people who have unique needs means special educators have unique needs. Because special educators are in a field that doesn't often receive general societal support. Because special educators can't even rationalize the physical and psychological costs of stressful careers by pointing to culturally applauded rewards such as money and status. Because special educators are exceptional people in an exceptional people profession who are "used up" more often than necessary at the close of the day.

The energy and dedication for the following pages came from a strong personal respect for the moment-to-moment experiencing of individual life and a personal commitment to touching the education professional. I believe that no moment of life is expendable, that no experience—including every contact with a student, client, colleague, supervisor, or written report—functions separately from the stream of events that determines personal character and the capacity to experience life pleasurably.

Here is where the unique, potentially stressful, characteristics of special education become apparent. You will be changed by the career you have chosen. You are changed dramatically over the span of a career and you are changed a little every day. You are different when you come through the door of your home in the evening than when you left through that same door for work in the morning. The question is, how are you changed? Are you changed in the direction of increased vitality and internal richness? Are you changed toward increased interest in self, others, and your world? Or, are you changed toward decreased curiosity about yourself, others and your world and are you just tired, just glad it's over, and just older? Chronic stress on your job can mean that the ways you are changed each day serve to take away from who you are, who you are becoming, and thus, the quality of life you will experience.

I do not consider the special education profession a hopeless source of career stress. If that were true, this book would focus on escape techniques for changing fields—and it does not. To the contrary, particularly because the helping professions are richly laden with sources of social contact and opportunities for individual creativity, I believe that special education can be a good place to be, that special education can be a positive source of personal growth and a source for developing an increased capacity for enjoying moment-to-moment experience. However, while such may be possible, it isn't always working out that way.

I have spoken to the needs of special educators because too often the potentially stress-producing realities of the profession are treated as temporary difficulties that can be overcome with new programs, brief training, or by making available a mythical, super-class of miracle-working staff. When these difficult realities do not go away, the cry is given for more new programs. Worse still, special educators are made scapegoats for the distress experienced by people who still want retardation cured and who want handicapped persons with progressive disabling disorders treated and released from public care. Working in special education means working in a career in which small steps and the joy of participation are goals. Yet we function in a culture in which giant strides, speed of accomplishment, and acquisition are goals. The stress management guidelines for other professions do not always work for special educators.

Accomplishing management of job stress in special education means moving beyond the process of merely coping with situations and events. A stress-managed workstyle involves a changed relationship with self, others, and the special education environment. Such changes do not come easily or quickly. That is why reading lists of stress management suggestions in newspapers and magazines rarely results in lasting improvements in the quality of job experience. The simple solutions of such superficial applications do have their appeal in our busy lives. So we feel better while we are reading each item on the list and we feel much improved while we recopy the lists and tape them to the bulletin board or the refrigerator. But nothing of substance changes. Something more extensive, more involving, is needed. This book brings together studies and programs that have resulted in improved experiences for special educators throughout the country—those very special people who have altered their responses to everyday events, who have altered their habits of everyday physical care, and who have smiled at times when before they would have stressed their bodies and their minds.

BRD

Chapter 1

Inside Special Education: How Long Is the Rope?

1

The special education teacher from Charlotte Springs, Texas was a tall man with blond curly hair and an impressive air of strength. Right now, as he sat across from the principal behind his desk, that air of strength was tinged with frustration, discouragement, and below the surface, anger.

"But, it seems like I've tried everything to make this situation work—everything I was taught in college, everything I've had in in-service training, and plenty of what I've read about what to do. Maybe I'm just at the end of my special education rope. I asked the principal to call you out here as a consultant because I don't know what to do. But if I did—even if you could show me—I'm not sure I have the energy or patience to do what you might suggest."

I had already spent a couple of my very best consultant-from-afar suggestions on how to work with difficult students. The child under discussion had the disconcerting habit of hitting or screaming every two to three minutes he was without individual attention. I tried to look as though I was about to come up with something brilliant and the principal tried to create the same impression by noisily rearranging the student's test report pages in the manila folder on his desktop. The special education teacher didn't wait patiently. Unlike the principal and myself, he was going to have to face the real situation in ten minutes when the bell signaled him back to action. He pushed again for the help he needed.

"I wonder sometimes how I'm supposed to keep going in that class. Maybe some of your ideas would help, Dr. DeShong, but it wouldn't change things that much. Do you realize that sometimes I have 28 kids in that 12 by 20 room along with 2 aides who are too terrified of the students to be of any real help? Maybe we should just forget this conference. If it weren't for this particular student's problems upsetting everything, it would be something else!"

3

My special educator friend leaning forward in his chair was not the first person in the field to point out that no matter what new and ingenious techniques we came up with he was still going to find himself in troublesome situations characterized by the unpredictable appearance of new "challenges" and requirements. And, like the others, today he was out of the energy, faith, and whatever other qualities he was supposed to have in order to keep doing his job the way he set out to do it. The tall, strong, and now exhausted special educator in Charlotte Springs was asking what to do about a reality for which he had not bargained. That reality was stress.

Special education can be hazardous to your health. Of course, so can accounting, homemaking, or carpentry. But the mounting collection of data on stress, along with the day-to-day and hour-by-hour requirements of special education indicate that the special educator is an especially vulnerable target for stress and for all the complications that accompany the stressed condition.

Consider the evidence that high rates of job stress have been noted among persons whose jobs require them to have responsibility for the welfare of others without the authority or resources to adequately manage that welfare. "Responsibility for people" has been shown to result in more job stress than "responsibility for things." Work situations in which there is more to do than one can do well result in higher rates of stress. Workers in careers with high rates of change in the work environment also have increased potentials for stress. Other elements of the career situation found to encourage high stress include: isolation from colleagues, low status attached to the job, unpredictability of job requirements, high rate of involvement with people who are ill, lack of guidance and training, and, lack of recognition (Selye 1976; Maslach, 1978). One study, completed by Alfred Bloch at U.C.L.A., is of particular note. Bloch investigated a stress-related phenomenon occurring among teachers in the Los Angeles area. After evaluating the career situation of 252 teachers referred for psychiatric evaluation between 1971 and 1976, he concluded that these teachers showed signs of "combat fatigue" similar to signs found in soldiers at war. Two aspects of the job situation were given top honors for contributing to the disorders experienced by Bloch's subjects: (1) educators have little control over their job; and (2) the teaching situation lacks an outlet for educator frustration (Bloch, 1978).

FRUSTRATION

Why would a special educator need an outlet for frustration? Special educators *should* be able to handle all situations and emotions without negative feelings or tiredness. Everyone *knows* that special educators are rarely bothered by frustration, that special educators are never impatient, discouraged, or disillusioned, that special educators are never angry, jealous, cowardly, or afraid. Special educators are hurt rarely and never feel themselves hurtful. What kind of special educator would have these unacceptable feelings and, particularly, what kind of trained, sincere helping professional would have angry, or hopeless and helpless feelings toward exceptional students? As a special educator, you are able to handle situations that would break other people because, like all other special educators, you have a Magic Coping Skill.

At least you're expected to have a Magic Coping Skill. Of course, the portrait drawn above does not accurately describe you or any human being, particularly a person working in a complex, trying situation. Yet because the public has imbued special educators with magical competence in the matter of emotional control, the idea of providing stress management training in this field has come slowly to prominence. And, if you have accepted the public's projected belief in your possession of supernatural coping powers (that is, if you too, believe in the Magic Coping Skill), you may find the idea of a stress management program for yourself difficult to accept. An important element of the stress problem experienced by educators results because many of us (if not most) have accepted the idea that we are *not supposed to have* undesirable feelings and thus these feelings are suppressed unsuccessfully. Because the feelings we are not supposed to have are held down with only partial success, we punish ourselves for experiencing them, a process that intensifies personal stress. The unsuccessful suppression process has a second painful consequence. Along with numbing our awareness of the negatively charged, doubtful feelings we experience, we block our access to positively charged, hopeful, and energy-giving emotions.

The concepts of emotions and energy as related to stress will be key throughout this book. Your thought-induced emotions are the major contributors to deciding your own style of handling stress. Assessment of your moment-to-moment available energy is one easy measure of how well you manage stress. As we examine the situation of the special educator, keep in mind that while the focus on solving stressful special education situations has long been on providing educators with additional technology and procedural skills, the provision of these environmental improvements and alternative techniques does not provide sufficient means to manage special educator stress. Stress can never be explained or solved in terms of management of the environment and other people. Stress is an internal event, affecting and affected by the most critical element in your special education experience, your internal *quality of life* experiencing. This aspect of the educator's experience was labeled "emotional life" by Herbert M. Greenberg when he stated in *Teaching With Feeling* "that within the teacher's emotional life are the forces which most powerfully affect the entire teaching process" (Greenberg, 1969). This is not to say that environmental changes and skills development are not important elements of special educator stress management. Both are needed and will be discussed in later chapters. But the thinking and emotional aspects of your special education career have proven to hold the greatest potential for both creating a special education workstyle of damaging stress or creating a style of healthful enrichment on the job.

WHAT IS STRESS?

Stress is a physiological experience affecting you in physical, emotional, social, intellectual, and spiritual ways. Most special educators do not think of stress as a bodily experience. When stress is mentioned in seminars for special educators, the immediate stress level of almost everyone in the room is raised as technicolor visions of the plentiful situations that encourage stressful discomforts crowd into view. It is these situations that are seen as stress. It's not difficult to translate the general characteristics found to result in high stress levels to the specifics of the daily experience of special educators. It's not difficult to define stress by reviewing the typical situations of special educators. Below is a partial list of situations special educators have shared that define stress for them.

Stress is:
- "having to deal with parents who want me to teach their child to not be retarded."
- "isolation from (and by) the other 'regular' teachers."
- "never having any reinforcement for what I do."
- "getting my paycheck and realizing how little I'm getting paid for this."
- "trying to teach students who don't want to learn."
- "having a student with handicaps I'm not trained to handle."
- "when the regular classroom teachers refuse to followup the resource room programs."
- "having so many different people to answer to who all seem to have different priorities."
- "when the principal wants one thing, my area supervisor wants something else, and the parents want something different from either of them or from what I see as best."
- "when more paperwork comes in and I am already hopelessly behind."
- "being expected to be a vocational training expert, a parent, a baby-sitter, a personal hygiene trainer, a counselor, a nurse, and a teacher."

- "working on schoolwork in the evenings while my children are left out."
- "that one child I am unable to help."
- "needing to go to the bathroom and being unable to leave my students for even a minute without supervision."
- "being transferred without any prior notice."
- "so many kids with so many different problems that I just can't take it, that's all."
- "no money for special requirements of my students."
- "the dangerous student, the one who hits the others and throws things."

Of course, the list could go on and on. You have your own image of the particular situation that "gets you" or a particular unsmiling face that has meant uncomfortable stress for you in the past. But, regardless of the powerful effect these situations have had on you, no external situation can be defined as *stress* and no environmental circumstance can be credited with all the physical, emotional, social, intellectual, and spiritual damage that is the very personal final result.

Environment Is Not the Whole Problem

This title is not to suggest that the realities of your situation are not of the kind or degree that have proven to result in high stress levels. Of course they are. But if these circumstances were wholly responsible for the damaging stress in your experience, your only choice would be to change fields or, impossibly, to attempt to eradicate stressors from the special education environment. Fortunately, the entire problem cannot be attributed neatly to the real environmental stressors of the situation.

If stress is not the outrageous situations in which you sometimes find yourself, what is it? Before continuing, it is important that you have a clear picture of the stress "creature." Stress is described here as a body-invading creature to help you visualize the sometimes malicious nature of its effects. The taming of this creature is the goal of stress management as runaway, chronic stress is proving to be a major health hazard of our century.

Stress management for special educators is designed to counteract the hazards specific to the field. It has the goal of guiding special educators toward a healthy approach to the profession and toward the people, papers, plans, and hopes that are the reason special education exists. Stress is ultimately a bodily response resulting in personal and environmental changes.

With the recent flourishing interest in the topic, numerous descriptive definitions of the creature have been put forth; several of these have relevance here. Of greatest import is the definition of stress provided by endocrinologist Hans Selye, who is rightfully titled the father of stress research. Selye defined stress as the "physiological response of the body to any demand made" (Selye, 1976). Other researchers have elaborated on his statement focusing particularly on the psychological involvement that is part of the stress reaction. Robert Woolfolk and Frank Richardson have emphasized that it is the individual's *perception* of the "demand" as being dangerous that is the critical variable in determining resultant stress. In *Stress, Sanity and Survival,* Woolfolk and Richardson (1978) write,

> they (the demands made on the individual) must also call into question the degree to which the individual believes he can respond with success and comfort . . . thus for a stress reaction to occur the individual must perceive a demand which is of importance and which calls into question his or her ability to cope successfully and painlessly (p. 6).

These researchers go on to say that the arousal of stress is more than physiological. As they view the response, the arousal is behavioral, intellectual, and emotional as well. While discussing anxiety and tension rather than stress as a specific response, Eugene Walker (1975) in his book, *Learn to Relax: 13 Ways to Reduce Tension,* gives two definitions of the stress creature inhabiting our special educator bodies. Walker defines anxiety as "the reaction we have to a situation where we believe our well-being is endangered or threatened in some way" (p. 3). He goes on to define tension as "chronic, usually low level, anxiety that is experienced as part of an ongoing situation in which we are involved." (p. 3). The stress creature is thus an invader of the elusive structures of our minds as well as our bodies. Taming the creature will require management of your mind processes and your physical self as well as management of your surroundings.

Stress Is Physiological

Imagine that you are at home preparing to sit down with the newspaper and a soothing cup of hot herb tea. You receive one in a series of nighttime phone calls from an outraged parent, Mr. Elmwood, who is convinced you are an incompetent special educator and are mistreating his child. You complete the call and on replacing the receiver, you experience that ultimate result of the unmanaged creature—physiological distress. Actually, you were experiencing plenty of physiological symptoms during the conversation and maybe even from the moment the phone rang and you wondered who the caller might be. The reality of the situation is that if you are like most of us you would be experiencing low level stress even before the phone rang. In the back of your mind you would be dreading the phone call, just in case it occurred.

This worry or apprehension over the possibility of the call would in itself be enough of a perceived *demand*, or perceived threat to invite the stress creature whose ultimate bodily invasion would probably be described by us as fatigue or a vague headache. The obvious discomforts experienced in this limited situation are merely symptoms of the more complex, more involving, and more dangerous, full-fledged stress response.

The stress response (the response your body makes to any demand made on it) begins with an electrical impulse alerting certain parts of your brain to attend to the "dangerous" situation. This impulse usually comes from one of your sense systems, such as the messages sent by way of the optic nerve whenever you see a potentially threatening situation. Many sources can send your brain "alert" messages at once. As you stress yourself while attending to the phone call described above, your brain would be receiving alert signals through your hearing, and through messages from your tightened muscles. Most importantly, messages will be sent in a circular, repeating pattern to and from your own thinking system as you "talk to yourself" while walking toward the phone, while listening, and after hanging up. Cyclical thinking patterns serving as alert messages are likely to include rehearsal of internally spoken statements about how unfair and upsetting it is for this parent to call, and how things like this make it impossible to do your job, and how maybe this whole problem is your fault because you should be able to handle it better. Your brain is thus alerted to help you, having been told by various channels that your well-being is endangered, that your ability to respond with success and comfort is in question, and that you need for your brain to move your body into a state of heightened readiness to deal with this danger.

The human body has been developed beautifully through many thousands of years to best enable us to survive among creatures stronger and faster. The response your body now begins does an excellent job of readying you to either fight the attackers that you encounter and have some hope of defeating or to help you run from those attackers that you have no hope of subduing. Unfortunately, you can neither "beat up" nor run from Mr. Elmwood. (At least you are not likely to choose these alternatives.) The efforts of your body designed to help you survive, designed to assist you in dealing with the danger presented by Mr. Elmwood, are not just ineffective, but are actually counter-effective to desired resolution of the problem. Your physical, emotional, social, and intellectual stress response in the situation on the telephone (and in most of the potentially stressful situations you encounter), is not helpful because the stress response is a physiological solution to what is usually a socio-psychological problem.

Once the "alert to danger" message is received in your brain, your body is stimulated into readiness. The hypothalamus and pituitary gland in the lower part of your brain act on your "alert" orders by secreting hormones designed to organize your body for an upcoming battle or a fast retreat. A number of substances enter the blood stream at this time but the one demonstrated to be of central importance is the adreno-cortico-tropic hormone (ACTH) that, once in circulation, has its most profound effect on the adrenal glands situated on top of the kidneys. Other glands in the endocrine system (in addition to the adrenal glands) are affected so that blood levels of various hormones such as testosterone, estrogen, thyroxin, and others are shifted to out-of-balance emergency concentrations. But the subsequent actions of the adrenal glands, particularly the outer portions or the adrenal medulla, are the most critical and can be seen as the functional "heart" of our creature. Once this "heart" goes into purposeful action your body is changed profoundly from the top of your head to the ends of your now cold toes. Of major importance in carrying out this change are the hormones adrenalin and nor-adrenalin released by the adrenal glands to relay your "danger" messages to the rest of your body systems.

What happens between the top of your head and the tips of your toes as you stand, telephone against your ear, sending your brain repeated warnings of impending danger while Mr. Elmwood rages on the other end of the line? Starting at the top of your head, your skin is altered, constricting the surface blood capillaries so that in case you are cut in the upcoming struggle you will have less surface bleeding. Your brain waves change to a pattern of increased alertness that has been shown to improve your capacity to complete simple tasks such as identifying the presence of a light flash on a wall. However, it will also decrease your capacity for more complex tasks such as creative thought and accurate perceptual processing. Blood flow to the brain changes. In most cases the flow is significantly increased, which in turn dilates blood vessels, a condition which, if maintained, often results in the well-known *tension headache*. This aspect of the stress creature, headaches caused by tension, is accepted readily as a "normal" part of a working day by many special educators. This acceptance of an imbalanced situation in the body as normal and unavoidable has been taught to us through the media. Advertisers are allowed to portray headaches as unavoidable consequences of unpleasant situations and as a condition to be treated by deadening the symptom. Similarly, stress-caused digestive disorders have been presented to us as normal consequences of daily living in order to accelerate the sale of antacid tablets and fizzes.

Composition of the blood in the dilated vessels of the brain and throughout the body changes as body organs functioning to balance the blood levels of several critical ingredients are alerted for involvement in the emergency. It is this change in blood ingredients that is most clearly related to the increased likelihood of artery and heart disease for persons whose workstyle or approach to work is designed to include certain deadly stress-prone characteristics. Considering that through the stress response, your body is preparing to be of the best possible service in your upcoming battle or escape, the changes in blood composition follow a logical, but undesirable pattern. Your blood serum level of fats increases, including increases in levels of cholesterol. The storage organs release into the bloodstream blood platelets, fibrinogen, and other pro-clotting substances to decrease the clotting time of your blood, again in case you should be lacerated in the upcoming struggle. And, of course, your blood pressure and heart rate increase.

Noting the most obvious changes in your body (below the brain) as the stress creature gains control of your body—and you lose it, the muscle and other tissues through your neck area tighten including those surrounding your windpipe and esophagus. This results in well-known problems; we lament that we have a "lump in the throat," or that we can't eat because our throat is too tight. More people than admit it, "can't breathe" because a mysterious clutching sensation (the creature) affects their throats. Then there is the "pain in the neck" syndrome describing tightened muscles across the back of the neck. The pain in the neck syndrome is usually ascribed to another person rather than accepted as our own response to that person. The tightening of muscles is an important logical aspect of the stress creature's preparation for battle. This tightness hardens your body surfaces so that, in case you are hit in the upcoming struggle, your more delicate internal body systems will be better protected. The muscles and systems of the trunk of your body undergo an array of alterations too complex to describe completely here, including a series of adjustments that results in lowering the functional capacity of your immunology system. The encompassing effects of impaired immunological responses, perhaps more than any other single aspect of stress, highlight the hazardous internal environment of the stressed person.

Simply stated, the body muscles designed for combat and running tense for action while vital internal systems each adjust in an individual effort to best serve the same purpose. The heart rate increases. Breathing changes, usually to accommodate more oxidation at first and then the chest walls tense and breathing actually becomes more shallow and less functional. Stomach acid increases and the rhythmic digestive processes of your digestive tract slow down or cease as energy and oxygen providing blood is diverted to systems more critical for struggle. The results of these changes are heartburn, ulcers, colitis, and constipation. The liver and pancreas become active in supplying the blood with their stored products of sugar, fats, and blood clotting agents. Like the rest of the body, during stress, vital organ systems give up balance and continuation of smooth running functioning to serve your demand for resources and attentiveness to the threatening situation.

Now, if our Mr. Elmwood on the phone was a roaring lion poised to strike you as you made your daily trip foraging through the jungle looking for berries, your body would be in peak performance readiness to effectively handle your environment. However, Mr. Elmwood is not a lion but an accusing voice, projected for miles by wire. Since the situation includes no genuine threat of bodily harm, this physiological solution to your socio-psychological problem does not prove to be helpful. In fact, this very response can prove disastrous to your health if it is inappropriately forceful in an acute situation and/or if it is chronically present. Your health, your happiness, and your very competencies as a special educator are threatened. While no threat of bodily harm existed, your body prepared you for combat in response to your perceived genuine threat to well-being. With each stress response, your body prepares you for physical combat because that is the only way your body knows to help you. Mr. Elmwood's actions constituted a psychological threat involving fears about self, fears relating to others, and fears about the future. Socio-psychological threats of this nature are the lions, cobras, and tigers of the special educator's environment.

The Stress Response Backlashes

Our physiological solution to the socio-psychological problems (perceived threats) in special education is not only ineffective, but it is counter-effective. While the counter-effective results within our bodies are the first level of the creature's damage, keep in mind that in the pattern of stress, self-destruction includes changes in your emotional functioning, your general self-care behavior, your interpersonal functioning, your functions of thinking and reasoning, and changes in your overall spiritual self. Landmark studies that show the undeniable physical damage linked to the presence of chronic stress are responsible for calling attention to stress as a legitimate concern worthy of study. Until now, it seems that those of us working in jobs loaded with stress-inducing characteristics have been satisfied to accept (and have been expected to accept) the emotional, social, intellectual, and spiritual pain of stress. These had become unavoidable elements of expected "suffering" on the job. Now that the evidence is in to show that these conditions are accompanied by invisible and visible health damage, we're paying attention.

Given a powerful enough stress inducing situation, one thing we know is that everyone eventually breaks down (Selye, 1976). The breakdown is usually physical and not consciously attributed to stress by the suffering individual. We are likely instead to "blame" our stress-induced difficulties on particular environmental complications since most of us have never learned to understand the relationship between our environment and the management of our internal selves. Hans Selye describes the path to breakdown and the stress response as having three stages.

1. Alert: Your body is signaled into heightened functioning.
2. Resistance: Your body remains at a high pitch to "fight" the situation.
3. Exhaustion: Resistance energy is gone and breakdown occurs. (Selye, 1976).

The exhaustion state occurs when our limited amount of resistance or adaptation energy is depleted and physical symptoms become apparent. No organism can be continuously maintained in a state of alarm. This book is not the place to list all the disorders, disabilities, chronic, and fatal body diseases that have been shown to result from the stress creature. Several detailed surveys of findings are available and are listed in the bibliography (Levi, 1971; McQuade & Aikman, 1974; Selye, 1976).

For our purpose let's take a look again at what is happening within your body as you stand listening to Mr. Elmwood, phone against your ear, asking yourself over and over why this had to happen to you. Because we are interested in the effects of chronic stress, let's assume that you have not learned how to manage stress creature, and that, this being the case, Mr. Elmwood's call has added to an already high stress level blamed on a hard day at work. When you allow stress to work on you in an unmanaged or chronic manner, the adjustments made by your body begin to cause damage. These damages take their toll during and after Mr. Elmwood's call. The increased blood supply to your brain causes a headache. Your alerted muscles become twisted and unbalanced, resulting in backaches, shoulder pains, and more headaches. McQuade and Aikman (1974), in their general audience book on stress, detailed the dilemma of muscle adaptation in this way: "Everyone expresses feelings muscularly" (p. 81). Changes in your vascular system are among the most critical imbalances engineered by the stress creature to help you survive. Your raised blood pressure, no longer a temporary source of improved functioning, becomes a dangerous chronic condition. Your irregular, increased heart rate leaves your vascular system with confused and dangerous messages.

Exploring the effects of chronic stress within the interior of your vascular system, your blood with its composition altered to better enable your body to win against the threat that started this whole reaction, contains high levels of substances which, when they are present chronically, are known to have deleterious effects. The more blood fats you have circulating through your system, for example, the greater the opportunity for deposits to build up and to constrict your arteries. Of particular note are the blockages that clog the coronary arteries supplying the four chambers of the heart muscle. The build up of deposits and blood clots encouraged by the jagged edges of these deposits is a major cause of "heart failure" and premature death. The high concentration of clotting factors that accompany the ACTH stimulus also serves to encourage blood coagulation in dangerous places.

Your digestive tract (which basically takes a back seat during stress to allow for maximum blood supply to the skeletal muscles) inadvertently ends up with problems, too. The lining of your stomach increases production and release of hydrochloric acid. Over time, instead of digesting food this acid serves to digest and to burn holes, or ulcers, in your stomach lining. In order to create a need for a frequent use of over-the-counter medications, our media systems have worked hard to convince us that the over-acid condition is a normal, to-be-expected element of everyday living for busy, important people. We are taught to react to the heartburn *imbalance signals* of our body by popping an alkaline (anti-acid) product that often causes further imbalance to the gastro-intestinal system. To add to gastrological problems caused by stress, the diversion of energy sources in preparation for the struggle require that the lower regions of your digestive tract halt or slow down the smooth muscle parastaltic process; these movements are not critical to immediate survival. The way your body's digestive system handles the cholesterol you ingest is affected by stress and is a critical element in determining the cholesterol level in your blood throughout the day. The digestive process which is responsible for breaking down cholesterol molecules into more easily absorbed substances occurs in the upper part of the intestines. When the lower digestive tract cuts back functioning to support an impending emergency, the digestive process stops breaking down cholesterol. This means higher levels of ingested cholesterol remain in the blood for longer periods. Interference with cholesterol digestion is one reason that research on the efficacy of cholesterol in the diet has been so confusing and even contradictory. The amount of cholesterol moving through your system at any one time is the result of two important factors: how much cholesterol you've eaten and how willing your system has been to digest that cholesterol. The latter factor is controlled by the delicate endocrine message network.

This description of your body's eventual situation is not all-inclusive. It is meant to alert you to the reality that regardless of how diligently you ignore the manner in which the stress creature damages your enjoyment of your job and your ability to function competently therein, your body will not be denied its reaction. A very personal reminder of this occurred several months ago when during one of those hectic weeks we stress-prone work-types are wont to arrange, I woke up several mornings in a row with an earache. Between out-of-town consultations on stress management I squeezed in an appointment with my regular neighborhood physician. Once on his paper-covered table, he began punching and poking around and I felt more comfortable. Soon he would give me a prescription to fix my discomfort. But, instead of concentrating on my ears, he began poking around my jaw. Before long he found the sore spot and I winced with the pain of what I was sure was a serious infection. He nodded with confidence at having located the difficulty. To my surprise and secret embarrassment, the doctor I was so sure would just give me a pill to bring my body back into operation, smiled an understanding smile and asked me if I knew anything about stress and the physiological effect that could be caused by stress. It seems I had been clenching my teeth together during my sleep causing an inflammation of the jaw that I had misinterpreted as an earache. I politely informed him that, yes, I was familiar with the literature on stress and that perhaps I had been experiencing stress because of overscheduling myself (with stress-management workshops).

Stress Is More Than Physical

One reason for dealing first with the eventual physical damage wrought by stress is that it seems to be easier for adults to make changes for health reasons than in the interests of general well-being. In a culture where guilt is a mainstay for motivating behavior, individuals find it hard to draw the line on work conditions and personal workstyle habits that are emotionally, socially, intellectually, or spiritually damaging. This is especially so if these conditions and habits are viewed as admirable or to be expected. While it is the threat of actual physical harm that usually provides justifiable cause for making a workstyle change to reduce stress, the other damaging results of stress are an integral part of the overall experience. Imagine again the picture of you poised in your house with the telephone against your ear and Mr. Elmwood raging on the other end. While your body changes to meet this threat to your well-being, your emotions will be undergoing changes as well. Feelings such as joy, satisfaction, and comfort, which were predominant back when you were settling yourself down with the evening paper, now give way to fear, anger, dissatisfaction, and perhaps a vague sense of fatigue. Of course, fatigue is not supposed to be an emotion but a state of physical being. The "sense of fatigue" or loss of energy that often accompanies stress is closely tied to emotion and so quickly affected by emotional change that it is grouped here with the emotional alterations resulting from creature inhabitation. Emotional shifts are easy to notice; usually we tell others (in case they didn't notice) that our "mood" has changed. In following the concept of stress as related to emotions and positive energy availability, we can say that before the phone call, energy was available for pleasurable care-taking of self and others, and after the phone call such energy was "lost."

Social or interpersonal changes follow logically from changes in emotions so that when experiencing acute or prolonged stress the likelihood of having pleasurable, growth sharing experiences with your family and friends is altered. Before you might have listened with sincere concern to the problems of a friend, your spouse, or a child. Now "caught" in your own stress pain, you are more likely to have less patience with others and perhaps even less desire for involvement in planned socializing. In interacting with others you are likely to be either more silent than usual or more talkative, particularly on the subject of your phone call. Others may notice your distress and try to help. You may notice how your distress is showing and regret that you're not coming across well with others and enjoying their company.

Whether or not you have people available to you with whom to discuss (lament and cry about) your distress is an important factor in stress management. The internal pressure brought on by the creature presses for expression and this changes our freedom of interaction with others. Some persons have learned not to share distress with others, either because others in the past have not set an example by sharing their feelings or because the distressed individual considers these feelings to be proof of personal inadequacy and therefore best kept hidden. A person living alone has no one with whom to immediately change the pattern of interaction once the stress creature is in residence. Here the person will likely interact differently with the next phone caller and the television or a book.

And since we are changed by everything we touch, your future patterns of interaction will be affected by your telephone experience. The extent to which the phone call will influence your future experience depends on the degree to which you react or overreact to the present situation. Extreme invasions of the creature, characterized by all-night tension and anger or by fear and worry, may result in letting the phone go unanswered in the future or teaching the children to say you're not at home. When back-to-school night arrives, you may decide that some parents are too threatening and you may interact differently with all parents who come to meet you. If you have children in school you may find that your style of talking with their teachers has been influenced by your experience with Mr. Elmwood. The beliefs you maintain about yourself and other people may be altered by the stressful experience. You are changed interpersonally once the stress creature is in control of you. Your behavior with others on both superficial and intimate levels is changed in logical ways to accommodate your body's concern with survival.

Your changed mood and changed patterns of interaction are the result of alterations taking place in a more central process. When you have shifted your body into stress gear, your cognitive or thinking processes, in fact, your overall intellectual functioning is affected. Under the creature's influence your thinking is likely to take the course of magnifying the problem, lavishing out doses of self-recrimination, and initiating a one-person campaign against the unfairness of other people in the world. These processes are characterized by silent repetition of self-statements such as, "This situation is unbearable," or, "I should be able to handle this better," or, "He has no right to accuse me of such things when he doesn't even understand the situation!" Self-statements that guide thinking during stress are products of beliefs, critical components that determine the eventual stress experienced in each situation encountered. Later chapters will focus on specific procedures for identifying and changing self-statements to manage stress as a major technique to tame the creature. While self-statement rehearsal is primary in examining the intellectual effects of stress, other cognitive process changes occur during stress. Tunnel vision (an overfocus on only certain aspects of the environment) and selective perception (seeing only what we want to see) take prominence so that we are unable to accurately perceive the environment. Unable to accurately perceive what's going on around us, we are crippled in our efforts to respond reasonably. When experiencing stress, the capacity for synthesizing information, examining evidence, and coming up with creative solutions to problems is diminished. In fact, the person under the rule of the stress creature is characterized by a pattern of trying old, ineffective solutions over and over again in the same problem situations. The chronically stressed person's problem solving style is characterized by blind rigidity.

In a general sense, your behavior toward yourself, others, and your environment will change once all your body systems are in a defensive posture. Even before Mr. Elmwood's call, if you are apprehensive about the possibility of the phone ringing, you will change what you do and the degree of enthusiasm with which you do it. When the phone rings, your speed of movement toward the phone is altered by the well considered possibility of an upcoming confrontation. During the phone call, your expectations are fulfilled and stress will be evidenced in what you do with your hands, lips, teeth, and breathing. Your voice and posture change once you are prepared for combat. When the "danger" has passed your behavior continues to be affected. The soothing cup of hot tea you were going to have while savoring the paper is now exchanged for the slice of cake you resisted earlier and a more powerful beverage. The idea of leisurely reading the paper is less appealing and either the television is turned on or someone is sought out to hear your tale of woe. When you experience prolonged or acute stress, your daily routine behavior and even your overall lifestyle will change away from the style and activities you would choose when you are feeling comfortable and unthreatened. Many people who express a vague dissatisfaction with the way they spend their evenings and weekends are actually expressing discomfort with being caught in so many habitual, but ineffective activities. These activities have been picked up because they were handy when the tension and the fatigue of stress were the greatest.

Stress-induced changes in actual, observable behavior are essential in determining your competence as a special educator and your healthful or unhealthful functioning as a person. The overstressed special educator is likely to display a sense of hurry in tasks that could be better accomplished in a calm fashion and to display direct or indirect hostility toward others. For the stressed person, patience with self and others is short; organization and creativity lose ground. Behaviorally speaking, the stressed person is likely to accompany these changes in career competence with self-damaging habits such as drinking too much, overeating, underexercising, driving too fast, and setting up negative interactions at home. The behavioral changes accompanying stress that occur in both the professional and personal setting lessen our capacity to conceptualize special education as a personality enhancing experience.

To state that the experiencing of stress changes a person spiritually may seem a bit strange in a book designed to provide special educators with directly applicable skills. What is meant by the term spiritual is left to your interpretation. For our purpose, it is sufficient to say that when the stress creature takes over, you are less likely to make decisions based on the central values guiding your life and more likely to be drawn to solutions based on perceived immediate survival needs. Your behavior is less likely to reflect your priorities and goals. You are more likely to feel hopeless and less at peace with yourself and others. The concepts of hope and hopelessness as related to stress and survival have been the focus of research done by Douglas Richter (1957) at John Hopkins. Richter's early experiment was a simple one designed to test the importance of perceived hope in efforts toward survival. He allowed two healthy rats to drown in a vat in his lab. To learn something about the power of hope, Richter simply dropped the first rat in the water and timed how long the rat swam before giving up and sinking to the bottom. Rat number one swam for about six hours before giving up. The second rat was treated differently. Before dropping rat number two into the vat of water, he held the rat tightly until it gave up all efforts to escape. He then dropped the stilled animal into the deep vat of water. Rat number two struggled only a few minutes before sinking and drowning. This simple project served as a beginning for many studies aimed at showing that a "broken spirit," if you will accept this term, can result in a lessened capacity to cope and maintain positive functioning.

Going back to our scenario of your interaction with Mr. Elmwood, we can understand the physical, social, intellectual, psycho-emotional and spiritual changes that occur and the alterations in energy and enthusiasm are now quite logical. When you realize that all these changes stem from one phone call or even the anticipation of that call, what defense can you have in your special education environment? Every potentially stressful situation will have similar consequences. Defense and even personal and professional growth is possible in your potentially stressful special education environment because the physical, social, intellectual, emotional, and spiritual changes described above do not result automatically from the phone call. For that matter, these responses do not result *automatically* from any source. Every stress reaction you experience is more than just the result of environmental circumstances. The occurrence of stress and the extent of its damage is determined by three factors. The stimulating event is only one factor and not even the most important one.

WHAT CAUSES STRESS?

The working realities of special education and its service environment are not usually complete surprises to those of us going into the profession. After all, the salary and status limitations were apparent before college was completed. The hours required were not unexpected. Most special educators, once out in the schools and agencies of special education, are not surprised by the requirements and unique challenges of the students and clients assigned to them. The surprise comes when we discover that the feelings and enthusiasm we brought with us to the job are insufficient to motivate us through the year, the week, or sometimes even the day. The surprise comes from within ourselves. When we launched our careers in special education, we didn't know how we, as emotional and growing people, were going to respond to the realities of the working environment. Particularly we did not know how we were going to respond to the stresses and strains that are an integral part of the experience of working with seriously handicapped people. Damaging stress is experienced by special educators for two basic reasons. First, these careers possess characteristics that are known to create potentially highly stressful conditions. Secondly, our preparation has not included learning to produce good, healthy emotions, while functioning in an unpredictable, sometimes difficult, and always changing environment. The result is unmanaged stress.

The eventual stress you experience in any situation and the intensity, duration, and frequency of stress experienced daily is the result of the interaction of three elements: (1) the characteristics of your environment, (2) your cognitions or thinking responses, and, (3) the condition of your body. While on the phone with Mr. Elmwood it is the interaction of these three variables that will determine whether or not you, as the imaginary recipient of Mr. Elmwood's rage, experience physical, emotional, social-interpersonal, and intellectual changes. The interaction of these three variables would decide the severity and longevity of the stress experience.

Characteristics of the Environment

You can learn skills to remain unstressed and energized in almost any situation, but it is certainly easier to maintain serenity and enthusiasm in some situations than it is in others. The special educator environment is replete with conditions known to result in high stress levels. Education as a whole is shedding its unrealistic public image as a haven from the stresses apparent in the rest of our culture. The awareness of this change was well stated by the 8,000 National Education Association (NEA) delegates attending the July 1979 National Convention. In a resolution to the full membership these delegates stated: "The National Education Association believes that the dynamics of our society and increased public demands on education have produced adverse and stressful classroom and school conditions. These conditions have led to increased emotional and physical disabilities among teachers and other school personnel. The Association urges its local affiliates, in cooperation with local school authorities, to develop stress management programs that will facilitate the recognition, prevention, and treatment of stress-related problems. The Association further urges that the harmful effects of stress on teachers and other school personnel be recognized and it demands procedures that will ensure confidentiality and treatment without personal jeopardy (National Education Association, 1979)." The reality of a tough environment exists. Special educators would not experience as much stress if we had the power to change our working conditions and to meet certain painfully obvious needs (and it wouldn't hurt if we could also reach inside certain of our students and help them to change).

We began with the premise that your stress response is initiated by a threat to your well-being and that the threat is often some aspect of your special education environment. In order to fully understand the relationship between the environmental event and your response, the extent of that threat needs to be considered. If Mr. Elmwood is politely restrained while making his accusations and demands, the potential threat is not perceived as being as great as if Mr. Elmwood yells uncontrollably, is personally abusive and refuses to listen to any counter discussion. Whether or not Mr. Elmwood is an influential person with your supervisor and the community will influence the degree of threat. If Mr. Elmwood accuses you of being imperfect in areas in which you, too, have suspected yourself to be lacking, the environmental stress takes on added strength. If instead of calling, he makes his point by presenting himself raging on your doorstep, the stressor can be considered to have higher potential, stress-inducing power than would be encountered over the phone. Whether or not he closes the conversation with plans for continued and accelerated harassment makes a difference. If Mr. Elmwood happens to remind you of someone in your past who treated you badly (perhaps a parent) the stress potential of the encounter will be higher.

The specific characteristics of your special education situation at any given time will play a part in determining the ease with which you can apply stress management techniques and remain calm and feeling good. Your situation is unique and falls somewhere on the continuum from possessing very few stress-inducing characteristics to being a living exhibit of the "adverse and stressful classroom conditions" discussed by the NEA delegation. Just where your situation falls on that continuum will make a difference in determining the frequency, duration, and intensity of stress you experience as a special educator.

Your Cognitions or Thinking Responses

I have lied. Intentionally, and in good faith, of course. And only because the innocent part-truths written above were for the instructional purpose of demonstrating the essential problem in describing the "three-factor determinant" model of stress. You see, whether or not Mr. Elmwood yells rather than speaking softly really doesn't automatically effect the stress you experience. It could be that yelling is a style with which you are comfortable, perhaps more comfortable than you are with a soft-spoken approach. Whether or not Mr. Elmwood is an influential person with your supervisor doesn't automatically change the stress potential of the situation and neither does it matter whether Mr. Elmwood chose to have a face-to-face encounter or to say his piece through a telephone wire. The grim yet hopeful truth of the matter is that Mr. Elmwood's action does not automatically constitute a cause for stress at all. With the exception of situations in which physical harm is present, stress is not an automatic consequence of circumstances but rather a result of perceptive and interpretive reactions to these circumstances.

In the encounter with Mr. Elmwood, as in all situations, your interpretation of the situation is more important in determining your eventual stress than are the specifics of what happened. In each special education situation it is your interpretation of the situation that guides your internal physical experiencing. These interpretations are direct products of your beliefs and are expressed during your encounters with the environment as internally spoken sentences. Just how your beliefs and internal sentences affect your emotions during stress was discussed previously. Beliefs that are of critical importance is managing your moment-to-moment stress level as a special educator are those beliefs regarding certain core ideas you maintain about your *self* and your self-worth, about other people and their relationships to you, and about the basic hostile or benevolent tendencies of the environment. Special educators with stress-prone workstyles tend to operate from a set of beliefs that prevent the job from becoming an ongoing, personality enhancing experience that can be characterized by energy and enthusiasm. The beliefs underlying stress-prone behavior spring from early teachings regarding the need to be or to appear to be perfect, the need to struggle against other people, and the undependability of the environment. An examination of alternate, nonstress-producing beliefs and procedures for "catching" and trying out new hypotheses about yourself, others and the world constitute an important message in following discussions. Special educators are encouraged to recognize the power we have in difficult situations that comes with increased control over habitual ways to approach environmental realities of the field.

Part of the reason we are unable to produce healthy, positive emotions in the unpredictable, sometimes troublesome, special education environment results from preservice and inservice education. Such training continues to apply technology and behavioral skills to problem situations that require a deeper commitment to the process in order for meaningful behavioral change to occur and to be maintained. To alter your beliefs about yourself, others, and the environment in order to reduce the stress-inducing nature of your perceptions throughout daily functioning will require more from you than would be required to learn a new instructional "technique." But the resultant improvements in your special educator quality of experiencing will be immediate. For example, note how your internal experiencing, your stress level, would be different than that described in the Mr. Elmwood encounter, if you happened to believe that irate parents are to be *expected* occasionally since you can't please everyone all the time. Suppose you believed that, while you have not been effective with Mr. Elmwood's daughter, this evidence of less-than-perfect competency as a special educator does not have anything to say about your basic worth. Believing these ideas, you are not likely to invest yourself in a series of self-recriminating and other-person recriminating interpretations of the situation. If you happen to believe that Mr. Elmwood, like everyone else, is a concerned, vulnerable person dealing with his painful feelings in the very best way he knows, you are not likely to experience accelerating stress as you expound to yourself and others on the inappropriateness of Mr. Elmwood's actions and ideas. If you happen to believe that you deserve to enjoy a comfortable and relaxed evening even though someone else is quite displeased with you, you are more likely to spend the evening without a full-fledged creature invasion.

If, however, you have learned well the lessons taught many "successful" educators, you are likely to invite the stress creature for a rather troublesome and lengthy stay. Examples of commonly held beliefs that contribute to interpreting reality in stress-inducing ways include the belief that other people are always supposed to behave according to identified standards, the belief that somehow situations like this shouldn't occur, and the belief that you should be able to conduct yourself at all times to match a mythical "ideal self," constructed during the fantasy life of your childhood. These beliefs, a sampling of some of the major ideas that serve as standard bearers for the stress-prone educator, result in interpretive self-statements. They are a part of the intellectual changes you experience during a stress response initiated by a threat to self-esteem. Probable self-statements in the Mr. Elmwood situation would include, "Oh, no. This is a terrible situation. I am terrible for letting this happen. Mr. Elmwood is an unbearable, impossible person. Having a parent call me at home and remind me of school problems just ruins my whole evening. I shouldn't have to put up with this. It is unfair for him to complain about my treatment of his child when it is his child who is mistreating *me*. I won't put up with it. Oh, now I can't be as comfortable and relaxed as I was before this awful thing happened." Such interpretations serve to accelerate the stress reaction.

Woolfolk and Richardson (1978) conclude that for an event to result in stress, the demands of the situation must be perceived by the individual as threatening: "Stress is a perception of threat or expectation of future discomfort that arouses, alerts, or otherwise activates the organism" (p. 6). Stress-prone special educators maintain a core of beliefs that result in a perception of the world as replete with threats to their well-being. To clear the record as we progress in a description of the stress-prone special educator, let it be known that I include myself in this group and we are not "bad" people. We are, instead, people who learned to overreact to imperfections in ourselves and others. We are people who have learned to interpret much of our environment as threatening because during the time when we were forming our beliefs, we were taught to fear ourselves and our own mistakes, the motivations and feelings of others and the structures of the environment. We stress-prone people interpret an excessive number of events as threatening because we were taught to be afraid. This makes it hard to relax.

The Condition of Your Body

Both the characteristics of the potentially stressful situation and the interpretations or cognitions you rehearse regarding these characteristics make a difference in determining the eventual stress you experience. Another important factor is the physical condition of your body. Stress is ultimately a physical response. Thus when the changes called up to prepare you for survival occur, it matters how able your body systems are to manage the unbalanced stimulated conditions. There are two levels at which your physical condition can determine the duration, frequency, and intensity of stress you experience. First, you will be helped in your efforts at managing stress if your body is in an overall healthy state. When changes setting off the balance of your body systems occur, you will be better able to avoid a breakdown in these systems if they are otherwise strong and well-cared for. If you are overweight, rises in blood pressure caused by stress will likely cause you more difficulty than for the normal weight person. If you smoke and already have a diminished breathing capacity, shallowness of breathing will cause more severe symptoms. The term stress is taken from the science of physics where it describes what happens when sufficient force is applied to an object or system to distort the system. The distortion your body experiences is partly determined by the strength or health of your body system when the forces of stress are applied.

Many factors contribute to the maintenance of your overall physical condition including nutrition, exercise, and certain lifestyle behaviors. Educators, and stress-prone educators in particular, seem to neglect these areas due to a lack of time and a sense of pressure generated by the intensity and variety of demands from people whose needs seem even greater than our own. Stress-prone workstyles often include purposeful neglect of procedures necessary for maintenance of good physical health. Frequently stress-prone workstyles encourage and result in lifestyle habits directly harmful to body health such as overeating, poor nutrition, drinking too much, and hurried, accident-prone behavior. After all, we tell ourselves, what matters is getting the job done. If we gain a few pounds, lose our muscle tone, or ruin our lung tissues with smoking in the process—so be it.

Your physical condition at an immediate, moment-to-moment level is also important in determining how much stress you experience. When Mr. Elmwood calls, it matters if you, as the listener, are hungry, tired, or have a cold or any other sort of illness or disorder. If your body is already in a weakened condition, the invasion of the stress creature will be more easily provoked. With your body in a weakened state, your "perceived threat threshold" is lower. You are more likely to overreact and interpret situational characteristics as threatening and as having a greater importance than you might if you were in a state of good health, comfortably nourished, and feeling reasonably energetic. The period from 5:00 p.m. until supper is known for its high probability of family squabbles. During this stretch of time, family members usually meet the major criteria for heightened susceptibility to stress, that is, hunger and fatigue. (Many special educators tell me that they experience these conditions during most of their school day.) A temporarily lowered perceived threat threshold, due to a weakened body condition, means that not only are you likely to respond to more situations as threatening, you will also be likely to respond to whatever "realistic" unpleasantries that exist with more stress and discomfort.

Your Environment, Your Mind, and Your Body

A few weeks ago an article appeared on the front page of a local newspaper headlined, "What's Up Doc? TLC for Rabbits." It was a small article that filled up the lower right hand corner and received no mention on other media. But the findings reported therein synthesize concisely the interaction of the three components of stress reaction. The article began, "Ohio State University researchers report that treating laboratory rabbits with 'tender loving care' seems to greatly reduce the risk of heart disease, even for animals fed abnormal amounts of cholesterol." In fact, the laboratory report said rabbits that had been especially well treated "interpersonally" developed only half the cholesterol circulatory damage as compared to rabbits fed identical diets but given no special treatment. The article goes on to describe the essential difference between the TLC treatment versus the non-TLC condition. During the period of the study the rabbits in the TLC group were visited four or five times a day by a laboratory assistant who talked to them and cuddled them next to her while the unfortunate rabbits in the other group received no special attention. The small article concluded saying, "the rabbits that received tender loving care presumably felt less stress than those that did not" (p. 1). This experiment, while not the most remarkable in the area, in its simplicity and clarity says something significant to those of us who are experiencing painful, daily stress as part of special education and who are trying to rationalize our way out of doing something about it.

The eventual results of chronic stress involve more than undeniable physical damage. You most likely began your stress-filled pattern of working as part of a sincere desire to do a good job, out of genuine dedication to something in which you believed. (I haven't found anyone yet who went into special education for money or power advantages.)

Unfortunately, in addition to immediate and eventual physical damage, chronic stress results in sabotaging the very energy and love that attracted us to the field in the first place. Stress-prone special educators have a hard time accepting this because we are so sure that we *should be able* to overcome stress in much the same way we have attacked and quelled the many other challenges of our work. But, whether we want to look at it or not, chronic stress eventually results in reduced energy, impaired relationships with others (including those we were attracted to helping), restricted creativity, constriction of personal growth, and reduced enjoyment in your job. All of this means a reduced enjoyment of the time you have been given to live and grow.

In the later stages of chronic stress we call "burnout," symptoms include acceptance of fatigue, headaches, lingering colds, and other evidences of lack of wellness as normal for special educators (aching exhaustion is *not* an automatic and essential result of spending a day in the profession). Along with physical dragging, the burned-out special educator begins to feel alienated from colleagues and the profession. If your stress has reached these proportions you may feel abused, as though "everyone wants a piece of the action and you're the action." Being burned-out means sensing an increase in cynicism. One doubts that one's work, and perhaps the work of special educators as a group, has any real meaning or effect in our world. Boredom replaces relaxed enthusiasm. Self-esteem drops as work that once sparked a sense of self-meaning begins to threaten and becomes a stressful event wherein well-being is endangered on a daily and regular basis. The advanced stage of chronic stress known as burnout can last a week or 20 or 30 years. Just because we're miserable doesn't mean we do anything about it. After all, many of us are convinced that the pain comes with the special education territory. In fact, if you are not experiencing these symptoms there are those among us who would suspect you are not dedicated enough to the cause.

THE CHOICE FOR STRESS MANAGEMENT TRAINING

The welfare of the infants, children, and adults served in special education is, of course, our first concern. In this helping profession you must learn to manage stress and to deal comfortably with the environment if you are to effectively provide for the care and growth of others. Many special educators have difficulty with this idea because most educator training programs have taken for granted what must be learned. That is, it has been taken for granted that special educators will know how to manage their internal selves when faced with the realities of the job. When something that must be learned is taken for granted, quite often everyone behaves as though they know whatever it is that is expected. Internally they are chastising themselves for being the only person who doesn't know whatever it is that everyone else seems to know. Special educators are expected to possess the Magic Coping Skill. Not meeting the expectation, we turn our doubts on ourselves and eventually our impatience is felt by those we serve. Later stages of chronic stress include a tendency for the burned-out person to see the needs of students as threats (stress inducers), since at this point the special educator has little energy available to meet those needs. The continual energy drain caused by stress gradually results in objectification of students and detachment from the job, a result that is diametrically opposed to our plans when we started as special educators. A first step in stress management is the recognition that you must manage your own stress before you can help others and that means learning new ways to react, new ways "to be" in old situations.

Beyond Coping

Your body's stress response is a response to a perceived crisis. There are "crises" in special education situations, but these crises do not need to be totally negative occurrences. The stress crisis message is a signal that change is needed, that the way things are being done or have been done in the past is not sufficient to the present situation. The Chinese symbol for crisis is composed of two elements, one meaning danger and the other representing opportunity. Special educator stress is both a signal that we need to re-examine our special education situation (and to alert the public as NEA has done) and a signal that old ways of dealing with situations are no longer functional. The signals of personally felt stress indicate opportunity for change as well as danger.

This book will focus on the three components of special educator stress: (1) the cognitions or thinking habits of the special educator, (2) the special education environment, and, (3) the physical health of the special educator. We will provide procedures for stress management within each area. Strongest emphasis will be on the mediating component of special educator stress, cognitions or thinking habits. Second in emphasis will be the unique special education environment in which you function. Throughout, the focus will be on acquiring the skills of stress management that have been expected of special educators. Now that you are in special education, you must learn effective ways of relating and being in that world, ways that could not have been learned before you understood and became a part of the field.

Coping is something that works to get you through a transient situation. The trying realities of your special education environment, though changing and unpredictable, are not temporary. Mark Twain is attributed with observing that "life is one damn thing after another," which pretty well describes the stimulus-filled, everchanging situation in which you work. If you focus only on environmental change, as soon as you "fix" one element to your liking, several new difficulties will appear in its place. In fact, a first step in stress management involves giving up the illusion that someday the externals of special education will change sufficiently to solve special educators' stress problems. An effective program in stress management thus must go beyond coping to helping you in designing an ongoing workstyle that functions not just in response to crisis but serves as a central guide for behavior at all times. The idea of a program based on coping would give tacit validity to a concept that in itself accounts for a great deal of stress. This concept involves the belief that work-happiness or enjoyment results from the absense of problems and unpleasantries. If you've worked in special education more than a week, you're aware that if work-happiness is the absense of problems, such a happiness is not to be had in your profession. Thankfully, this concept is merely another illusion to be shed as we begin a program of stress management that extends beyond coping.

Beginning a program that extends beyond coping means it will be necessary to examine what's going on now in your work situation, how you think and behave everyday. Going beyond coping also means retrieving some of that special irrational glow that brought you into this unique and, I believe, very special world of special education. Stress management involves giving up an acceptance of the half-alive structures suggested by the term "coping" and moving toward a special educator workstyle based on personality enhancement, energy, and enthusiasm.

NOTES

Associated Press. What's Up Doc? TLC For Rabbits. *Austin American-Statesman*, 1979, p.1.

Bloch, Alfred. Combat Neurosis in Inner City Schools. *American Journal of Psychiatry*, 1978, 135(12).

Greenberg, Herbert M. *Teaching with feeling*. New York: Pegasus, 1969.

Levi, Lenart (Ed.). *Society, stress and disease, volume 1: The psychosocial environment and psychosomatic diseases*. New York: Oxford University Press, 1971.

Maslach, Christina. Burned-out. *Human Behavior*, September, 1978.

McQuade, Walter & Aikman, Ann. *Stress*. New York: Bantam Books, 1974.

National Education Association Reporter.

Richter, Curt (1957) cited by Douglas Colligan, That helpless feeling: The dangers of stress. New York, July 14, 1975.

Selye, Hans. *Stress in health and disease*. Boston: Butterworth Publishers, 1976.

Walker, C. Eugene. *Learn to relax, 13 ways to reduce tension*. Englewood Cliffs, New Jersey: Prentice-Hall, 1975.

Woolfolk, Robert L. and Richardson, Frank C. *Stress, sanity and survival*. New York: Signet Books, 1978.

Chapter 2

The Stress-Prone Special Educator

2

Would you agree that for you there is never enough time to get things done? Do you feel frequently impatient with your administration because they don't get things done fast enough? Do you feel vaguely guilty when you "do nothing" for a few days, hours, or minutes? Do you end each work year scheduling more and more to do in the same time frame? Do you expect yourself to work harder than other people? If any of your answers to these questions is affirmative, you are an active member in good standing of the stress-prone group of special educators. The most exciting research in the area of stress has identified the behaviors and thinking habits of the person whose characteristic workstyle and lifestyle results in chronic stress problems. As difficult to accept as it may be for those who are accustomed to blaming internal feelings on the external complexities of special education, the stress we experience in our careers is more a result of our personal workstyle than it is a result of long hours, low pay, weak supervision and administration, or difficult students and clients. Hard work, a hectic pace, and long hours do not a stressed person make. Stress is an internal response that is mediated largely by interpretations. Only you can stress yourself by your workstyle approach to the special education environment, a setting that is, admittedly, wrought with potentially stressful conditions.

Before describing the characteristics of the stress-prone workstyle, note again that stress-prone types have learned this approach out of a desire to do a good job and to have other people see we're doing a good job. It grows out of a belief that this workstyle is the only way to be successful special educators. In fact, the person with the extremely stress-prone workstyle, the person answering "yes" to all the above questions, is still the ideal worker and is usually held as representative of responsibility and success in our culture. During the past year pictures advertising the *Wall Street Journal* on the fronts of newspaper stands across the country have shown a young man with a furrowed brow and clenched fists flinging himself and his briefcase ahead of two other well-attired men with similar briefcases, furrows, and clenched fists. The young man in the picture, his expression pained and his body captured in the motion of running desperately, symbolizes the self-dissatisfaction and insatiable drivenness of the stress-prone person. We stress-prone special educators learned our workstyle by exposure to models like this one and through admonitions since childhood that keep us afraid to try any other approach.

One special education teacher, after a recent consultation, shared a motto he had learned as an undergraduate. "A good special education teacher goes home each day happily dissatisfied." Special education is an ideal career situation for those with tendencies to throw themselves into stress-prone behavior and worrisome thinking habits. After all, in your special education environment, there is always something more you could be doing, something more you could be learning, and a slightly better way of doing everything you're already doing. Special education waits with open arms for people with unrealistic goals, perfectionistic expectations of themselves, and commitments to the impossible, because in special education there *are* genuine, unending needs waiting to be met. Fortunately, those needs cannot be met by an onslaught of stressing behavior but by special educators with a relaxed, stress-managed workstyle approach.

Early desires to do our job perfectly (because the children we serve in special education cannot afford our mistakes) and to do more and more in less and less time, backfire because we end up making cruel and unreasonable demands on ourselves and others. The stress-prone workstyle eventually destroys our vitality and diminishes our inner resources and our spontaneity. Our ability to provide instantaneous responses in line with our professional knowledge and creativity are reduced. The stress-prone pattern erodes our ability to respond to new challenges in other than ritualistic or stereotypic ways. A most painful result of being a stress-prone special educator is that only limited aspects of our personalities receive all our energy and attention. Our energy and attention are focused on survival abilities, and on whatever will help us to move faster and faster against our own design of dissatisfaction with ourselves, others, and the world. This means that other developing elements of our personality are neglected. These neglected areas of self-care and self-development are needed to build an effective and enhancing workstyle. These neglected areas are needed in order to model a whole person for those you work with, if you are to respond and grow in your role as a special educator. Designing a stress managed workstyle as special educators is not easy since we often treat ourselves as skill possessors instead of people, and sometimes we are treated as such by the public and administrators. This is apparent when curriculum assignments, class assignments, and in-service assignments are made without review of the whole person being asked to absorb these tasks. Even though we stress-prone types may have machine-like expectations of ourselves, we are not machines. The overwhelming evidence regarding the physical damage that can result from chronic stress in difficult situations at last has freed us from viewing ourselves as other than vulnerable humans.

The Problem with Positive Thinking and Trying Harder

The stress-prone workstyle is the result of an attempt to heroically surmount insurmountable problems, problems having to do with perfection, unreasonable self-made demands, and unrealistic reactions to circumstances. However, the very behaviors and thinking habits we adopted to solve our special education difficulties, to surmount the unsurmountable, end up being our most serious problems. This situation—wherein the behaviors a person institutes in order to solve a problem result in becoming the problem—is often evident in behavior problems posed by students. A young person unable to complete reading assignments in the time allowed starts interrupting and bothering others and slows down the group. The disruptive behavior rather than the student's reading difficulties is identified as the major problem requiring attention. A handicapped high school student who suddenly doesn't "know how to talk to girls" develops obnoxious and inappropriate speech during class. The inappropriate classroom behavior is the identified problem. So it is with the stress-prone workstyle problems of special educators. The original problems still exist (those genuine and unending needs both within ourselves and in the environment), but the behaviors we have learned in response now pose health risks and threaten our satisfaction and competence. Stress management allows us to back away from our first well-taught methods of solving the realistic problems in special education and to find healthier responses.

Healthier responses and solutions will involve going beyond working harder and positive thinking. After seminars on stress management for educators, the more stress-prone in the group plead, "I've read dozens of 'how to' books and heard even more 'inspirational speakers' but it doesn't seem like I can ever do enough. I start out on a cloud of energy, but end up more discouraged than ever." I wish changing toward a better solution for special educators could be as simple as reading a book, but changing requires altering basic assumptions regarding yourself, other people, special education, and how all these elements fit together. Too frequently "how to" books and speeches are designed only to teach new ways to work harder and faster, to gain on your own unrealistic demands for perfection and power.

For example, I received in the mail the other day a brochure for a new book that guarantees: "100 percent pure power techniques for the persuasion and control of people! Pure domination power, pure convincing power, pure authority power, pure command power, pure persuasion power, pure controlling power." The brochure goes on to promise, "a carefully designed set of words and actions that make you into an immediate *somebody*." What special educator wouldn't like to have that? Even books published ostensibly to provide stress management techniques are sometimes based on the theme, "work harder, think positively in order to have the right to feel relaxed and good about yourself." A recent stress management book for executives promised that "you too can be a human dynamo . . . you can tune up to a 'concert pitch' at all times and always be eager to turn in an A-1 performance." The whole idea that being a human dynamo is better than being human was the attitude that got us into our original stress difficulties.

It may be difficult to give up the struggles encouraged by such programs. Stress-prone special educators are people who have motivation to work hard and think positively in sufficient quantities to last several lifetimes. The problem is that these methods do not lead automatically to a rich, satisfying and *effective* special educator experience. These methods (coupled with the illusion that if we work hard enough and are good enough long enough, we can work ourselves into a safe, trouble-free life) result in the behavior and thinking patterns described in the next section.

ARE YOU A STRESS-PRONE SPECIAL EDUCATOR?

Two cardiologists, Meyer Friedman and Ray H. Rosenman (1974) followed the extensive work of Hans Selye. Through their research and their popular book, *Type-A Behavior and Your Heart*, they have helped to make the medical community and the general public aware that certain personal characteristics or personal styles of working and thinking result in greater and more frequent eventual physical stress than do other personal styles of behavior and thinking. Friedman and Rosenman labeled the person with the stress-prone behavior style as *Type A* and the person with the nonstress-prone behavior style as *Type B*. The stress-prone special educator exhibits the Type A characteristics as well as corollary characteristics identified in research since the Friedman and Rosenman book was published. To avoid confusion between the original Type A and Type B syndromes and the unique stress-inducing workstyle of the special educator, the Stress-Prone Special Educator will be defined and referred to as SPSE Type. The other group (off somewhere lying on a quiet beach by the sea instead of reading this book) will be the Nonstress-Prone Special Educator Type or the N-SPSE group.

One, way to tell whether you have SPSE tendencies or N-SPSE tendencies is to note your behavior when you work as a special educator. The observational method is not totally reliable, however, since stress is an internal response that may or may not be expressed by individuals in the same fashion. In fact, since Friedman and Rosenman's identification of typical Type A behaviors, other researchers have noted additional stress-prone behavioral styles that include the quiet, inwardly raging stress-prone person whose internal pain goes unnoticed by friends and coworkers. These are the persons whose friends and coworkers exclaim with surprise when the quiet ones have a "breakdown" or are diagnosed with bleeding ulcers. These persons "never let anything upset them." But the most frequent stress-prone behavioral style is the more typical Type-A hyperactive type. The hyperactive type SPSE is known to possess at least several of the following habits:

1. talks too fast
2. walks too fast (runs into things more often than the N-SPSE)
3. speaks in staccato bursts rather than fluid, soft tones
4. squints
5. blinks eyes rapidly
6. nods head while another is speaking
7. gestures even when someone else is speaking
8. interrupts others
9. finishes other people's sentences
10. engages in polyphasic activities (tries to do more than one thing at a time)
11. sits on edge of the chair
12. finds it difficult to refrain from talking about his or her own interests and concerns; when conversation goes to others, the SPSE pretends to be listening but is preoccupied
13. is hypersensitive to criticism
14. finds it difficult to remember sensory details (has a poor memory for how something felt, smelled, or tasted)
15. neglects to allow for contingencies when scheduling activities
16. maintains a semblance of surface organization, but beneath outward appearances, there is clutter (in drawers, closets, and so on)
17. sighs often
18. lifts eyebrows rhythmically while talking or responding nonverbally
19. engages in tuneless humming

20. jiggles feet or legs while sitting at desk or in meetings
21. strums fingers, taps with fingers
22. clicks teeth
23. maintains a frozen smile while interacting with others
24. clenches fists

These are the obvious, outward signs of the inward pressures that propel SPSEs. By separating people into Type A and Type B groups using Friedman and Rosenman criteria, solid evidence has been provided that links the behavior pattern of the individual to one's likelihood of suffering artery and heart disease. Numerous studies have demonstrated that the Type A pattern increases the likelihood of most *diseases* of both traumatic and mildly irritating natures. While we can separate people into groups for study using these observable criteria, the behaviors obviously are not what causes eventual breakdown. No one has yet been diagnosed with a terminal case of head nodding or a heart failure attributable to interrupting others. These behaviors do not directly *cause* accompanying changes in our emotions, interpersonal actions, and intellectual functioning.

These behaviors in and of themselves do not dramatically reduce the special educator's competency or job enjoyment. Conceivably, you can tap your fingers, squint, nod frequently, clench your fists, and still do an excellent job while experiencing satisfaction and enjoyment. Such is not usually the case, however, because these behaviors are usually symptoms of more powerful and detrimental drives. Your face and your body serve as reflections of what is going on inside. The SPSE not only presents an outwardly different appearance while working than that presented by the N-SPSE. The SPSE also has a different internal experience from the N-SPSE. Unlike the N-SPSE, the SPSE is unable to find a comfortable, personality-enhancing way of relating with the special education environment.

SPSEs experience uncomfortable internal pressures as a result of particular beliefs that we maintain about ourselves, others, and our environment. These beliefs direct our observable behavior and stimulate our internal stress. It doesn't matter whether the beliefs held by the N-SPSEs or the SPSEs are the true beliefs; there is no way to prove the case for one side or the other. What matters is that the set of beliefs guiding stress-prone types leads to self-destructive stress, ineffective work practices, and decreased job and life enhancement. The beliefs generally held by nonstress-prone types have been found to be corollated with relaxed behavior, job satisfaction, positive interpersonal relationships, and longevity. Examining and altering attitudes and actions stemming from the SPSEs' belief structure is the core of a successful stress management program.

THE FOUR CORE BELIEFS OF THE
STRESS-PRONE SPECIAL EDUCATOR

SPSE Core Belief Number 1

Work in special education (like the rest of living) is a struggle. For the SPSE in special education, work is a struggle with time, other people, and events. The key word here is *struggle*. In contrast, N-SPSEs can be said to view their jobs in special education as a game, and not the kind of superficial, highly competitive, cruel game that is often mentioned in sales management programs. To the N-SPSE, work in special education (like everything else) is part of a cooperative, never-ending game that is played by benevolent people doing their best to develop and adhere to just rules. The game, of course, is unpredictable, ever-changing, and often unmanageable, but such is the nature of a game. The SPSE, in order to maintain a pose of constant alertness to the struggle, sends a regular stream of messages to the brain that result in chronic stress problems.

To determine whether you have a struggle approach to your job, ask yourself which of the following descriptions fits you. As you pull out onto the street to begin your journey to work each day, are you thinking to youself, "Here I start out on another exciting day in the game of special education, another day in my adult work experience. I wonder what will happen today?" Or, are you more likely to sigh, grip the wheel tightly (bracing yourself for battle), and say to yourself, "Well, here goes another day in the struggle of special education. Another day with too much to do, another day with uncooperative students—not to mention the lack of clerical assistance. That means that I won't have the help absolutely necessary in order to complete the minimum number of units for each of my students. I wonder if they've fixed that cranky air conditioning system or if it's going to be unbearable again." The thinking habits of the N-SPSE and SPSE on their way to work reflect the differences that permeate the work day. On the way to work the N-SPSE plans, watches the scenery, and notices people in other cars. On reaching work, the N-SPSE focuses attention on the children raising the flag and notices and waves to a parent dropping off a student. On the journey to work the SPSE worries about plans already made, speculates about whether or not a slight sore throat means a cold is coming on, and notices other cars only when they become objects in the way. On reaching the agency building, the SPSE focuses attention on whatever is slowing their way into the proper parking spot.

Whether you are mostly a SPSE or mostly a N-SPSE, your beliefs determine the constant communication you have with yourself. It is the nature of this communication that largely determines the stress you experience.

To further understand the struggle approach, consider that the stress-inducing self-talk of the SPSE follows corollary beliefs or *sub-beliefs* that stem from the struggle orientation. The belief that our work in special education is a struggle is really a package of beliefs which, taken together, builds a case for struggle that becomes airtight, if you accept the following chain of assumptions.

SPSE Corollary Belief 1a

Work is supposed to be suffering. This concept has its roots in childhood when we were told that we were not to receive payment for anything we enjoyed. We learned to see work as that unpleasantness preceding pleasurable activity. We were warned about people who were lazy, who "couldn't take" the necessary suffering of work and who were therefore worth less and not deserving of respect from others or deserving of postsuffering relaxation. Since we were sometimes taught that the more we suffered, the more we should get paid, we learned to complain loudly and to set ourselves up to be the target of overwork and suffering. We learned to pat ourselves on the back, not for doing a fulfilling, relaxed job, but for surviving difficult situations and persevering against the odds. We expect our work to be a struggle because we are being paid for doing it and because SPSE types have been raised to be dissatisfied and pressed.

SPSEs have accepted the dichotomy presented in the following scheme.

Work is:	*Play is:*
suffering	freedom from suffering
tension	relaxation
stress	stress-free
everyone else's needs are met	our needs are met

Dichotomous or black and white thinking is a problem habit of SPSEs anyway. SPSEs are frustrated frequently because the world is not a matter of black and white, right and wrong solutions, but rather a matter of infinite gray areas. The dichotomy of work as suffering, and play as enjoyment is a particularly destructive thinking habit that contributes to the struggle approach to special education. Note the other elements of the dichotomy. All the pleasurable side effects of activity are on the non-work side of the dichotomy while the effects of battles go on the work side. This representation agrees with research showing that stress-prone individuals are more likely than nonstress-prone persons to insist on a clear break at a definite time each day when work stops and play begins. Nonstress-prone special educators are less likely to insist on such a separation between work and what comes afterward because, to them, no dichotomy exists between the two. The N-SPSE, rather than seeing a split between work and play, realizes that all the characteristics listed under work and play can be interchanged and mixed together to become a single list.

But SPSEs balk at the idea of work and play being one and the same. To play means to drop our guard and then to be overwhelmed by the opposing forces of time, other people, and events. To play means to be noncaring and irresponsible in our job. To play means to attend to our own experiencing of enjoyment as well as the experiencing of others. To play means to be relaxed, and SPSEs all know that relaxation, if allowed, leads directly to irreversible laziness. So we strugglers have learned our workstyle in special education largely because we were never allowed (and have never allowed ourselves) to consider an alternative, more relaxed approach. Perhaps more importantly, we were discouraged from demanding that the work-play dichotomy be closed, discouraged from demanding the right to be involved in work that is personality enhancing as well as productive.

SPSE Corollary Belief 1b

The end product is more important than the experience. This belief is often used to justify the miseries of our struggle approach. It's not too difficult to see how one picks up the idea that the end product is all that counts since most of us in education received messages throughout our pre-college and college training that it didn't matter how much we felt isolated from the experience as long as we eventually ended up with credentials. Becoming involved in the process, expecting personality enhancement, could even have resulted in that most feared circumstance—it could have slowed us down.

So now as we approach our special education work day we estimate our end-product successes and begin to long impatiently for the time it will be all over. All we have learned to respect are the end products of the day rather than the experiencing while there. SPSEs have the sad habit of trading the here and now for the there and soon, which results in tossing away many opportunities to enjoy and grow. But then part of the concept of the struggle approach is that the special educator is supposed to put up with all the suffering and stress because of some belief that the end products will be worth it.

This idea breaks down in a couple of important respects when we study the behavior of the N-SPSE. You see, SPSEs focus on end products rather than journeys because we have been taught that to do otherwise would endanger our chances of collecting our end products. Also, SPSEs have been taught that if we pay attention to the here and now we will lose our forward propelled motion. These two attitudes go a long way toward explaining why the person experiencing chronic stress loses his or her sense of humor. Who can afford to laugh at strange twists of words and life when these could delay or distract us? Fortunately, the SPSE belief that attending to the experience will destroy progress doesn't hold true.

Seeing the collection of end products as the goal in special education sets up the SPSE for a stressful experience; once we establish our objectives and our deadlines, the path is cleared for fighting our way to completion. The job becomes a matter of going from one spot to another on the calendar, one spot to another on the test score profiles, and one spot to another in the reading progress package. This is not to say that having objectives and goals is, in itself, a harmful practice. But, rather, the approach to such practices is important. The SPSE's worship of end products over experiencing contributes to a loss of ability to relate to students. Whether we specifically say so or not, they know where our priorities are and they know what it means when we do not have time for distractions and delays. SPSEs lose the ability to creatively use present experiencing to blend into our lessons, our therapies, and our programs. We become frustrated when we're behind on deadlines and are more likely, in behavior problem situations, to hook into repeating stereotypic responses that have not proven effective in the past. Remember, when things go wrong SPSEs are more likely to do what we're already doing harder and faster rather than wasting time by regrouping and reconsidering the situation.

The N-SPSE counterparts are interested in end products, too. It's just that N-SPSEs consider end products to be the nice results of productive experiences. Nonstress-prone special educators do not view the special education job as necessary but painful labor that precedes end products. The experience itself is important. The experience is important because the experiencing of time in the here and now is important to the N-SPSE. Stress-prone types have learned to measure time against rate of accomplishment rather than against the value of present happenings.

SPSE Corollary Belief 1c

Doing and having are more important than being. SPSEs believe that end products are more important than immediate experiencing because we were taught to measure ourselves by our achievement and to measure ourselves by other people's judgments of our achievements. We learned a hard lesson: a person is valuable because of what one can *do* or because of what one *has* and not for who one *is*. In fact, severely stress-prone educators are unable to describe the differences between what one does and has and who one is. It's as though it's been so long since any unconditional self-acceptance was felt that the end products of doing and having have taken over the internal space designed for meaningful personal growth.

Of course, special education is going to be a struggle if you are constantly in the process of piling up numbers, successes, trophies, and deserved possessions in order to earn the right to feel worthwhile. It's not difficult to see how this process gets started since we are bombarded daily with hundreds of commercials that tell us that doing and collecting are the ways to bring smiles, attention, and therefore, we incorrectly assume, relaxation and enjoyment. I have yet to see a commercial encouraging inner peace, knowledge of oneself, and celebration of the okay-ness of the person without the person being pushed to achieve, and/or buy something. It's not that doing and having things is bad; it's just that the person with a tendency toward stress pressures is likely to swallow the concept whole to the detriment of their overall personality.

The self-command to gain the right to worthwhileness by doing and having is an insatiable demand. Having insatiable demands on oneself results in a sense of struggle, deprivation, and tension. There's always something more to do, something else that's needed. The N-SPSE is involved in doing and having but these are not as important as one's internal comfort with larger goals and principles. The N-SPSE is free to sacrifice achievements and objects to protect state-of-being values. Having learned well that state-of-being values have little market value, SPSEs choose to sacrifice them. The result is that essential elements of the personality are neglected, elements that are needed later. Meyer Friedman, in reviewing methods used at his clinic to rehabilitate Type As relates that one thing each participant is asked to do is to ask himself or herself each evening, "What have I done for my soul today?" This is one way of getting the stress-prone, end product devotee to focus on the importance of his or her state of being.

These three subcategories of SPSE Core Belief #1 are general statements that spring from the basic belief that one's job is a struggle with time, other people, and events. It is very likely that you can retrieve statements from your own learning that serve as additional and corollary statements to this belief. Others suggested include: (1) It's a jungle out there, and, (2) All that counts is the bottom line.

SPSE Core Belief Number 2

There is not enough time to get everything done. Usually when I make this SPSE belief statement to a group of special educators, many people in the audience nod their heads in strong agreement—agreement that there really *isn't* enough time to get everything done! As far as stress management is concerned, it does not matter whether in reality this is the case or not! The point is that with SPSEs this belief becomes a powerful directing force in daily behavior. Much of the stress-prone person's behavior and discomfort can be traced to time consciousness or what Meyer Friedman calls *hurry sickness*. Once you have accepted that your worth is tied up in doing and having and once you become accustomed to the tension and deprivation that accompanies this belief, the battle against time is an obvious course of action. There seems never to be enough doing and having to feel okay. Therefore the only hope is to force more and more doing into less and less time in an effort to gain on the problem. This approach does not work and results in a powerful sense that the problem is not in our basic approach to self-worth but in the belief that there simply is not enough *time* to do and to collect what we need in order to have the right to relax.

The hurry sickness of SPSEs is characterized by reduced openness to interaction with others, increased accidents, and decreased satisfaction with other people and the job. This belief about time gives SPSEs the appearance of propelling themselves forward. It is a subtle hint to others at work and at home that "there isn't time for you." Irritability and lost enjoyment are rationalized because, "I just have so much to do right now," or because, "I'm irritable but I'm behind in my schedule and I'm tired." Because, "I should have finished this task a long time ago," or because, "I can't take the time right now to listen." The SPSE says *right now* but the hurry sickness is a habitual way of functioning. Throughout the day there is an internal tension. No spare moment goes unused and no time is allotted to anything as "unproductive" as personality and workstyle enhancement. One characteristic of Friedman and Rosenman's Type As is that they are unlikely to seek medical or psychological help when they need it. After all, "Who has 60 extra minutes a week? Who has time to go to the doctor everytime they get sick?" Because of time mania, SPSEs are not likely to involve themselves in exercise or relaxation programs. As one principal in Tulsa, Oklahoma put it after we had agreed as a group that each of us would walk 20 minutes that evening, "Well, I'll do it. But I don't understand why anyone would waste time doing *unproductive* exercise." Often during seminars I will teach participants a simple 20-minute relaxation technique. After the session, many of the more stress prone will take me aside to inquire hastily, "Who has 20 minutes a day to spend on something like this?"

It is important to note that in reality each of us has the 20 minutes. We have just learned to feel guilty about using 20 minutes for something that does not directly contribute to our achievements or our collections.

Stress-prone special educators are fiercely impatient. Improvements never happen fast enough. And while we huff and puff around in response to internal pressures we reassure others we're only angry, pushy, irritable, and so on, in efforts to help the situation. Lines at the bank, at the grocery, at the county clerk's office are unbearably long. We rationalize our discomfort by pointing out to others that "people just shouldn't have to wait." I have found that SPSEs tend to be late to meetings because they have planned too many things to do in the space between their last activity and the meeting. Also SPSEs prefer to be late rather than early because, "Who has eight minutes to spare waiting for a meeting to get started?" Nonstress-prone special educators believe that there is enough time to get everything done that is important. The reality of how many tasks you have to complete in whatever impossible time span is not particularly important in determining how you approach your special education career. Your relationship with your environment and your approach to time are much stronger factors. SPSEs caught up in painful hurry sickness are easy to spot. The face of the SPSE is set with an expression of life and death seriousness. Whether taking time out to go to the lounge or going in late to keep a court appearance appointment, the SPSE always walks at a fast clip. You can tell the genuine N-SPSEs too.

The expression on the N-SPSEs face is different, more relaxed, more inviting. What goes on inside the body of the N-SPSE is different, too. The N-SPSE maintains an internal balance and comfort that allows relaxation and an easy availability of energy. Interactions with others are pleasant since other people and their needs are not seen as obstructions in the race against time. Interactions with the self (internal conversations) are more pleasant as self-made errors are not seen as unbearably time-consuming and are not met with internal overreactions. The internal conversations of SPSEs, on the other hand, are likely to include silent warnings such as, "You'd better hurry or you'll never make it and that will be disastrous. Don't linger listening to others; you have too much to do. Stop wasting time and get going. Oh, you're never going to make it." Self-statements such as these are key phrases to keep the stress cycle in action. Many are the beliefs about time that keep the SPSE tense. Three of the most frequent are presented below.

SPSE Corollary Belief 2a

Quantity is more important than quality. The SPSE is obsessed with numbers, test scores, projects completed, numbers of parents called, piles of papers graded, years accumulated in one system or another, and years left to go in one system or another. Again this distorted attention to only one aspect of experience comes from learning that quantity is what other people will notice and what other people notice is what gives one the right to feel okay. A teacher shared this story about one of her students who had, the day before, participated in the 100-yard dash at the Special Olympics. At the beginning of school he excitedly appeared at her desk holding up a fourth place ribbon. The teacher, a stress-prone type, responded by saying, "Hey, that's great. How fast did you run?" The student looked up confidently and explained, "As fast as I could." Not stress-prone himself, he responded as though she had inquired about quality rather than quantity.

Concerned with numbers, SPSEs take on more to do than can be done well, or with high quality. Pride is taken in being able to do more than one thing at a time (polyphasic activity). Satisfaction is lowered since quantifiable goals are the only source of good feelings, and these occur only occasionally. In addition, overall quality of accomplishment is reduced in the hurry to do so many things at once. Interpersonal relationships suffer since building quality relationships requires much time and the results are not quantifiable.

However, I've heard many an SPSE try to use numbers to describe the quality of relationships. Such an effort is apparent in statements such as, "I don't see how she could say they don't love each other. After all, they have three children, a lovely four-bedroom, $100,000 house, and they've been married 17 years!" Stress-prone special educators are concerned with how many lessons can be completed in one day, how many children can be tested in two hours, and how many gold stars can be pasted on the book chart.

Nonstress-prone special educators want to know how everyone felt during these experiences and whether what they learned had any meaning for them. The N-SPSE is concerned with whether he or she enjoyed participating in these activities since *life-time* was passing during these hours. Because N-SPSEs believe that by focusing on the experience, end products will come, and they are then free to focus on the quality of activities. This means a freedom to focus on the internal quality of personal experiencing as well as observance of the external quality of activities. Because N-SPSEs expect not only to produce but also to enjoy themselves while producing, they have a much less stressful and more enjoyable internal experiencing during each special education work day.

SPSE Corollary Belief 2b

People in a hurry are important people. This belief has simple beginnings. We were taught not to bother people who had a lot to do because they were needed for more important things. We were taught that people who weren't very, very busy weren't being highly sought by others. (We didn't learn that some people had learned to establish priorities and to say no.) We heard significant others talking about the unworthiness of nonbusy people—idle hands being the devil's workshop and all. The idea of giving up the hurry sickness is frightening because SPSEs have learned that to do so will put us in the category of persons not in a hurry. And we were not taught to respect those persons.

SPSE Corollary Belief 2c

The only way to be successful in my job is to be in a constant state of hurry. One reality that serves as a bitter pill for SPSEs is the fact that Type As do not necessarily get more done than do Type Bs. At first such a possibility may seem unreasonable. But think about it a moment. Take the situation of a SPSE and a N-SPSE both on the road on their way home from attending an out-of-town, in-service meeting. The SPSE, being quantitatively oriented, decides before leaving just how much time will be allowed for the trip. Just how fast he or she will need to drive to make it within the arbitrary deadline is decided. Then our SPSE pulls out onto the road and quickly speeds up to the "necessary" speed. Let's say that speed is 60 m.p.h. During the entire trip the SPSE stares closely at the speedometer to make sure the car does not, under any circumstances, travel more slowly than the "necessary" 60 m.p.h., an event that would throw him or her off schedule (and we know what that means . . . or do we?). Once out on the road our SPSE invariably finds himself or herself caught behind a car going 58 m.p.h. Well, this car *must* be passed since to stay behind it would mean getting off schedule. So with much effort the car going only 58 m.p.h. is conquered. Two miles further down the road another car is encountered going 58 m.p.h. After several tries this car also is passed. Meanwhile an N-SPSE leaves the meeting for the same destination. The N-SPSE has a general idea of how long the trip will take and makes sure there is plenty of time for contingencies. Our N-SPSE glances at the speedometer only infrequently since, when one is driving slowly, there are plenty of cars passing to let you know you're doing fine.

Now after both have been out on the road for about ten minutes, our SPSE reaches a small town and stops for a school bus to unload and then for two lights in the middle of town. You know what happens while our hurried, harried, SPSE sits waiting for the second light to change. Of course. All the cars he or she strained to pass drive up casually beside and behind the car of the SPSE. Most of us have learned to look cool and to stare straight ahead when this happens since it's embarrassing to have blown five extra dollars on gasoline for the privilege of being first in line at the stoplight. The same phenomenon happens in our special education environments. Those among us who started out as Type Bs or who have overcome their hurry sickness manage somehow to accomplish as much in essential areas as do Type As.

Real strugglers and quantifiers may succeed in actually completing more tasks of a repetitive nature since we are likely to have extreme standards in areas that are not critical to our work, such as neatness and to-the-letter punctuality, and we may be quite compulsive about the placement of materials in our classrooms. But, as far as the essential, creative aspects of our work, we can even be outdone by N-SPSEs since they are more likely to have an energy supply that burns slowly but steadily while our sprint style of energy burning finds us lacking before the day is finished. When special educators list the priorities in their job, taking care of the needs of those we serve is always at the top. One would assume, then, that meeting that first priority would determine much of a special educator's success. Without further explanation, which of the two, the SPSE or the N-SPSE, would be best able to do this, assuming that the SPSE lives by the belief that the only way to be a successful special educator is to be in a constant state of hurry?

These beliefs having to do with hurry sickness are compounded in their effect by the third core belief of the SPSE.

SPSE Core Belief Number 3

Whatever worthwhileness I have achieved has been possible because I am willing to work harder and faster than other people. In other words, not only do SPSEs hurry, but they believe that it is this very quality that has enabled them to gain whatever worthwhileness they now possess. Because of this stubborn belief, giving up one's hurry sickness requires a supreme effort of the kind that is difficult for those used to putting that supreme effort in the opposite direction. One process that can be helpful when you find the hurry syndrome seductive is to review your priorities and remind yourself of the physical, emotional, interpersonal and intellectual costs of keeping stress-prone behavior. The whole point of hurrying is eventually to have more time. Only it doesn't work. Hurry sickness is not something that happens once in a while. It is an important element of the SPSE's workstyle approach.

As ample research has demonstrated, stressful workstyles actually shorten one's lifetime, and that means the whole process is not working. The death rate is still 100 per cent.

SPSE Corollary Belief 3a

Making myself is more important than discovering myself. Clark Moustakas (1969) made these statements,

"Every person is, by nature, a potentially creative being with a unique destiny and with resources for genuine encounters in the world. Yet in spite of these capacities for individual and communal growth, men have turned away from themselves and from each other . . . Often the individual is unaware that he, as a unique, growing person, has been cancelled out and that in place of his genuine self is a concept, a definition of what should be; and that definition has been pieced together and executed in such a way that what the individual has become lacks substance and identity, which alone can give meaning to his life" (p. 1).

Moustakas goes on to say that only through sensitivity and recognition of genuine self can a person become all that he or she can be. What do you think is meant by "all that he or she can be?" Because of the context and because of the basic tenets of Moustakas it seems that when he refers to "all he or she can be," he is referring to full development of the uniqueness of the person in whatever direction that uniqueness takes them. This is not the meaning attributed to this phrase by many SPSEs; the phrase is interpreted as describing a process of struggle and ambition to make use of all opportunities to excel and to win the approval of self and others. SPSEs are prone to encourage people to "make something of themselves." Moustakas is speaking of a process of discovering undertaken by a person who *already is* something—something unique, something special. The struggle of *making* oneself into something leads to an approach to working that doesn't necessarily add to self-discovery, but rather hides oneself away.

Meyer Friedman has described three reasons why people work: (1) sustenance; (2) status and power; and (3) personality enhancement. He described Type As as working for status and power even though most will claim to be working for sustenance. The person working for sustenance and for personality enhancement is not going to experience the stress as will be experienced by the person struggling through special education to "make themselves," to earn the right to value themselves. Of course, we don't usually think of special education as a field rife with status and power. Yet, when we approach special education with exalted demands on ourselves for perfection and exalted demands for superpower, we are working to maintain status even unto ourselves. We are making ourselves perform rather than allowing it to happen. If the concept of "allowing your energies to happen" or working as a special educator for the personality enhancement seems strange and confusing right now, take heart. The next several chapters are devoted to letting go of the stress prone beliefs which keep us from trusting and growing as special educators.

The concept of your job as personality enhancement and as an opportunity for growth and discovery is a major focus in stress management. To consider how this idea fits with you, determine how your workstyle approach fits with either of the following descriptions.

Working to make something of yourself involves:

- Locating rigid goals that receive praise
- Working harder and faster (than others) always
- Ignoring functioning of self as whole person—ignoring non-productive elements (those that do not further approved goals) of the self
- Reaching for proof of okay-ness from others
- Working in fear that you haven't done enough, are still making mistakes, and could have done better

Working for personality enhancement involves:

- Finding work that suits your sense of growth
- Discovering new aspects of self by trying new ideas
- Looking for goals in line with self
- Reviewing each day as it fits with self
- Feeling lucky on the job

You may need to be further into this book before you can conceive as feasible the idea of trusting yourself to work without using threats born of the work for status, power, and approval. Threats such as these are common in the internal conversations of stress-prone persons: "If you don't get better at this, you are hopeless. You'd *better* hurry, what else have you got going for you?" Some morning (if you live in a town of 20,000 or more) watch the faces of other people in their cars on the way to work. Notice the lack of smiles and the furrowed brows. It's no wonder that work for special educators has been set in opposition to enjoyment. The workplace becomes the chief proving ground for self-worth and that means it is a source of stress. Remember, once you have bought the idea that you must "make something of yourself," that you must achieve and collect things to have the right to relax, this need will be insatiable. The results are tension and stress.

Ruben (1975), in his book, *Compassion and Self Hate*, described the healthfulness of a relationship this way: "Any relationship, professional or otherwise, that ultimately reduces self hate and enhances compassion contributes to a long term and possibly permanent therapeutic effect." The same statement can be made regarding your relationship to your work in special education. How does your work change you?

Okay, so if you aren't going to use judgment of your performance and the approval of others to establish your self-worth, what are you going to use? The next chapter will speak to this issue.

SPSE Corollary Belief 3b

It is more important to keep moving than to have a clear idea of where you're going. Arthur Coombs (1969), the well-known educator and educational researcher from Florida, studied the characteristics of effective helpers versus ineffective helpers. His studies showed that good helpers concerned themselves with larger goals and the poorer helpers concerned themselves with smaller goals. In looking at SPSEs, many are certainly effective helpers. It is better said that problems occur not only as a result of focusing on smaller goals but in trying to attend to too many goals at once. The SPSE uses the "scatter-shot" approach to goal development. That is, because of habitual patterns of trying to do everything, of trying to respond to every need presented, of putting goal completion ahead of experience and quantity over quality, SPSEs feel themselves pulled in many conflicting directions at once. The central goals that originally attracted SPSEs to this profession are often lost in the shuffle.

The SPSEs hurry sickness adds to the problem. When you're always pressed for action, who has time to review priorities and to attend to values other than the value of getting more done in less time and to do it better? And SPSEs are not used to determining our own values and demanding the right to live by these. The goals of the SPSE are often goals set by other people, people who must be pleased.

Something very special attracted you to special education, some feeling, some sense of value. To maintain that special something and to manage stress, you will need to match your energy investments with your values. The special education environment is a constant demand situation. If you do not decide where you stand, it will devour you.

SPSE Core Belief Number 4

Other people cannot be depended on. This belief is one of the most painful to examine. After all, SPSEs are not recluses. In fact, we are usually quite verbal and we can be depended on at a moment's notice to expound on the importance of trusting others and delegating responsibility. After all, we didn't start out with the idea of alienating others, but with the idea of helping others. It's precisely because we're so anxious to cover all the bases in meeting the needs of others that we end up not trusting other people. SPSEs suspect that other people can't be trusted—not because they're bad people, but because they may not be as intense as we are or as willing to subvert energies from all other areas to attend to whatever it is we need to trust them to do. We reach a point of not trusting other people to help us because in the process of rejecting ourselves as okay without performance and approval, we learn to not trust ourselves. Not trusting ourselves, we project our fear of being overwhelmed and our desire to relax onto others. We believe in our hearts that others cannot be relied on to ignore quality of experience and focus on end products.

You will not be able to relax and depend on others until you have settled the trust problem with yourself. Eric Fromm (1956) in *The Art of Loving* says it very well:

> ". . . the logical fallacy in the notion that love for others and love for oneself are mutually exclusive should be stressed. If it is a virtue to love my neighbor as a human being, it must be a virtue— and not a vice—to love myself since I am a human being too. There is no concept of man in which I myself am not included."

Because self-trust and self-acceptance must come first, the next chapter focuses on this issue. Finding a nonstressful way of dealing with others comes afterward.

The connection between the belief that other people can't be depended on and the struggle context of the stress-prone workstyle is easy to see. When other people are not seen as willing to help, when other people are not seen as capable (or as capable as we are)—who can relax? Time and energy must go into extensive supervision of people less dedicated than we are. Other people become obstacles. The needs of other people are seen as threats to our forward progress toward wherever we are heading at the time. In our efforts to be good, people-oriented, special educators, we become fiercely impatient with others. And it doesn't take much for that impatience to turn to anger.

More and more, evidence demonstrates that the *self-fulfilling prophecy* is an essential concept for understanding behavior. Simply stated, the evidence indicates that whatever we believe to be true about our environment strongly influences that environment. To look at a most basic example, some of the earliest studies investigated how the self-fulfilling prophecy operated in experiments in which rats were taught to run a maze. The "rat trainers" were told that certain of the rats had been bred for intelligence while others were selected at random for the experiment. Actually, all the rats were selected randomly. True to form, study results demonstrated that the "specially bred" rats learned the maze structure significantly faster than did the other rats. We see what we expect to see; we make happen what we expect to happen. Afraid of errors, bothered by the reality that other people do things differently, SPSEs rely heavily on the self-fulfilling prophecy to support our beliefs about others—and it works.

One corollary belief fits with SPSE Core Belief #4.

SPSE Corollary Belief 4a

If I want it done right I have to do it myself. What a tiresome and tiring notion. This idea stacks up right next to stress-inducing beliefs such as, "I cannot afford mistakes," and "Everything with which I am involved must be superior." The only way we can make absolutely sure that every project follows these standards is to do everything ourselves. Other people might not know just the right way to accomplish what needs to be accomplished. Usually when SPSEs decry that we have to take over tasks because other people are not doing things right, what we really mean is that other people are not doing things "our way." And, of course, as we step in with our tired expression, we assure everyone we are "just trying to help."

The "I have to do it myself" belief damages relationships and inhibits progress in the workplace. Students, clients, and coworkers learn not to extend themselves since there is no hope of ever operating on an equal plane with the "do it myself" SPSE. Communicating the "I have to do it myself" belief to others lets others know where they stand. Students and clients are likely to either withdraw and make jokes about the tyrant or to buy the play for superiority and feel sorry for us because of our burdens while feeling badly about themselves for being inadequate and adding to the load. And, of course, we resent the "fact" that we have been given all this superior knowledge and diligence and now must be responsible for everything when other people could pitch in and do things right (our way) if they wanted to badly enough.

WHY IS THE SPSE AN SPSE?

After seminars I am often asked the question, "Can a stress-prone person ever completely change into the classic nonstress-prone type?" My answer is that while many changes can be made, I don't think currently that a complete and unwavering transformation from stress-prone to nonstress-prone is possible. This shows my general background and perhaps bias toward developmental psychology. The SPSE workstyle approach results from being a child who was taught either overtly or covertly to be afraid—to be afraid of trusting the self, afraid of trusting others, and afraid that without constant performance and approval, the individual is "worth-less" and won't be cared for by others. Clark Moustakas (1969) describes the losing of self-trust this way, "Often, the individual is unaware that he, as a unique, growing person, has been cancelled out and that in place of his genuine self is a concept, a definition of what he should be; and that definition has been pieced together and executed in such a way that what the individual has become lacks substance and identity, which alone can give meaning to his life." SPSEs chronically experience stress because the loss of appreciation of self leaves us in a combat stance, trying to prove ourselves amidst the plentiful "external judgments and cues" in special education.

In growing up, SPSEs were frightened into hurrying ("If you don't hurry you won't get enough done."), frightened into going overboard in competing ("Watch over your shoulder, other people want to overtake you."), and taught to be dissatisfied with ourselves ("Yes, this is a good report, but it's not as good as you *could* produce."). Dissatisfaction motivation, never quite doing things fast enough, becomes a driving force for the SPSE. Because our parents, friends, teachers, and mentors were afraid we would quit trying if they indicated satisfaction with us, stress-prone types learned to be uncomfortable with anything less than perfection—a goal, of course, no one ever achieves. Carl Pickhart (1979), educational consultant and writer, has described job burnout as partly the result of adherence to certain culturally accepted ideas. These ideas, as he defined them, are presented below. These beliefs were the cornerstones by which SPSEs were raised.

- New   is better than   Old
- More   is better than   Less
- Different   is better than   The same
- Better   is better than   As well
- Fast   is better than   Slow

We learned that no matter what we do, it will never be enough, and the result is chronic stress and dissatisfaction. Remember, we believe we have achieved whatever success we have achieved by being able to make ourselves work harder and faster than others. Being like the others would never do. Usually we were also heavily reinforced as children for intelligence and diligence above all else.

As for N-SPSEs, these rare folks received the confidence as children that they were okay already and that what was necessary for a fulfilling adulthood was to allow that okay self to grow and develop. Persons without chronic stress problems learned a powerful benevolence toward themselves and others along with a seemingly endless supply of enthusiasm and wonder toward people and the environment. Believing work is not a struggle, N-SPSEs expect to enjoy their work and do just that. Believing there is enough time to complete what is necessary these special educators are not tense and harried (a characteristic that drives SPSEs up the wall). Believing that whatever success they have achieved has been the result of personal uniqueness and a benevolent environment, N-SPSEs are open to new experience but feel it would be silly to strive blindly for product-only success. Believing other people to be dependable, N-SPSEs find a great deal of support and help available from others.

Oh, how nice it would be to go back, grow up again, and this time learn these core beliefs. But rather than be dismayed, remember that we SPSEs picked up our behaviors because we wanted to be good, because we believed these behaviors would bring us the success that seemed to be what everyone valued in children and adults. And change is possible. You can, like myself, be an SPSE working toward becoming an N-SPSE.

In Conclusion

Your workstyle approach is determined by the health of your mind which in turn determines the health of your body. The working of the mind is complex and resistant to change, so there is no easy way to reduce the chronic work stress of special educators. Change will require a genuine commitment on your part that sometimes only happens when stress has reached such proportions that an immediate, voluntary Acapulco, leave of absence or a lengthy involuntary hospital stay is required. But pain is certainly an okay reason to try a new approach. If you need another reason, consider how your service as a special educator is being affected by your stress and how your ability to serve others has been affected by whatever behaviors you have developed to cope with the problem.

The frequency and extent of the eventual stress you experience will be determined by: (1) your environment, (2) your cognitive approach to the environment, and, (3) the condition of your body. Management of stress can be accomplished by working with any or all of these factors.

Specific procedures for managing stress include: (1) altering your environment, (2) altering your cognitive approach, and, (3) altering your physical behavior. Of course, making changes means making choices. Making choices is the core of your uniqueness. Special educators who insist they have no choices in their special education environment, in their cognitive approach to special education, and in their physical behavior, disenfranchise their own power, lose energy, and are candidates for burnout. To integrate stress management with your special education work, your first choice will need to be in the direction of considering your job as an opportunity for experiencing creative values, as an opportunity to grow and enjoy. That statement may sound as though you are being asked to blindly follow "the path of the heart" and in part you are. But there's more. To manage your stress, to treat yourself with benevolence rather than as a machine, trusting the path of the heart will be an essential but not sufficient step. You will also need skills to follow through, which is what stress management is all about.

Altering Your Environment

1. Review your daily schedule of activities to determine if you regularly take on tasks unnecessarily.
2. Consider lowering your standards for neatness and punctuality in areas where these are not essential.
3. Since development of your stress management program will require solitary attention to your role as a special educator, design a private place for yourself somewhere in your work or home environment.
4. Plan some time during each day to spend alone considering your stress management program. (A tough one for super-SPSEs who already have *no time.*)
5. Purchase or check out from the library at least one book that can be considered "lasting literature" (not in the field of special education!) to begin your program of awakening neglected aspects of yourself.
6. Purchase for yourself one of the following this week:
   a. a picture or photograph that "says something to you" to be hung wherever it "feels right."
   b. a record album of a type of music you find relaxing and inspiring to be listened to during private time.
7. Begin to review your environment for nourishing stress-reducing activities you used to enjoy but have given up because of the time problem or for activities you have always wanted to try but for which you never had the time. (Following up on this initial review will come later.) Make notes of ideas for increased enjoyment as they occur to you.
8. Establish a three-joke-a-week minimum for yourself. This means that you actively seek out riddles, funny stories, and jokes to bring humor and its accompanying stress-reducing effects into your work. Use at least two structured bits of humor in your work each week.
9. Begin to re-establish the 360 degree environmental vision you had before being a "super-special educator" claimed all your attention. When you feel yourself tensing up, take three deep breaths and momentarily redirect your attention. Notice an aspect of your surroundings ordinarily ignored—smells, plants, sounds of insects, the crazy shapes of leaves rolling across the sidewalk, or the unique structure of a child's ear lobe. The reinstatement of "wonder" can also be practiced when

you have purposely set out for a "relaxing" activity such as a walk outside or even a jaunt to the local shopping mall.

Altering Your Cognitive Approach

1. Before leaving for work (I've found the best time to be just after brushing my teeth) stand in front of the mirror and repeat slowly to yourself:
   a. "I have before me another day in the game of special education. I wonder what it will bring."
   b. "There is enough time to do whatever is necessary. I am too precious to hurry."
   It can be helpful to print these statements onto cards and tape them to your mirror until you have learned them by memory.
2. Stop holding out for a time when you can relax. Remember Mark Twain's statement, "Life is one damn thing after another." Holding on to the childhood plan of being relaxed and satisfied when no problems exist means holding out forever. An adult can recognize that being stress-free does not mean having no problems, inconveniences, or unpleasantries with which to deal. It means being able to stay comfortable in the midst of imperfect reality.
3. Whenever you notice yourself becoming impatient because of lines, late meetings, overdue plans, and so forth, repeat to yourself: "Time is only wasted if I'm miserable, and only *I* can make myself miserable."

Altering Your Physical Behavior

1. Notice when you are hurrying—walking too fast, talking too fast, eating too fast. Pause for three deep breaths and purposefully slow your pace.
2. When you are conversing with students, clients, and others, make a purposeful effort to listen to what is being said for both the feelings communicated and the content. One excellent method of increasing this skill, slowing yourself down *and* widening your horizons is called the *two-question technique*. This means anytime anyone talks to you about something that interests them, ask them not one but two questions about the subject. Everyone asks one question to appear interested, but asking two questions requires more attention and adds flavor and depth to the interaction.

Examples:

One Question

Ms. Daniel: "Where'd you go for vacation?"
Sue: "To Mexico."
Ms. Daniel: "Oh, that's nice."
Conversation flattens. Ms. Daniel may or may not have heard.

Two Question

Ms. Daniel: "Where'd you go for vacation?"
Sue: "To Mexico."
Ms. Daniel: "Oh, that's nice. Did you travel by car or did your family fly?"
Sue: "We went by car to Laredo, then we took a plane to Mexico City where they had that big crash. Then in Mexico City we rented a car and . . ."
Conversation is open and rolling.

One Question

John: "Mr. Acres, I bought my dad the best birthday present I ever bought for anybody."
Mr. Acres: "That sounds exciting. What did you buy him?"
John: "A radio."
Mr. Acres: "That is a special gift!"

Two Question

John: "Mr. Acres, I bought my dad the best birthday present I ever bought for anybody."
Mr. Acres: "That sounds exciting. What did you buy him?"
John: "A radio."
Mr. Acres: "A radio! What kind of radio did you buy for him?"

John: "Well, I was going to get a big one with
                 numbers for a clock but then I decided on
                 a real small one so he could put it by his bed.
                 I got a red one. He likes red the best."

Notice how the interaction feels differently when two questions
are asked.

3. Begin to review your environment noticing physical activities you
   used to enjoy or might enjoy. In considering possible options do not
   neglect the simple inexpensive physical activities such as walking,
   gardening, and puttering.

4. If you have a history of overeating at times or eating too much of the
   wrong things, notice how this behavior is related to the internal
   pressures of stress. Eating is an appropriate and healthful behavior
   in response to only one stimulus—hunger. Responses other than
   eating must be found to stress, tension, and fatigue if overall body
   condition and healthy weight are to be maintained.

NOTES

Coombs, Arthur. *New light on the helping relationship.* Paper presented at the University of Texas
at Austin, Spring, 1969.

Friedman, Meyer and Rosenman, Ray H. *Type A behavior and your heart.* New York, Knopf
Publishers, 1974.

Fromm, Erich. *The art of loving.* New York: Harper & Row Publishers, 1956.

Moustakas, Clark. *Personal growth: The struggle for identity and human values.* Cambridge,
Mass.: Howard A. Doyle Publishing Company, 1969.

Pickhart, Carl. Presentation made at the Region XIII Education Service Center, Austin,
Texas, Fall, 1979.

Rubin, Theodore Isaac, M.D. *Compassion and self hate.* New York: Ballantine Books, 1975.

Chapter 3

Overreacting to Special Education Realities

3

Picture the following scene: You arrive at work in a pleasant mood, collect the mail from your box, and sit down at your desk for a few minutes of repose before the day's work begins. Among the other papers is a notice from central office marked "private mail." The notice explains that as of today all special educators must henceforth record individual student and client progress in a separate file to be kept in the main office of each agency. Records are to be updated every day. These progress accounts are to be kept current without exception and will be audited without notice. This announcement is likely to stimulate an outbreak of stress among those who will be held responsible for this new task. But not all special educators involved will experience the painful effects of stress to the same extent. Some educators will react with extreme anger, some with depression, some with a fear of what's to come. Some will react so strongly that they are able to think or talk about little else. Tempers are likely to run short and isolation from those educators who are not required to complete the new special records is likely to increase. But whether any particular special educator has a short temper or becomes isolated from others will be a matter of that individual's characteristic responding *style*, the physical condition of each special educator, and the extent to which this new environmental contingency actually affects each person.

Research concerned with the experience of pain and stress has shown conclusively that the degree to which the individual feels pain and stress is largely determined not by the characteristics of the external event that "causes" the pain or stress but by certain mediating events (Mahoney, 1974; Davidson, 1976; Woolfolk & Richardson, 1978). Up to now these mediating events have been referred to as thinking patterns or cognitive habits that are the product of certain core beliefs such as the Four Core Beliefs of the SPSE. Because these mediating events are central to learning an effective plan of stress management, and because these mediating events are not easily altered, this chapter will provide a structure for understanding the connection between (1) your immediate environment, (2) your cognitive habits, and, (3) your behavioral and physical responses.

Some of the most definitive research on stress has been concerned with the interrelatedness of these three aspects of experiencing. Repeated studies have shown that changes in your external environment (such as a change in routine suggested at the beginning of this chapter) affect your physical self, and particularly your stress level (Holmes, 1967). However, even the research that carefully and numerically predicts changes in individually experienced stress resulting from changes in environmental circumstances has been under fire. Attempts have been made to replicate the predictability of physical stress in relation to environmental changes. Studies have shown that the degree to which changes in the individual's environment will cause stress cannot be determined simply by identifying potentially stress-inducing events. Mediating events, cognitive habits, or basic thinking approach styles (stress-prone or nonstress-prone) intervene to largely determine eventual stress. The importance of mediating events in the management of body responses has been recognized for centuries. In certain cultures men have walked across burning coals as part of religious ceremonies and have been observed to suffer none of the normal painful effects. Self-regulation of heart rates and blood pressure is accepted as common knowledge. Controlling physical stress through management of internal mediating events is accepted practice in these cultures.

Experiments have demonstrated that by simple external suggestion, people are able to alter their heart rates, blood pressures, and skin temperatures in specified parts of the body with relative ease (Brown, 1974). Brain waves, too, can be altered through suggestion. Donald Meichenbaum and his associates have demonstrated the role of mediating events in the perception and control of pain. In Meichenbaum's studies, overtight blood pressure cuffs were clamped around the arms of subjects who were requested to put up with the pain as long as possible. When the person indicated that the pain was too much to bear, the cuff would be released. The variable to be measured was the length of time between the point when the clamp was first tightened and the point when subjects perceived the pain as intolerable. Prior to training on the influence of mediating events, subjects were able to tolerate the pain for an average of 12 minutes. After brief training in order to understand the role of mediating events and a rehearsal of a variety of behavioral and cognitive coping techniques, subjects were able to extend their pain toleration time to an average of 32 minutes (Meichenbaum, Turk, & Burnstein, 1975). The point here is not so much to note that difficult situations in the special education environment can feel like you have a blood pressure cuff clamped on your arm, your head, or your chest, but to point out that the same mediating processes which so strongly affected Meichenbaum's subjects are the processes by which you manage your stress level.

CHRONIC OVERREACTIONS AND STRESS

The idea that mediating events (rather than external situations) are largely responsible for eventual stress responses is difficult to incorporate during early learning. Instead we learn to blame our stressful feelings and our feelings of relaxation on the luck of circumstances. If our students behave during class, if no extra paperwork is assigned, if everything goes well we have learned to say that we are not stressed *because* of these things. If fate is not with us and behavior problems abound, new requirements for accountability are assigned and the weather takes an unfavorable turn, we accept that our stress is caused by these events. This direct cause and effect association between external events and internal experience is an action-reaction theory that oversimplifies the brain function. The brain that controls your stress responses is not a reflexive organ. Your brain is an *active structuring mechanism* that uses your beliefs and resulting attitudes to design your responses to your environment. Before going further, make note that we are not preparing to launch into a plea for blind positive thinking. If you must be either a blind optimist or a blind pessimist, being a blind optimist would probably be to your mental and physical advantage. Stress management, however, is not based on either approach. Effective stress management for you, as a special educator, includes understanding the basic structure of the mediating process and learning to *react* in emotionally healthy ways to the imperfections, unpredictability, and ambiguity of your special education situation. Stress management also includes learning not to *overreact*.

Stress-prone special educators overreact habitually to imperfections in themselves, other people, and the environment. Overreacting characterizes the SPSE's style since guiding beliefs make the SPSE particularly afraid of the disruptions and difficulties that are an integral part of the special education situation. When imperfections and inconveniences happen to someone who is already engaged in a desperate struggle with other people— someone who is already convinced that not enough time exists—these imperfections and inconveniences become blown out of proportion. Difficulties and unexpected occurrences are seen as threats and unfair obstructions that may cause us to do the unforgivable, that is, cause us to lose time, lose our place in the race with others, and lose in our constant battle to bring complete order to our surroundings.

We need to better grasp the difference between stress-prone overreactions to evidences of imperfections in self, others, and the environment and nonstress-prone reactions to these evidences. It will be helpful to describe fully the mediating processes occurring in the period between the instant the disruptive evidence is noted by an individual and the moment that person's observable reaction begins. The explanation presented below is a condensed version that is drawn from extensive research and writing of psychologists who specialize in the study of mediating processes and behavior. Particular credit is given to Albert Ellis (1962, 1970, 1971), whose prolific and entertaining essays have focused the behavior change spotlight on the importance of cognitions, and to Donald Meichenbaum (1970) and Michael Mahoney (1974), whose research has provided a solid base of positive data to the study of mediating events. The exact details of *how* thinking determines responses remains to be discovered through research. However, the contributions of these scientists and others allow us to state that cognitions are the critical variables in the experiencing of stress.

One can encounter an environmental stressor or one can produce a mental stressor, such as when you remind yourself how hopelessly behind you are or how unfair it is that a particular child has little hope for a productive life. The stress that results from either stressor does not happen through a simple action-reaction process—a once-popular notion based upon a simplified version of the *stimulus-response* theory of behavior. If the stresses you experience were purely a response to the characteristics of your environment, your stress quotient could best be viewed as a beaker of water that is crystal clear when you start out the day and that changes color as a result of every encounter with environmental stressors. Whether or not your beaker (your bloodstream) is hopelessly muddied or relatively clear at the end of your special education work day would depend solely on whether or not events had gone your way. If the action-reaction model accurately described the mediating process between events and reactions, your only hope for reducing stress would be to carefully control your students, your clients, your administrators, and the world so that no unpleasantries and imperfections would come your way. No one who has worked in this field could long maintain a fantasy that special education is going to be cleared of its share of imperfections and surprises. The surprises in human nature are a mainstay of our profession. Fortunately, the stress you experience as a special educator is the result of a more complex mediating process. Making changes in this process will be the focus of the next several chapters and, especially the *Altering Your Cognitions* guidelines at the end of many chapters.

Between the occurrence of the potential stressor and your eventual stress reaction, three mediating processes occur: (1) perception, (2) elaborative interpretation, and (3) feeling. After and as a part of these three, you react internally (stressfully) and externally (behaviorally). Lest this complex and interactive process be seen as explainable in a one, two, three simplistic process, it is important to note that the steps of mediation do not occur slowly or separately from one another. There are no definite lines between what constitutes perception and what constitutes interpretation and there are no lines to separate either of these processes from the process of "feeling." The mediation process happens quickly and continuously with the various steps interacting in intricate cyclical patterns. In the example of being unexpectedly saddled with a time-consuming, new accounting procedure, the resulting feelings (anger or hopelessness) would serve to stimulate new perceptions and interpretations. These, in turn, would then intensify, de-escalate, or change feelings that stimulate new perceptions and interpretations, and the cycle continues.

To follow the steps of the mediating process, let's return to the scene at home in which you have just received that disruptive evening phone call from an irate parent. The first requirement in order for you to initiate a full blown stress response is to *perceive* the occurrence of the event. Now this may seem to you an unnecessary step since most of us are accustomed to believing that, "Of course, we perceive our environment at all times. It's the environment we're reacting to!" However, perception is not so simple a matter; your brain is an active structuring mechanism. This means you do not respond to reality as an absolute and definable entity. You respond to the environment as you design it. Sometimes you respond internally and externally to threats to your well-being that are not there and sometimes you do not perceive and, therefore do not respond to, actual dangers. In the situation with the phone call, if you had been asleep and had never heard the telephone ring, no inward stress would have been experienced. If you didn't answer because you were sure it would be for one of your three teenage daughters, or had answered but had been distracted by other issues, such as a movie on television or a family argument, you would not have perceived the danger. Perception plays an obvious role in the effectiveness of behavior change systems.

Consistent punishment for misbehavior and reinforcement for desired behavior is usually difficult. On those days when we are in a good mood, and are pleased with ourselves, other people, and the world, we simply do not see minor disruptions and rule infractions. On those days when we are not so pleased, even the smallest infraction of the rules is immediately obvious to us. Several guidelines from *Altering Your Environment* involve the occasional arrangement of your schedule to avoid unnecessary perception of potential stressors. For example, if you are terrified of flying or heights, there is no sense sitting next to the window on planes. If you find it difficult to relax on the weekend, going away can separate you from the buildings, books, and papers that remind you of upcoming struggles.

Assuming you have perceived a potential stressor, it is the second process, elaborative interpretation, that determines whether what you have allowed into your realm of attention develops from a *potential stressor* into a *stressor*. As you recall, for an event to result in stress, the perceiving individual must interpret that event as threatening to his or her well-being. To judge whether a potential stressor meets this criterion, it is necessary to interpret the situation based on your experience. Those in the group of SPSEs have had certain real and imagined experiences that lead us to interpret behavior and the events of our environment as threatening to our well-being, as threatening to our right to feel good about ourselves. SPSEs would be more likely than N-SPSEs to interpret the irate parent's phone call as threatening and more likely to experience physical, emotional, interpersonal, and intellectual stress.

Once you have begun the process of interpreting the personal meaning of an event, you next have feelings about the event and then you react externally and internally in accord with your interpretation regarding the positive, negative, or neutral nature of the potential stressor. While listening to the irate parent your level of stress fluctuates dynamically in accord with your changing interpretations of the situation. If Mr. Elmwood makes a statement indicating he is softening, you will likely interpret that as reducing the threat, unless, of course, you interpret his softening as the "quiet before the storm." As Mr. Elmwood accelerates his demands, your ACTH and adrenalin levels will climb *if* these changes in Mr. Elmwood's behavior are interpreted by you as increasing the threat. It could be that in your prior experience, people who are irate on the phone are harmless off the phone, or that people who appear to be reasonable are usually waiting to cause a greater disturbance. Your outward behavior will change continuously to coordinate with your fluctuating perceptions, comparisons with past experiences, and interpretations of the unfolding event. Bodily changes occurring during a stress response interact with behavioral responses so that when adrenal levels are high, you are capable of moving more quickly, striking harder, and running faster. At the same time creative thinking and listening to others becomes more difficult, forcing you to base interpretations more and more on past experiences and less and less on reality factors of the event. Because your feelings, internal responses, and external behaviors stem from your active and continuous interpretations and your special education environment, and since some responses and behaviors are healthier and more effective than others, additional attention to the structure of interpretations is needed.

The Interpretive Structure of a Stress Reaction

Let's suppose you have just received notice that, due to a change in state regulations, your class or case load will be increased by 30 percent during the next two weeks. Most special educators do not believe themselves to be underworked, so it can be assumed this turn of events would serve as a potential stressor. After first perceiving, interpreting, and feeling a typical external reaction might be increased irritability. You might make frequent negative statements about state regulations, state officials (and perhaps federally elected officials), and local central office staff. Energy output would likely decrease along with positive actions. "Dread talk" with colleagues would increase. If eating and drinking behaviors relieved stress in the past, overeating and overdrinking are more likely to occur. Willingness to take part in agency-wide or region-wide activities is likely to decrease. Behavior with students and clients is likely to change as an expression of internal pressures. And behavioral adjustments to interpretations of the troublesome events will not be restricted to the realm of work. Irritability and other distress behaviors are brought home. Typical internal changes are those that represent the body's efforts to deal with social crises by physiological responses.

But these behavioral and physiological reactions can only occur if the potential stressor, for example, the newly imposed regulation, is changed into an actual stressor by your interpretations of the event. The stress behavior(s) will occur only if you actively engage in a continuous process of alerting your brain to danger. This is accomplished by repeating the threatening interpretations to yourself in the form of *self-statements*. Remember the technique described in the Altering Your Cognitions section of the last chapter in which you were directed to repeat certain calming sentences to yourself in the mirror. This is one way to affect your self-statement system. Like everyone else, you maintain an ongoing conversation with yourself that directs your feelings, your external behavior and, to a large extent, your internal reactions. The exact content of your conversation with yourself is influenced by the core beliefs you maintain about yourself, other people, and your environment. The self-statement patterns of SPSEs are different from the self-statement patterns of the N-SPSEs. The self-statement patterns of the SPSE stimulate stress because those statements are based on beliefs that encourage fear, urgency, and struggle. To see how the structure of the self-statement patterns of SPSEs and N-SPSEs differ, it will be helpful to discuss the contrasts between general self-statements that guide overreaction and general self-statements that guide reactions.

The Three Levels of Overreaction Pain

Anytime you involve yourself in a stress-inducing overreaction, you experience three levels of pain: (1) *reality pain*, (2) *omnipotent demand pain*, and (3) *exaggeration pain*. The second two levels are the most destructive and stress-inducing and these are stimulated by self-statement habits not by external events. The first level, *reality pain*, consists of the actual, observable inconveniences, unpleasantries, and difficulties resulting from the stressor event. If a new regulation is instituted that will require you to take on a higher student load, certain quite real and observable difficulties will accompany the regulation. Class arrangements will need to be adjusted. Additional time will be required for planning lessons and staffing meetings. Management systems will need to be reviewed and perhaps altered. Working arrangements, objectives, and activities for present students may need to be adjusted. These additional duties or inconveniences constitute actual results of the event which, since they are not usually conceived as pleasurable, can be labeled the reality pain accompanying the event. Some self-statements regarding reality pain in this circumstance would be similar to these:

- This new regulation will cause my room to be more crowded.
- The new regulation will cause my schedule to be more crowded.
- More time for staffing meetings will be needed.
- I will need to spend more time helping process records or spend less time on the records of each student.
- I will need to reduce my individual time with present students.

If all special educators had to deal with were the inconveniences and difficulties of reality pain, we would still not experience chronic stress and burnout. The frustrations of reality pain come with the territory. Chronic stress and burnout result from acceleration of reality pain into omnipotent demand pain and exaggeration pain.

Reality pain requires only the perception element of mediation. Omnipotent demand pain and exaggeration pain involve interpretations of the event as presented in two specific types of self-statements. *Omnipotent demand pain* results when the reality pain of an imperfection in ourselves, others, or the world becomes evident and that realization is met with our insistent interpretation that whatever has happened *should not* have happened, or that whatever exists, *should not* be the way it is. *Exaggeration pain* follows and is a magnification of omnipotent demand pain. Whatever the actual imperfections of the real event, the magnification of resulting inconveniences and difficulties diminishes our own capacity to tolerate the imperfection. To understand the overreaction process as a learned, habitual responding style for SPSEs, a brief sojourn into child development theory is required.

Each of us learned our stress-prone or nonstress-prone style of responding to imperfections when we were children. As children we did not have the data we now have about ourselves, others, and the world, nor were we very powerful in comparison with others in the environment (especially adults). As a result, in our ignorance and innocence we learned to overreact to reality. As very young children, then, we developed certain mistaken beliefs, particularly those regarding perfection and power. Having no reason to believe otherwise, we believed that perfection was possible and within our power and the power of others. As we moved into the later stages of childhood, evidence against the perfection theories began showing up. Undeniable imperfections were made obvious when others outstripped us in certain areas and adults were seen to be much more skilled in most every area of accomplishment. Not long after we gained some mobility, the limits of our power started to become obvious as well. Other people picked us up, put us down; put us in the bathwater, took us out of the bathwater; gave us treats and let us be with the others—all when the big, powerful people wanted to do so. As we developed and gathered more data about the world and our place in it, our plans for perfection began to look less possible.

Stress-prone individuals do not easily give up beautiful fantasies of perfection and power. We have high hopes for ourselves (and usually so do our mentors and parents) and refuse to settle for less than the pure and ultimate goals plausible to us as young children. In fact, to accept a less-than-perfect self and others became abhorrent. We saw such an approach as the downfall of others not willing to try as hard as we to make perfection a reality. Throughout our growing years, evidence was plentiful to shed doubt on our perfectionistic world view. We rationalized an acceptance of present levels of imperfection and powerlessness by insisting that these were merely conditions of our youthfulness. We assured ourselves that once we were beyond the common trials of immaturity we would be able to realize our plans. As children, we may have been confused, imperfect, inconsistent, and unable to design a perfect self and a perfect environment. But *someday*, we firmly insisted, we would do it.

Of course, we never fulfilled our ideals of perfection and power. Such aspirations were only possible because of the limited information of early life. The differences in the workstyle approach of the SPSEs and the N-SPSEs are products of differences in adjustment to this reality.

Just because imperfect reality is all around us does not mean we SPSEs are willing to accept it! Rather than change our childhood omnipotent standards we developed chronic stress-prone workstyles replete with unrealistic demands on ourselves, time, other people, and events. Nonstress-prone special educators develop workstyles more in line with the possibilities and the limitations of reality. SPSEs do not cling stubbornly to childhood ambitions because we are evil or cavalier. Rather, we are afraid that if we don't, we will not be successful in our pursuit of happiness.

Omnipotent demand pain and exaggeration pain characterize the internal conversations of persons with chronic stress. Pains are direct products of developmental insistence to prove perfection and power. Omnipotent demand pain consists of a series of furious and clear self-statements that only those still hoping for omnipotence can understand—statements insisting that realities we do not like simply *should not* be happening. Relying on our belief that perfection is possible, we are righteously angry when an imperfection has occurred. Something, therefore, is *wrong* and *should be* different. Typical omnipotent demand or *should statements* the SPSE might rehearse covertly in an increased class load situation would include:

- This should not be happening.
- Our local administrative officials should have prevented this from happening.
- Our local administration should have warned me that this was going to happen.
- The general public shouldn't be allowed to elect officials who are going to determine such policies because they don't know anything about what is really happening.
- The people who decided on this regulation should spend a few days with my schedule.
- This should not happen to a professional.
- So much money should not be spent on highways and state office buildings if budget cuts are necessary.
- The other teachers should volunteer to take over some of my other duties since this has happened.
- My college professors should have given me a more realistic picture of the demands on a special educator.
- My father was right; I should have married someone rich so I wouldn't have to worry about this.
- I should be able to handle this better.
- I should be able to handle this without getting upset.
- I should not have to put up with this.
- I should have had the good sense to go into some other kind of work.

Once we have metaphorically stamped our feet and begun our *should statement* campaign, the stress that was born of the original circumstance is rapidly accelerated. *Should statements* reflect an unwillingness to accept our limited power as well as our unwillingness to work comfortably with imperfection. The use of the term *should* implies that one is rightful and deserving of the power necessary to change things into what they *should* be. *Should statements* carry a stress-stimulating intensity born of our SPSE belief that we should be able to completely control our own development and our changing surroundings. We learn not to trust ourselves and others enough to consider accepting anything less than total control. Concomitant with omnipotent demand pain, we rehearse descriptive magnifications of the imperfection. The self-statements that account for exaggeration pain are most easily referred to as *it's terrible statements*. The purpose of this self-talk is to punish ourselves and sometimes others because things "should be" different. *It's terrible statements* express (repetitively) our outrage at this evidence of limited power and perfection. Energy is unleashed equal to the degree to which we have been afraid of anything less than complete control and predictability. With a discomforting situation facing us, we reject soundly an imperfect reality and choose instead to believe that whatever it is that has occurred is unacceptable, and even unbearable.

We proclaim that we "cannot stand" the situation and, if others will listen sympathetically, we can put together a heart-catching horror story describing the devastating characteristics of the event. Typical exaggeration statements to accompany *should statements* about the imposed class load increase might include:

- This is terrible!
- Special education is a terrible field to be in.
- This is unfair!
- This is unbelievable.
- Those people who did this are terrible.
- I cannot stand for this to happen.
- This is unbearable.
- My supervisor is terrible for not warning me.
- My college professors are terrible for not warning me about special education in the real world.
- I am awful for getting myself into this mess.
- I am terrible for overreacting like this.
- I can't stand the way I feel about myself.
- My day is ruined.
- My work is ruined.
- My year is ruined.

Once you have accelerated reality pain into a genuine self-stimulating stress cycle through *should statements* and *it's terrible statements*, your body-mind is out of balance and primed to help you struggle physiologically against the social enemy. Your capacities for competency and positive feelings are reduced. Once the overreaction cycle is under way, external behavior changes so that we do not behave in ways we would choose otherwise. Our hurry behaviors intensify to match our desperation or we clench our fists, talk too loud, eat too much, and alienate people with whom we need to maintain positive relations. But overreacting does involve making a choice. Nonstress-prone special educators do not have the cognitive habit of hurling *should statements* and *exaggeration statements* at unpleasant realities. As a result stress, as well as their general sense of satisfaction, remain at more comfortable levels.

Although early learning may prevent a full-fledged SPSE from becoming a total N-SPSE, there is hope. We can examine the characteristic ways we overreact and in a stepwise relearning process we can practice and habituate to new ways. This means learning to rehearse the kinds of self-statements N-SPSEs rehearse already as a result of functioning from a gentler core of beliefs about themselves and the environment. Procedures for beginning to change in this direction are described in the Altering Your Cognitions section at the close of this chapter. More explicit procedures will be given in the same section of each subsequent chapter as the specific issues of reacting to imperfections in yourself, others, and the environment are treated individually.

Altering Your Environment

1. Make note of the potential stressors in your special education situation to which you are particularly vulnerable. Vary the intensity of your responses to potential stressors from mild to extreme in order to heighten your awareness of the personal control you have in managing stress. Specific steps for reducing stress acceleration will follow in the next section and later chapters. But you can begin to alter the balance of control between your environment and yourself by purposely varying your reaction responses in both directions.

Altering Your Cognitions

1. Practice substituting *preference statements* for *omnipotent demand statements, antiexaggeration statements* for *exaggeration statements.* To use this procedure to manage cognitively inspired stress, you will need to actually write your way through the stress reduction, self-statement changing process. Before working through an example, note first the essential differences between *omnipotent demand* or *should statements* and the N-SPSE's *preference statements* and note the differences between *exaggeration* or *it's terrible statements* and the N-SPSE's *antiexaggeration statements.*

- *SPSE's should statements* (1) imply a demand that things be different than they are, (2) involve an intensity bordering on or concomitant with anger, and (3) imply that if the situation is not changed, the should statement maker cannot be comfortable and relaxed. *Key phrase:* These statements include in some form the use or implied use of the word "should."

- *N-SPSE's preference statements* (1) imply that the speaker is not pleased with the way things are, (2) imply a desire for change in the situation, and (3) do not imply that the speaker will be upset and uncomfortable if change does not occur. *Key phrase:* These statements include the stated or implied use of the term "I would prefer."

- *SPSE's exaggeration statements* (1) express outrage and anger at the situation, (2) are loaded with emotionally charged dramatic adjectives, (3) are usually spoken in a loud or strained voice accompanied by gestural expressions of stress and distress, and (4) usually include phrases that overplay the effect of the situation or condition on overall functioning. These phrases are designed to assure the listener (oneself or others) that the strength does not exist to tolerate the undesirable situation or condition. *Key phrase:* These statements include in stated or implied terms the adjectives *terrible, awful, unfair, unbearable, infuriating, intolerable,* and others.

- *N-SPSE's antiexaggeration statements* (1) downplay the potential unpleasant emotionality of less than desired situations or conditions, (2) are loaded with neutral and mild adjectives, and (3) include phrases that reinforce personal abilities to internally and externally adjust to undesired situations and conditions. *Key phrase:* These statements include in stated or implied form the adjectives, *unfortunate, unpleasant, inconvenient, less than perfect, disappointing,* and others.

Note the following example describing the self statements made by an SPSE and a N-SPSE in the same less-than-perfect situation. For one example, let's suppose that both special educators have just completed making an intensive, well organized presentation of instructions to three students working together on a team reading presentation. On walking away from the trio, the educator overhears the students closing their workbooks and planning to ditch the project as soon as the "general" starts in with the "dumb reading group." Both the SPSE and the N-SPSE react to the same event, but the self-statements directing internal and external behavior are quite different.

SPSE's Reacting Statements	N-SPSE's Reacting Statements
This should not be happening.§ They should not be so disinterested in learning.§ They should not be disrespectful of my efforts.§ I shouldn't be so concerned about them anyway.§ I should be able to	I wish this weren't happening.§ I would definitely prefer to have seen this coming.§ I would like it if things like this never happened.§ I would like it if students were always interested in what I taught.

maintain their interest better.§I should have been more aware of how they really felt about the project.§I should know the right thing to do right now.

This is terrible, unfair, and ridiculous. § This is humiliating, and infuriating.§I cannot stand to be treated this way.§This is awful and ruins my whole class.

This is a less-than-perfect situation.§This will mean inconvenience and perhaps more unpleasantries.

Perhaps the phrases of the N-SPSE sound stilted and even funny to you. That's okay. The idea is to familiarize you with the terms used and to help to make you aware of alternatives to typical SPSE overreaction habits. At this stage in your stress management program, you can begin trading overreactions for reactions by transcribing the chart shown in Exhibit 3-1 to a large sheet of paper and completing each step of the process as explained. Use situations from your own environment.

Exhibit 3-1 Overreactions to Reactions

Step 1. Identify the stressor. What condition or event did you use as a trigger for the overreaction response?_____

Step 2. What kinds of self-destructive internal and external behaviors are you exhibiting?_____

Step 3. What *should statements* are you rehearsing?_____

Step 4. What *exaggeration statements* are you rehearsing?_____

Step 5. What *preference statements* could you be rehearsing?_____

Step 6. What antiexaggeration statements could you be rehearsing?

Altering Your Physical and Behavioral Approaches

1. Search out an N-SPSE within your agency and observe their reactions to imperfections. Note particularly:

- facial expressions,
- speed of verbal response,
- level of expressed hostility,
- level of expressed pain, and,
- length of reaction responses to less-than-perfect situations.

Imitation of others receives much bad press during childhood when being a "copycat" is of low social merit. We learn to be afraid that if someone else does something first, it's not honorable to follow their example. But much can be learned by adults who watch other adults and copy their actions. Locate an N-SPSE to watch and then for short periods talk at the rate the N-SPSE would talk, walk at the rate the N-SPSE would walk and respond to your students with an exaggerated calmness and gentleness.

NOTES

Brown, Barbara. *New mind, new body*. New York: Harper & Row, 1974.

Davidson, Park O. (Ed.). *The behavioral management of anxiety, depression and pain*. New York: Brunner/Mazel Publishers, 1976.

Ellis, Albert. *Reason and emotion in psychotherapy*. New York: Lyle Stuart Publishers, 1962.

Ellis, Albert. *Growth through reason*. Hollywood, California: Wilshire Book Company, 1971.

Ellis, Albert & Harper, Robert. *A guide to rational living*. Englewood Cliffs, NJ; Prentice-Hall, 1970.

Holmes, Thomas J. Social Readjustment Scale. *Journal of Psychosomatic Research*, 1967, (II), 213-218.

Mahoney, Michael J. *Cognition and behavior modification*. Cambridge, MA: Ballinger Publishing Company, 1974.

Meichenbaum, Donald; Turk, Dennis & Burnstein, Sam. The Nature of Coping With Stress. The University of Waterloo, Waterloo, Ontario, Canada. Paper presented at the NATO Conference on Stress held at Oslo, Norway, 1975.

Woolfolk, Robert L. & Richardson, Frank C. *Stress, sanity and survival*. New York: Sovereign Books, 1978.

Chapter 4

The Special Educator as Superperson

4

In spite of our best attempts to make advised changes and in spite of our own unfatiguing effort, special education is still loaded with potential stress factors. Usually, programs for reducing personal stress focus on identifying stressful elements in order to change them. But many times making such a change in the environment causes as much stress as it alleviates. (This reality is often experienced by special educators in direct service when new laws are passed to improve programs for the handicapped.) Frequently, situations exist as potential stressors which we simply have no power to change. To maintain control over stress levels in these situations, you must reconsider old ideas born of the stress-prone workstyle approach—ideas about the goals of special education and your own place and particular job within it. Eventual stress will be determined much more by your workstyle than by the specifics of your situation.

The cognitive habits that most constantly affect your stress level as a special educator are the thoughts you rehearse about *yourself*. The person you talk about most often, and the person that upsets you most often is yourself. You need to make a special effort to learn a healthy, nonstressful way to discuss yourself with yourself. You are likely to experience tension and stress if you rely on childhood standards for judging your right to relax and if you rely on cultural trends for judging the worth of individuals. Stress is a wearing force. Pain results when thinking habits keep us in a more or less continuous state of alarm. SPSEs have learned to respond to themselves in a state of continuous alarm.

THE SELF-WORTH HOAX AND STATEMENTS
OF SELF-DOWNING

Those experiencing frequent stress and tension have overlearned the childhood practice of continuous self-evaluation. As children we were taught and we believed that if we were good long enough and worked hard long enough our efforts would be evaluated and we would earn self-worth. We believed that through our own efforts we could guarantee a time when we wouldn't have problems or nagging doubts. It's important to remember that stress does not result automatically from working hard, working long hours, or working at a hectic pace. It is the driving force, the *motive*, behind your striving efforts that determines whether internal danger occurs. In many articles stress and the long- and short-term effects of stress have been treated as the automatic results of desiring and working to be successful in one's chosen field. It is seen as necessary if one is to achieve success. The result of such misinterpretations has been a flurry of studies demonstrating that successful people do not experience ill health any more frequently than do less successful people. For example, in an article in *Psychology Today* on the long-term results of the Terman study concerning the adult lives of persons identified as children to be exceptionally intelligent, the author writes:

> If Terman's people have not turned out to be that exceptional, however, their lives do offer some fresh perspectives on a few contemporary issues. As some stress researchers have been suggesting recently, it appears that brilliant, hard-driving, success-seekers do not inevitably succumb to early heart attacks or to other stress-induced ailments; indeed, the mortality rate of the least successful Terman subjects was twice that of the most successful (Coleman, 1980, pp. 28-54).

Actually these findings are just what could be expected from the stress research of Friedman and Rosenman (1974).

It is not hard work or success that causes stress. Neither does a stress-prone daily workstyle necessarily result in success. Success and stress are not related in the equivocal fashion implied by popular articles or simplified statements. Stress is a physiological event with emotional, interpersonal, psychological, intellectual, and spiritual consequences. This event is influenced to a chronic condition by a severe physical or environmental trauma or by a particular workstyle and lifestyle approach. There is no reason to expect N-SPSEs to achieve less success in special education and logically their efforts in this humanistic profession could result in gains that surpass those of us deep in constant struggle.

There are special educators who have worked through childhood demands for perfection and approval and who work hard and long from an intrinsic joy and personal style. How can one tell a high energy, nonstressed individual such as this from an SPSE? High energy N-SPSEs are not tense in their work and are not anxious about the future. They can be easily distinguished from stress-prone types by their relaxed facial expressions, the easy twinkle in their eyes, and the fact that these serene but busy folks aren't dashing about in a dither, and do not mind our interruptions. Those experiencing stress, whether working hard or merely worrying, are doing what we are doing in an effort to earn worthwhileness, out of a fear that we may not succeed. SPSEs can be spotted by furrowed brows, short patience, an inability to relax and an insistence on the pressure-cooker nature of our jobs.

SPSEs experience an internal sense of pressure in our work as special educators because we buy the idea that when and only when we accomplish worthwhileness will we have the right to be relaxed and comfortable on the job. This guiding idea provides daily impetus for our struggle attitude toward the job. Special education as a field becomes the battleground for acting out our fight to prove worthwhileness. In an earlier section it was emphasized that your body reacts with a stress response when you perceive your well-being in danger. If you believe you must have and deserve the right to be comfortable and self-accepting on the job (as determined by one measuring stick or another), you will perceive your well-being as threatened frequently, in fact, almost continuously. Caught in the "fight for worthwhileness" you will make unreasonable and insatiable demands on yourself regarding the level of performance you must provide and the level of approval from others you must have in order to abandon the internal, tiger-fighting stress response.

This idea—that you must struggle and then deserve the right to accept yourself, to be relaxed, and perhaps even to like yourself—is a well-accepted element of our cultural fabric that just doesn't happen to provide healthy living situations for adults. We do not start out as young children believing we must deserve self-acceptance. This lesson is taught to inspire us toward fulfillment of potentials and toward securing respectable positions in the overall economic system. Also, we are taught struggle behaviors because others feared for our safety and were afraid we would not be able to take care of ourselves. There is a drive behind the belief that self-acceptance can only be achieved by the continuous collection of successful performances and approval from others. It is the unreasonable fear other people in our past and present have that without these evidences either we "won't make it" (whatever that means) and/or that they will not permit themselves self-acceptance if we do not prove worthwhile.

The belief that self-acceptance must be won through performance and approval is the backbone of the *self-worth hoax* which, when bought by special educators, turns daily learning experience encounters into ongoing trials of worthwhileness. Caught in the self-worth hoax you as a special educator are perpetually in danger, your well-being is precariously balanced at best and if you are to survive in reasonable comfort, you must make no mistakes, must never let down, and must never have any "average" days. If any of these events do occur—whoosh—your self-worth is taken away, your well-being is threatened, and your stress response goes into protective action. This phenomenon is described as a hoax because self-worth by the very nature of the title presumably is concerned with what *you think of yourself*. In other words, self-worth is an internal cognitive function that is decided totally by mediating activities in your mind. Self-worth then is something your decide for yourself and something that cannot be decided by any standard measurement or qualified or unqualified opinion from another person. The hoax element is introduced when we recognize that, while self-worth is a product of our mind (or even our imagination), we have learned to give up our right to decide our value. We switch the meaning of the term self-worth from its logical origin and now define self-worth in terms of what other people may think we're worth and how we measure up alongside others.

Self-worth has become "other-worth." With this transition we have given up the precious right to accept and even to like ourselves, that is, to possess self-worth, unless we deserve it. Self-worth is constantly up for review as judged by apparent ongoing success. In our achievement oriented, consumer culture it may seem heresy to suggest that the most valuable attribute any special educator can learn is to accept and like themselves separate from their performances as special educators and separate from other people's opinions of these performances. The claim of heresy will be made because on the surface it looks as though goading ourselves and others with the discomfort of "never being quite good enough to relax" is the only way to keep ourselves and others working and progressing. Unfortunately (or fortunately, if you are ready to give up stress proneness), withholding self-acceptance contingent on performance backfires. Creative energy is transformed to anxiety and tension as we worry about the possibility that we do not perform well. We spend our on-task energy evaluating ourselves rather than being involved in the experience. The self-trust once guiding our behavior is pushed aside by fear; energy is turned to self-directed and other-directed hostility. Personal and professional goals based on an accurate assessment of individual needs are traded for goals imposed (probably not directly) from others since performances only count toward worthwhileness if they are in certain areas deemed admirable by others. And since working everyday with the inward pressures of self-dissatisfaction creates its own devastating brand of frustration, the ability to relate with others and our environment is reduced.

When you believe that you are an acceptable and worthwhile person regardless of how well you perform and regardless of what others believe about you, you are able to reach your best functioning as a special educator. This means taking back your right to decide your own self-worth which won't be easy and to which purpose the rest of this chapter is devoted.

To illustrate how personal energy and the right to feel good about yourself is affected by how you determine personal worth, imagine for a moment the following sequence of events. You and your colleagues are seated around a large circular table playing a game of poker. The poker game is actually the game of special education and the chips with which you are playing are "self-worth chips" representing the personal energy you invest in the field. As the game opens, you are aware that self-worth is clearly your own product. You are also aware that because of this, the number of chips you have to play with at any time will be completely up to you. This being the case you know you can manufacture all the chips you desire and that regardless of your luck in the game you will be safe as a person and comfortably loaded with chips. If your supply runs low you will need only to generate more from your infinite, cognitive self-worth storehouse. This poker game of special education is characterized by high energy, cooperation among players, and an overall sense of enjoyment of the experience. The experience is enjoyed in the present since it is irrelevant which player ends up with the tallest stack of chips. The game is not being played to find out which player is going to be worth more than any other player; such a concept is absurd in this game. In this game special educators play freely with the chips at hand. Loans to other players are made as needed, without second thoughts, and without requests to guarantee a return. (After all, who needs someone to promise to verify one's worthwhileness when you know you can do it for yourself?) Communication channels are open with players sharing information and providing helpful ideas for one another. As in most poker games, the procedure calls for you to bet that your hand is the best at the table. With each round of betting you receive an additional card and thereby have an even clearer idea of your chances of winning. Since you are confident of your ability to manufacture your own supply of chips, in this game you stay in every hand dealt. Round after round, even though your cards are not always very promising, even though each hand isn't the best, you invest energy and enthusiasm from your endless personal supply. You take risks and try new possibilities. This special education poker game is interesting for all and threatening to no one.

Now, let's imagine that you are in the same game of special education but someone now comes in and informs the group that you have been playing the game all wrong. You are informed that from now on each player is allowed to play with only the self-worth chips each *deserves*. Instantly stacks in front of you and those kept by the other players shrink. Defensively, players rush to protect the chips they do have. Now that the right to feel relaxed, the right to possess self-worth must be earned on a continuously observable basis, the texture of the game changes. The enjoyment of the experience is lost as players focus all attention on surviving the game with a reasonably-sized stack of chips. Attention goes to who is going to feel good *when it's over* rather than *what is going on*. Sharing is minimal since chips are so hard to come by. Communication is stifled since chips must be earned and are valued on a comparative basis. To let others in on vital information could lessen one's own chances for winning self-worth. Fear of losing what one has and dissatisfaction with oneself for not earning more chips are the predominant motivations in the game. Since being good and working hard are supposed to bring the evidence of self-worth needed so desperately in order to survive, each player focuses energy on personal inadequacies, imperfections, and tasks undone, seeing these as unforgivable lost chances in which chips could have been earned. No longer are you willing to take a chance on any hand. Instead, like the other players, you learn to fold your cards frequently before you have enough information about the hand. What was once a game has become a struggle. By now you know what that means: The habit of basing self-worth on the products of performance and approval is a critical element in the development of a stress-prone approach to working as a special educator.

EARNING SELF-WORTH THROUGH PERFORMANCE

Becoming *stress managed* does not mean that you do not care about whether or not you perform well as a special educator; of course you care. To be stress managed means that relaxation and self-acceptance do not depend on your ongoing infallible performance. Being stress managed means learning the difference between "preferring to" do a good job and "having to" do a good job. When you have to put on a continually outstanding performance, every mistake, every evidence that your performance is not perfect (or up to your self-imposed standard) will result in a threat to your well-being. Notice the differences between cognitions of the special educator *demanding* a continuously outstanding performance and the special educator *preferring* one.

Demander (SPSE)	Preferrer (N-SPSE)
I have to do this well.§I should do this well.§If I don't do this well, I cannot accept myself.§If I do not do this well, it will be terrible.§If I do not do this well, I cannot possibly be as comfortable as I was before.	I would like to do this well.§I would prefer to do this well.§If I don't do this well, I will be disappointed.§If I do not do this well, I will regret it, but there is no reason for me to be less comfortable than I was before.

Of course, as a professional you have a preference for doing a good job. Giving up basing your worth on your performance will enhance, not destroy that performance. In addition you will have greater freedom to enjoy your work. It's difficult to have fun when the outcome of what you are doing is going to be used to determine whether or not you are a worthwhile person.

Distinguishing yourself as a person separate from the things that you do or the labels you carry is the essence of ridding yourself of the performance trap. But don't expect this to be easy since in childhood few of us were encouraged to have confidence in making this separation. As children we were truly dependent on our performances and our abilities to win approval. If other more powerful people did not approve of our performances or approve of us in general, as dependent, unpowerful persons we could suffer greatly. Our freedom, privileges, and even our material pleasures depended on performance and approval-seeking skills. To a much lesser extent this is still true for adults. Along with being required to take over the responsibility of caring for ourselves, came greater privileges. However, the problem is that we overlearned our childhood lessons. To develop the internal cognitive freedom to choose how we will feel when performing less-than-perfectly is usually difficult. When we fail to throw off the childhood lesson that equates our worth with our performances, we, in fact, *become our performances*. This strips us of our unique humanity.

Labels are shortcut ways of talking about people with a common characteristic. While labels are convenient, the shortcut nature of labels lumps large numbers of unlike individuals together and leads us to assume that because these persons have one characteristic in common, they have many other characteristics in common as well. Separating your unique, worthwhile self from your special education performance will mean separating yourself from your special education labels. Throughout this book I have referred to the reader as a special educator simply because the major intended audience is special educators. But the use of even this label is regrettably limiting. To accomplish the skills we are now describing, one important task will be to work on viewing yourself not as a special educator (which defines you by your performance), but rather seeing yourself as a physical, social, intellectual, emotional, and spiritual individual who happens to be *doing* special education. At a recent training seminar with a large group of special educators, the specific topics presented were separating self-worth from performance and the importance of viewing oneself as a person doing a job rather than "being" a job. After the session I had a special rush of pleasure to note how the participants had filled out the attendance roster. Under the column labeled "Position" each participant had written "unique and exciting person doing special education." Now that was fun to read. Your job is something you do; it is not who you are.

Before going on to discuss self-worth based on approval it needs to be mentioned that for SPSEs, the realms of performance that must be up to standard before self-worth is granted are not confined to activities of the job. The dedicated, stress-prone individual demands an excellent performance in every area of living. The SPSE falls prey early in life to our cultural push for superiority in every characteristic and endeavor. As a result, SPSEs are not willing to settle for less than being an excellent special educator, spouse, parent, housekeeper, groundskeeper, cook, conversationalist, financier, driver, direction-finder, party-giver, shopper—the list goes on forever. Now, of course, being human we fail to meet our demands for superiority in all areas. But we cling steadfastly to the belief that the struggle we have accepted is the only way to ever gain the right to relax. The result is the dissatisfaction motivation that SPSEs use to spur themselves on into battle.

In the previous chapter the three levels of pain experienced in frustrating situations were described. To see how these relate to cognitions regarding oneself, let's examine several frequent overreaction habits that are rehearsed by the SPSE when encountering a less-than-desired personal performance. In this case, let's say the SPSE has just reviewed the progress made by a particular student and has discovered that training methods used over the last teaching quarter have not been at all effective in helping the student to improve. On receiving the bad news, the SPSE first experiences *reality pain*. There will be certain, tangible inconveniences caused by this situation. Immediately on the heels of reality pain will be the real stress producers: *omnipotent demand pain* and *exaggeration pain*. The SPSE is likely to react with statements such as "This shouldn't be," "I should have done a better job," and "I should have done something else." These statements directed toward denial of reality will be followed with exaggerations such as, "This is horrible," "This is ridiculous," "I can't stand this," and "I am awful for letting this happen." Compare this reaction with that of the N-SPSE:

SPSE	N-SPSE
Reality pain statement	*Reality pain statement*
Reality pain is the same.	Reality pain is the same.
Should pain statements	*Preference statements*
This shouldn't be. I should have done a better job. I should have done something.	I wish this hadn't happened. I would like it if I had done something earlier.
Exaggeration pain statements	*Antiexaggeration statements*
This is horrible. This is ridiculous. I can't stand this. I am awful for letting this happen.	This is unfortunate. While this is unpleasant and not what I had hoped, it is not a disaster.

Our stress-prone teachings warn us that if we do not feel awful about such evidences of less-than-superior performance, we won't try to improve. The N-SPSE is actually more likely to be able to make an energetic and sincere response to the problem because the N-SPSE is not going to be wasting energy fighting with himself or herself and the student. SPSEs have to find someone or some source for the internal pain we experience and often, after we attack ourselves, our students and clients are chosen as the targets. Free yourself from basing your stress level on your performance by considering the following reasons that you may be doing so now. When your stress level is based on your performance:

- Any time of comfort with yourself and your job must be tenuous and temporary because, at any moment, your performance level could drop.
- You will only feel positive and strong on those days when others choose to cooperate.
- Standards for acceptable performances are undependable. The more you do, the more you will demand of yourself before permission to relax is given.
- You will use performance standards to judge the right of clients and students to feel good about themselves as people.
- Mistaken and less-than-perfect performances will be exaggerated.
- Since you can only relax *after* proven performances, you will not be able to relax and do your best job *during* your performances.
- Since performances are usually evaluated in terms of how well others are doing, your relationships with others will be damaged as you compete for the right to be worthwhile.

EARNING SELF-WORTH THROUGH APPROVAL

Snell and Gail Putney (1974) describe the approval struggle in their sociology classic, *The Adjusted American.*

> The struggle to achieve indirect self-acceptance is a pervasive pattern of American normalcy—a very normal neurosis. Not all seek indirect self-acceptance in the same way, but wherever they are and whatever they are doing, adjusted Americans devote the major share of their time, energy, and assets to seeking the acceptance and approval of others. (p. 73)

Research into the characteristic behaviors of stress-prone individuals has shown that not only are such persons inordinately concerned with their performances but they are also inordinately concerned with other people's impressions of them. In other words, SPSEs allow criticism from others to upset them more than do N-SPSEs. Because of this tendency much stress is self-induced during an ordinary work day because SPSEs fear criticism. And as special educators responsible for others with conflicting needs, this hyper-susceptibility to criticism is most hazardous.

A simple study, reviewed by Meyer Friedman (1979) at the Houston Institute for the Advancement of Human Behavior Conference, demonstrated in measurable terms how this sensitivity to criticism results in stress problems. In the study, subjects were first divided into stress-prone (Type A) and nonstress-prone (Type B) categories. Each subject was then engaged in an electronic game of "pong" or electronic table tennis with an opponent whom they were told was another experimental subject. Actually, the pong playing opponent was in on the experiment and had been trained thoroughly to play the game with professional expertise. Needless to say, the true experimental subjects lost every match by large margins. Before playing the game each subject's heart rate, blood pressure, and blood serum levels of substances related to artery disease were taken. After the game measurements were taken again and, as would be expected, the stress-prone subjects registered greater increases in heart rate, blood pressure, and fatty substances in the blood. This finding relates to the SPSE's harsh self-treatment on noticing a less-than-desired performance. To test the differential effects of criticism, the experimenters repeated the experiment with an added factor. In this trial, not only did the "professional" pong player clobber every opponent but, rather than play quietly as before, this time the professional pong player harshly criticized the losing subjects' efforts. Again heart rate, blood pressure, and blood content measurements were taken before and after the game. This time the differences between the changes experienced by stress-prone and nonstress-prone individuals were significantly greater than before. The stress-prone individuals reacted significantly more strongly to the criticism than did the others.

How does this finding relate to the survival and pleasant experiencing of the special educator? Survival as a special educator depends on the availability of personal energy and the capacity of the job to provide a long term, positive effect for you. Personal energy is not easily available to special educators who frequently rehearse the omnipotent demand statement, "I should be approved of for everything I do." Constant attention to approval or to avoiding disapproval takes away from your ability to do your job. Again this is not to say you wouldn't prefer to receive absolute approval for everything you do, but that you don't *have to* have it to stay relaxed and comfortable in the job. To know the difference between preferring total approval and demanding total approval is a tricky proposition. Most of us grew up accepting compulsive approval seeking as normal and typical behavior.

Approval seeking as a special educator can best be viewed as seeking permission from others to exist without turning on yourself, without inducing damaging stress. Since special educators are trained to meet everyone else's needs before their own, it is fairly easy to see how we could get into the habit of stressing ourselves whenever anyone indicates dissatisfaction with our ability to do this. But this style of "holding our breath" until everyone is happy has a number of damaging results besides the eventual effects on our body. We become obsessed with details, obsessed with managing or hiding our weaknesses, and we begin to shrink from situations in which we are not absolutely sure of total approval. We do not try out new ideas and programs since we can't be sure of success. Demanding approval from everyone in order to be relaxed turns us into *feedback hogs* who always seek attention and gratitude from others. Overconcerned with feedback, our relationships with supervisors and coworkers become strained.

Of course, the greatest problem with basing your right to be relaxed on receiving continuous approval from others is that the process fails miserably and is extremely time consuming. The process fails because there are so many different people to please and they (the diagnosticians, the counselors, and the parents) require that you behave differently to each one in order to receive his or her continual and positive feedback. The process also fails because approval seeking is a fulltime job and I assume that you already have one fulltime job. Stress-prone special educators overconcerned with approval usually overburden themselves with "too much to do" since taking on all these tasks merits nods from others. Any refusal could bring with it that dreaded look of discontent from others. The "too much to do" burden is further complicated. We refuse to delegate tasks that could be done by others because we fear disapproval for the mistakes others might make, too.

The Four Core Beliefs of the SPSE relate clearly to the demand for absolute approval. Our struggle behavior, our hurry sickness, our lack of self-trust and trust in others all are partly due to a pressing inner need to be sure to do what's right and admirable in the eyes of others—even when others aren't around to watch. Managing our struggle and hurry approach won't necessarily mean becoming brazen nonconformists who do not care what others think of our behavior. Adopting a stress-managed workstyle approach means developing a strong self-trust. This enables us to discover the energy that comes with taking back the right to feel good about ourselves separately from the continuously received feedback from others.

Here are some reasons to abandon the practice of basing self-worth on other people's approval. When your right to be relaxed is based on approval:

- Your energy and actions must be dictated by the values and methods of others.

- Since other people in the profession are confusingly unique, what pleases one won't please another.
- You won't have time for anything else since approval seeking requires full time attention.
- Any relaxation experienced will always be tenuous and temporary since at any moment the dreaded disapproval could occur.
- Some people whose approval you work the hardest to gain will be too busy to supply your needs.
- Your permission to feel good will always depend on the moods of other people.
- You will be reluctant to try anything new, to risk.
- There will always be one or several coworkers, supervisors, clients, or students who will not be pleased.
- Approval seeking is tiring, leading to a particular kind of exhaustion that is known to turn into irritability.
- The pressure to receive approval is transferred to students and clients who then must progress in order to keep you feeling okay.

Managing your stress level in the face of disapproval will mean altering your habitual cognitive responses. Specifically you will need to alter your demand to always have approval in every situation in order to stay relaxed and satisfied. Note the following comparison of the SPSE's and the N-SPSE's responses to disapproval. For this example let's assume that the school principal observed this teacher's class on one of its bad days and the teacher noted that as the principal left the room, she shook her head and expressed distress.

SPSE	N-SPSE
Reality pain	*Reality pain*
Reality pain is the same.	Reality pain is the same.
Should pain statements	*Should pain statements*
I should have her approval at all times.§I have to have her approval now.	I would prefer having her approval at all times.§I would like it if I had gained her approval now.
Exaggeration pain statements	*Antiexaggeration pain statements*
I am a terrible, awful, hopeless person because I do not have the principal's approval.§I cannot stand this disapproval. Everything is ruined.§I can't stand this.§	It is certainly inconvenient to not have my principal's approval.§This disapproval is an undesirable experience that I know I can stand because I'm obviously still here.§

Now I cannot be relaxed and like myself.

It is unfortunate that I do not receive absolute approval when it would be so nice.§While having this happen is unpleasant, staying tense will not help the situation.

The statements of the N-SPSE may seem stilted or strange and are not meant to be repeated verbatim when you experience unpleasantries on the job. The hope is that you will be able to contrast preferences and demands and thus work on changing overreactions to your own reactions.

Self-Trust over Insatiable Ambition

Managing personal stress on the job in part means switching from a focus on dissatisfaction motivation and self-distrust to a position of self-acceptance and self-trust. This means refusing to base your self-worth or right to remain energetic and comfortable on the success of your performances and on others' expressed approval. The threatening, stress-prone, self-beating style of motivation decrees that if we weren't afraid of self-rejection and if we didn't degrade ourselves, we wouldn't accomplish anything. This attitude has to go. In its place the stress-managed special educator can rely on the motivation that comes from involvement in a growing experience, in an experience in which you can only bloom since your self-worth isn't on the line.

FIVE ENERGY DRAINING HABITS OF THE SPSE

Several energy draining habits of the SPSE, products of the other-directedness problem, deserve special attention. Without giving up the following five habits you are unlikely to be able to develop a healthy, self-trusting, relationship with yourself, others (particularly clients or students), and your job. The demands of these five habits are such that the side effects nearly always include: 1) a self-punishing inner dialogue, 2) a run-down physical condition, 3) a disintegrated, nonsatisfying environment, and 4) social deprivation.

The Habit of Expecting Perfection

As a mature individual perhaps you think you no longer have such an unreasonable expectation of yourself. But when was the last time you were surprised when you made a mistake? When was the last time you forgot something at home that you needed at work? When did you last drop or break something? If you handled a situation poorly, did you chastise yourself as though being less-than-perfect came as an intolerable surprise to you? Remember that as children, we believed that big people had it made and that big people could be perfect if they wanted to and if they tried hard enough. So why, then, do we keep making errors? Children are not as knowledgeable as we are about what being an adult means. Only as our knowledge of ourselves and the world increases, are we able to see that, regardless of our achievements, we are fallible. We have weaknesses as well as strengths. On some days or during some hours, our weaknesses are more apparent than at other times. This knowledge will not result in a stress-prone style unless we refuse reality and continue to overreact to every evidence of personal imperfection. The *stress prone plus* special educator views every evidence of imperfection as evidence of inadequacy as a person. When one's adequacy as a human being is threatened with every less-than-perfect experience (or every experience in which imperfection "could" occur), stress and tension becomes a painful, typical way of life. To alter the habit of expecting perfection from yourself consider altering your thinking from the typical stress-prone responses to the N-SPSE's responses as outlined in the example situations below.

SPSE Response to Mistakes

Reality pain
Reality pain is the same.

Should pain statements
I should not have made this mistake. (I'm grown up now. Why do I keep making mistakes?)

Exaggeration statements
It is terrible that I have made this mistake. I am terrible for having made this mistake.

N-SPSE Response to Mistakes

Reality pain
Reality pain is the same.

Preference statements
I would like it if I hadn't made this mistake. But, being human, I expect errors.

Antiexaggeration statements
It is unfortunate and inconvenient to have made this mistake.

SPSE Response to Being Late

Reality pain
Reality pain is the same.

Should pain statements
I should never be late. What is wrong with me? I should not be late now. There is no excuse for my being late.

N-SPSE Response to Being Late

Reality pain
Reality pain is the same.

Preference statements
I wish I weren't late. It would certainly be preferable to not be late. I would like it if I weren't late.

Exaggeration pain statements	*Antiexaggeration statements*
This is awful. I am awful. I cannot stand myself for doing this. I can't believe I've done this.	This is inconvenient at best. It is unpleasant for me to be late but it's not a disaster.

As you can detect, by not overreacting to evidences of imperfection, the N-SPSE maintains a steadier approach to the job which means energy flow remains even and strong instead of fluctuating wildly with the effects of overreacting. By not overreacting, N-SPSEs maintain their levels of energy control within themselves.

The Habit of Setting up Win/Lose Situations

Because SPSEs are perfectionists about our performances we are easy targets for student- or client-induced power struggles. We begin each day expecting a battle and as the day progresses the opponents we planned to find make themselves known. Stress-Prone Special Educators have learned to need to have things a certain way. When things do not go that "certain way," we often set ourselves up in unnecessary opposition to others and our environment. In other words, by approaching our work as a struggle throughout each day, we entangle ourselves in situations or battles in which the only outcomes are to win or to lose. And you know how we despise (are terrified of) losing! The process may well begin on the freeway on the way to work. We pull out on the road and pit ourselves against the clock and the other drivers. It's us against them. Those special educators with a nonstress-prone approach do not compete for position and speed. But with SPSEs win-lose entanglements continue throughout the SPSE's day. For example, what happens to us when a student or client defiantly refuses to participate in planned activities? The N-SPSE is less likely to take the other person's defiance as a personal affront (threat to adequacy) while SPSEs are likely to set themselves in opposition to the student while insisting that we have no other choice. Since the only way we can continue to like ourselves and feel relaxed is to maintain continued, acceptable performances and since the student's behavior endangers our performance, our well-being is endangered. Then comes the stress response. In situation after situation the SPSE approach sets things up so that one person is going to be the winner and one the loser. Our right to remain unstressed depends on our ability to win and as our need to win is perceived by our defiant student or client, an accelerating power struggle is under way. SPSEs are easy targets for those students and clients whose self-concepts have them looking for a fight and a put down. SPSEs may be the loudest and most commanding persons in these struggles but there is some question as to who is in control.

Giving up the habit of setting up win-lose situations is a major step. To begin, recognize that you are likely to fall into the power struggle trap whenever you believe your ability to respond competently and comfortably is in danger. There is usually some legitimacy in this belief; the stressor situation preceding the power struggle may present real questions regarding how to respond with comfort and confidence. The invasion of the stress monster comes when you overwhelm yourself by exaggerating the consequences of responding in a less than totally competent manner. Your perception of not knowing how to respond is the reality pain of this situation. You may not have the knowledge, the skills, or the power to respond effectively to the defiance of the student or client. The situation may result in genuine consequences such as a disruption in the activities of others, time away from programs or lessons, or more time spent later reevaluating the program behavior management system. The win-lose situation is not established by these realities. The win-lose, stress-inviting component comes into play once you begin rehearsing *omnipotent demand statements* and *exaggeration statements* regarding the behavior of the student and the effectiveness of your own response. These principal *should statements* dominate the internal self-talk of SPSEs caught up in win-lose situations: "He (she) should not have done this!" and "I should be able to handle this better (or keep this from happening)," and "I should not have to put up with this." Several of the more frequent exaggeration statements close on the heels of these omnipotent demands include: "He (she) is terrible and awful for doing this!" and "I am terrible and awful for letting this happen," and "I can't stand this." Once should statements and exaggeration statements take over, the energy and concentration with which to effectively resolve the situation is lost to useless demands that the situation should not be happening at all.

The N-SPSEs (whom we are working to be more like) avoid unpleasant and usually unproductive power struggles because, from the onset, such situations are not interpreted as "struggles" at all. Remember, only for SPSEs is the job of special education a struggle. The N-SPSE is more likely to view the student's refusal to work with a cognitive approach.

- Reality pain: Actual consequences of time lost and minor disruption.

- Preference statements: "I wish this hadn't happened. It would be pleasant and easier if I had more skills in handling situations like this. I wish I didn't have to deal with this."

- Antiexaggeration statements: "This situation is less than perfect. This is an unpleasant, temporary occurrence. While I have not performed as well as others might, this is not a disaster or an unbearable situation. I am not worthless."

The N-SPSE is in a better position to manage the potentially stressful situation. Blood pressure cuffs and heart rate monitors would not be necessary to determine which of the two special educators would be the more relaxed. When first working to reduce the frequency of the win-lose habit you may need to practice breathing and relaxation techniques that will be described in later chapters. The win-lose habit may be so well ingrained that you find yourself polarized easily by those who misbehave or who express opinions different from your own. If this is true for you, use each win-lose entanglement experience as an opportunity to complete the cognitive change techniques outlined at the end of Chapter 3. Part of changing this habit involves (1) accepting other people as different and (2) not taking these differences personally. This is a gigantic leap of faith for SPSEs who have a hard time accepting their own right to be unique and to have unique needs.

The Habit of Ever-Increasing Standards of Achievement

Woody Allen opened his movie *Manhattan* with a one sentence joke that expresses this habit rather well. He said (paraphrasing) "My problem is I wouldn't want to belong to any club who would be willing to accept *me* as a member." This joke points out the absurdity of the situation in which a person works very hard toward a desired goal and then, on achieving it, redefines the goal as not valuable since it was attained by such an undeserving person. The SPSE is often caught in a similar bind saying, "If I can do this much in my job and still be comfortable, anybody can. Therefore, I must do more." Thus, the spiral of demand for increasing achievements either in quantity or degree of difficulty is begun. For the SPSE with this habit, no achievement is ever enough. The satisfaction accompanying daily experiences in special education (the original reasons for taking the job) lose their meaning. The increasing achievements spiral is a direct outgrowth of basing your right to feel positive on winning the approval of others. Once you return that right to the realms of your own judgment you will be able to view your activities and achievements in terms of their potential for growth and satisfaction.

The Habit of Overdoing

An easily identifiable characteristic of SPSEs is our use of intense language, particularly in relation to personal expectations of work objectives. Our intense expectations result in the SPSE workstyle of insatiable ambition. By insatiable ambition I don't mean climbing the professional status and money ladder; anyone with those ambitions is not likely to be in special education. Insatiable ambition for SPSEs means the demand that *everything* we do must be superior ("I should be able to do this better!"). If we put together a program for parents we must have not just a good program, but a great one. If we set up a student gardening project we want a *great* garden, not just a good one. We expect our students to make *great* advances, not acceptable ones. And, of course, we expect to be a *great* special educator, not a good one. Needless to say, this habit results in much disappointment and frustration since little reminders of our fallibility keep popping up now and then.

This is not to suggest that we should not have high expectations for ourselves and our students. The value of expectations in directing behavior has been well established. However, if these expectations are born of a tension that anything less than superior performance will result in self-rejection, the likelihood of a stress-prone workstyle sets in. The habitual requirement for greatness in every project has the end result of limiting our involvements to safe projects. Sadly, when special educators expect continuous greatness, students and clients withdraw from us because they are afraid they will get in the way of our receiving the approval we seek from ourselves and others. Focus for a moment on the difference in your tension level when the following two styles to introduce a project are used. In this example, a teacher is explaining that a field trip is planned for the following day.

SPSE	N-SPSE
Students, tomorrow we are going on a field trip and I know it will be the best field trip we've ever had. It will be wonderful. It's going to be a *great* trip.	Students, tomorrow we are going on a field trip. I think it's going to be a very enjoyable trip. I'm looking forward to it and plan on having a real good time.

The use of the terms *great, incredible, unbelievable,* and so on, lend themselves to creating a temporary high for listeners that changes to a low when the first dissatisfaction occurs. Also when you use such lofty terms to describe upcoming events for which you are responsible, you place yourself in the pressure cooker position. You need to produce the feelings in others that you promised they would experience. When people are expecting something to be "very good," "enjoyable," or "pleasant" the positive elements can be appreciated and the less-than-perfect elements do not destroy the overall experience.

The Habit of Neglecting Simple Pleasures

Remember the SPSE is convinced that the safety of one's self-worth depends on being able to work harder and faster than others. So with working harder and faster as prime goals "who has time to talk for hours or to listen for minutes to someone else?" The SPSE's personal environment often lacks the organization and available nourishing activities needed for satisfying living because "who has the energy left to attend to such mundane details? Taking care of oneself through involvement in simple pleasures is something anyone can do and who wants to spend time and energy doing what *anyone* can do?" The SPSE's habit of neglecting simple daily activities goes along with our belief that every activity must have some relationship to one's overall productivity and progress. Since progress means movement or change, SPSEs are likely to gravely neglect the maintenance activities of their jobs and their personal selves.

The two energy users in your special education job are the activities of maintenance and the activities of change. Most studies agree that 90 percent of your energy is required to just maintain yourself and your students or clients, to just keep yourself, others, and the program functioning smoothly. The SPSE finds it almost impossible to devote sufficient time to basic maintenance since these activities seem so simple and self-evident. Thus the SPSE overspends in the areas of change. As stress-managed special educators, a return to appreciation of maintenance activities is needed. Programs for clients and students need frequent, patient review. Others need to be asked how things are going and to be heard patiently. Students, clients, coworkers, supervisors, and others have stories to tell you. Everyday paperwork needs your quiet, full attention. Your work environment needs care and redecoration. There is time for maintenance. Without maintenance we will eventually begin to break down. Our surroundings become unmanageably dilapidated and the morale of those around us begins to droop. As SPSEs working to become N-SPSEs, we can remind ourselves that sacrificing the quality of experience for the quantity of constant productivity reinforces the unhealthy pattern we are working to avoid.

HOW YOU PLAY THE SPECIAL EDUCATION GAME

Recognizing and changing your overreactions to your less-than-perfect performances and the evidences of less-than-constant approval from others will reduce the tension you feel while working. You will be better able to view your work in a nonstress-prone way, and since your self-worth is not on the line every day, you will be able to change your approach from one of struggle to one of expecting satisfaction and pleasure in every hour of your work. Stress management for special educators is, before all else, a matter of developing a constructive philosophy for doing special education. Regardless of how tempting it is to battle for the achievements that make us feel alright about ourselves, the pleasures of these are too short lived to be responsible for our feelings. In special education, your satisfaction, your stress level, and, largely, your competence comes down to how you play the game rather than how you fight the war.

The following guidelines are designed to improve your capacity to notice and to become a part of the living game of special education.

Altering Your Environment

1. Johnny Carson used to tell his audiences that every day on his way to the television studio he drove by Forest Lawn Cemetery in order to better appreciate his work. On contemplating the alternative Forest Lawn had to offer, he preferred to be doing what he was doing. The drive by the cemetery reminded Carson to examine the statements he was telling himself on his way to work and make sure they were conducive to enjoying the process of experiencing himself through his work. It is a good idea to use such techniques for regularly reminding yourself of the important energy-directing function of your current thoughts, particularly thoughts about yourself and your relationship to your work. Establish a place in your workspace and a spot at home where you can post reminders of the thoughts that provide you with relaxation and enjoyment. Whatever is posted needs to say something special to you so that every time it catches your eye, you are able to bring the priorities of your job and your workstyle into focus. I have several favorite reminders picked up over the years of doing Stress Management seminars and learning to develop some N-SPSE characteristics:

- "In the Tibetan Book of the Dead it is written that the quality of your thoughts will determine the quality of your reincarnation. So shape up."
- "Forgive yorself and forgive yourself and forgive yourself."
- "It is illusion to imagine your environment is 'happening' to you. You are creating it with your thoughts."

There are many others, of course, and you will have your own favorites. Cartoons sometimes express feelings well and provide a superior stress management technique—an ongoing chuckle.

2. Make sure each school day includes a provision for humor. So much emphasis has been given the damaging effects of the stress response, you may have the impression that anytime your body is not completely quiet, something bad is happening. Such is not the case. The same parts of the brain that initiate the stress response also stimulate the release of certain "feel good" hormones called endorphins and beta endorphins. Endorphins and beta endorphins have been labeled natural opiates because their release causes you to feel refreshed and pleasant. Naturally, since feeling good is of high interest, when the function of these hormones was discovered, scientists went right to work to find out how their release is stimulated.

Several activities have been shown to be related to the release of endorphins and beta endorphins. These include eating, being pregnant, and laughing. Reasonable limits have to be placed on the first activity, eating, since food is not always immediately available to special educators in direct service and because excess eating results in unwanted side (and front and back) effects. The second condition for stimulating natural opiates, being pregnant, is only sporadically available to special educators and males are left out of this "high" altogether. Laughter, smiling, and thoughts rehearsing joy, are, however, constantly available and completely without calories.

So you have at your disposal actual body substances that can increase your pleasure on the job! All you have to do is find an effective means to stimulating their release. You can reduce the stress level of students you serve and reduce your own stress level at the same time by making sure humor is a part of every working *hour*. One way of describing the difference between the daily reaction behaviors of N-SPSEs and the overreaction behaviors of SPSEs is to say that N-SPSEs maintain their sense of humor in difficult and unexpected situations. Nonstress-Prone Special Educators maintain the capacity to smile at what's happening and at themselves. An advantage we have in working in a people profession is that, given a half a chance, the people we serve will be glad to provide the humor we need.

3. Include in your work environment objects or pictures relating to activities you particularly enjoy and with which you identify. People in business have long recognized the importance of decorating wall and desk space with pictures of special people or sports activities or cultural activities of personal interest. These things remind us we are richly interesting and complete people who are "doing" special education rather than viewing ourselves as special educators. Having these reminders within your peripheral vision can help you in the process of reducing chronic job stress. Those with whom you work will appreciate sharing aspects of you other than the special education you do.

4. Arrange the activities of your job to include involvement in projects you particularly enjoy doing. In doing seminars with workers in business and industry, one instruction for enhancing job satisfaction is to encourage supervisors to let employees do more of what they find interesting. For those of us in education, arranging job activities to include particularly enjoyable activities can be easier because our day's schedule usually includes a wide variety of tasks. Also, quite often we can choose exactly what method to use in order to complete specific objectives. If you like to do role playing, find a place for it. If you like literature, find a way to include something about your reading in other activities. Just to bring in these special interests

and activities is more critical than how you bring them in. Your work as a special educator is an expression of both your constructive philosophy of living and an expression of you. The more pleasure you find in doing your job, the more energy, enthusiasm, and hope your students and clients are going to experience.

5. Refuse to take on impossible tasks or to set impossible deadlines or goals for yourself. Unlike the mythical picture of the special educator created by those who need miracles, we do not possess magic coping skills and we do not possess access to a mysterious source of endless energy. You are setting yourself up for a self-punishing overreaction session when you line up more than you can do in the time available and when you accept other people's expectation that you will work miracles. When discussing goals with colleagues and teachers, focus on realistic objectives and do not yield to the temptation of cutting short how long it will take to reach objectives even though the timeline may not fit the hope of those seeking your assistance. Keep in mind that one element of the SPSE's "hurry sickness" is the tendency not to allow for contingencies when setting goals and deadlines. This tendency results in our being even more stressed than usual when unforeseen contingencies occur. Of course, the N-SPSE is aware that the unexpected happenings that slow us in reaching our objectives are not "unforeseen" at all, since the world is unpredictable and since other people have their own sets of needs and plans. Contingencies are to the N-SPSE an *expected* part of every day.

As an SPSE who is actively working to become less stressed, I recommend that when implementing these guidelines, it is not enough to just set reasonable goals and timelines. I find that because I believe so dearly that *there is not enough time to get everything done* I cannot always be trusted to decide what is a "reasonable" goal or timeline. Therefore, in my daily scheduling agreements (a process described below), I agree with myself to complete one half of what I would set as a goal if I let my stress-proneness take over. And I set aside twice the amount of time that I believe in my little, racing heart I "should" need for each project. As a result, the next day when I'm happily at work on my objectives and someone calls or one of the children suddenly needs urgent advice, I don't feel clutched or inwardly throw up my hands exclaiming "What's the use? I'll never get everything done I planned on doing!"

Setting reasonable goals and timelines is an important step in the practice of being gentle with ourselves. Though SPSEs have been frightened into believing otherwise, we can be gentle with ourselves and be productive, too.

6. Carefully schedule your use of work time. When I first make this suggestion sometimes I am met with despairing stares from special

educators. After all, isn't a Stress Management seminar supposed to be all about relaxing and about getting away from clocks and schedules?

The evidence indicates, however, that scheduling is relaxing. So, rather than turn away from scheduling as you learn to manage the tension in your day, you are encouraged to tighten your scheduling policies. If one could see a visual read-out of the damaging self-statements made by SPSEs, these statements would usually include many chastisements for forgotten details and misplaced items. SPSEs often have what I call *surface speed* and *undercurrent drag*. Because we are living by the belief that there is not enough time to get things done, we often find our attention drawn from our goals to a series of details. In the process of hurrying through, we neglect the activities we need to do to complete our own larger goals.

The best scheduling for relaxation procedure I have found includes the following steps:

a. Keep a stenographer's notepad with you at all times or keep a notepad in several locations such as on your desk at school, the kitchen cabinet or home desk, at the telephone, on the end-table by your bed. Anytime you think of something you need to remember to do or anytime you receive a phone call or a message that requires follow-up, make a note on the available pad. Write down everything—even such details as returning calls, stopping at a store, finding an object needed for class, or mailing a letter. The more details you leave up in your head the less likely you will be able to relax. Having a large number of unfinished tasks stored in your mind will add to the feeling that there is no possible way to get everything done that needs to be done. Putting each item on paper reduces anxiety by making concrete items out of overwhelming general tasks.

b. Set aside 10 to 20 minutes each afternoon or evening to go over your lists(s). Compile a "to do" list for the next day and place this with whatever materials you will be taking with you in the morning. Sometimes your "to do" list will include items for which you have several days or weeks to complete but need to be kept in mind, such as Quarterly Reports or planning for upcoming parent conferences. This is fine. Just transfer these from list to list every day. This will keep you aware of the tasks ahead without your having to carry them around in your head tormenting you and adding to that stress-prone sense of being overwhelmed.

c. Take some extra time on one day of the weekend to go over the upcoming week in a general day-by-day way. Go ahead and start a "to do" list for each day in the week so that appointments and weekly details are noted. Anytime the Sunday afternoon Sag Syndrome starts creeping in, review your "to do" lists to reassure yourself that you can complete what needs to be done or make adjustments according to the "realistic goals and timelines" method described earlier. Scheduling your time to improve your overall organization is one method of increasing the number of positive statements you say to yourself about yourself. It feels good to make agreements with yourself to complete certain activities and follow through with your agreements. Writing down your schedule is the first step in making an agreement with yourself to do something.

7. Notice if there are specific identifiable aspects of your environment that trigger negative overreactions to imperfections in yourself. For example, some special educators have corners of their work area that regularly generate self-dissatisfaction because these areas are disorganized or under-utilized. To reduce the stress-producing potential of these areas, you must decide one of two courses of action: (a) accept yourself as less than you'd hope for in the skill of managing your total work area, or, (b) change the work area to meet your expectations. In one seminar when special educator participants were asked to identify one aspect of their environment that triggered negative self-statements a large number identified their automobiles as a frequent source of self-consternation. After some discussion of the alternatives, the group as a whole, decided to stop overreacting to the less-than-perfect car situation. It was agreed that internal statements when messy cars are encountered would not include the word "should" but would instead be statements of preference.

Altering Your Cognitions

1. Using the procedure outlined in the previous chapter, review and alter overreactions to imperfections in yourself, particularly as these imperfections relate to demands for continuous performance and approval.

2. Throw away your list of crimes. Many of us rehearse our errors and the trouble spots at work while we drive along in the car or while we drift off to sleep. The stress-prone reasoning behind this behavior is that we are constructively dealing with the struggle of our job by worrying about it rather than doing something foolish like forgetting about it for a while. Remember the SPSE has learned to be motivated by dissatisfaction. Therefore, it isn't difficult to see how a pattern of daily *crime rehearsal* could be used to maintain our pace and dedication.

3. Reflect at least once daily on *why* you are working in special education. If this is difficult at first, write out why you are *choosing* every day to work in special education. Sometimes the procedure will seem awkward or you will only come up with "funny" answers ("because in graduate school they told us we could get a better job" or "because if I don't work in special education I'll have to go back into regular education"). Start the practice of

altering your cognitions about your interactions with special education by listing the three main things you hope to gain from each day in your career.

4. Remind yourself at several points during the work day that your feelings determine your quality of life while working and that these feelings are determined by your ongoing chosen stream of thoughts. SPSEs try habitually to attribute their internal states of being to outside forces by pointing to accomplishments or to all the things they haven't done. We are fond of deferring responsibility for personal well-being by saying things like, "I can't be relaxed while there is such a need for more services," or "I'll relax when I finish this week." How much of your life are you going to give away by accepting the fact that you can only feel pleasurable and relaxed on weekends and during the summer?

5. Give up holding your breath until you get it *all* together. Stop waiting for the day when it's finally okay to relax. The reality of being human combined with the realities of special education make it obvious that regardless of how long and hard you work, regardless of your impeccable planning and organization, your performance is destined to be interspersed with errors and problems. Again, the key to stress management and to an enjoyable work experience is in how you react to these realities.

Altering Your Physical and Behavioral Approaches

1. Listen to yourself while talking with others and deliberately slow the *pace* of your speech. This is best done by slowing all behavioral activities with others, such as walking, drinking, and eating. The concept of pace is important as SPSEs "do" special education. Often the people we serve do not move at the pace accepted as typical. Their special needs mean adjustments on our part, adjustments focusing on the quality of each learning, growing experience rather than on progress in terms of quantity; that is, numbers and charts.

2. Take back the right to spend time and energy participating in simple activities such as gardening, sitting, cooking, and playing games with others. Those of us who have based our self-esteem on being busy, often fill our daytime hours with "constructive" activities and nighttime hours at home with day-to-day maintenance duties. Thus, time at home is not energy replenishing. When our weekday schedules are thus planned, we usually approach the Monday through Friday work week holding our breath and clinging to self-made promises of weekend relief. The holding your breath approach does not lend itself to teaching you to see your job as a personality

enriching experience. Each day, weekday or weekend, is received by the stress-managed person as a separate opportunity for learning and growing, not as one more 24-hour stretch of slavery before freedom is granted. Retrieving your right to enjoy nonhurried, simple tasks every day can help you return a sense of completeness to each day.

3. Find someone to talk to about the stress management changes you are working on; you will be able to collect feedback on your progress. When your confidante witnesses the stress-managed you serenely handling a situation that previously brought forth an outburst of anger or a headache, he or she will have an understanding of the principles of your program. Most of the time, others are positive about your enjoying yourself more, reducing unnecessary hurry, and reducing your irritability, particularly if you report on plans for yourself without pressuring others to change.

4. Practice finding humor in less-than-perfect situations resulting from your own imperfect performances. Rather than launching into the SPSE tirade of exaggerations, when you've erred try admitting it with a pleasant statement such as "Now that *was* a goof, wasn't it!" Or, "When I mess up I try to do a superior job of it." Or, "My group is trying for the most original technique award instead of the usual prize." Or, "It's a good thing I'm doing this job for personality enhancement because I'm not going to win any awards for today." By continuing to feel pleasantly about yourself during your less-than-perfect moments as well as your star performances, you will be managing your stress level as well as providing a model for persons who may need to learn to view imperfect performances in themselves as okay, too.

NOTES

Friedman, Meyer & Rosenman, Ray H. *Type A behavior and your heart*. New York: Knopf Publishers, 1974.

Coleman, Daniel. 1,528 little geniuses and how they grew. *Psychology Today*, February, 1980, pp. 47-48.

Hammerskjold, Dag. *Markings*. New York: Alfred A. Knopf, 1969.

Putney, Snell & Putney, Gail J. *The adjusted American*. New York: Harper & Row Publishers, 1974.

Chapter 5

If Only Certain Other People Would Change

5

Day by day, hour by hour, we misunderstand each other . . . We make the other people simply extensions of self, either through attribution of our own thoughts and attitudes to the other person, or by familiar decisions about his nature, after which we go on responding to him as though he were the character we have invented. (Hayden, 1955)

Special education is above all else a people enterprise. Most of us were drawn to the profession by the promise of working closely with others who need our help and the promise of working in association with other humanistic professionals. These same promised realities can and often do lead special educators to search the classified ads on Monday afternoon (circling jobs in fields we've never even heard of) and going back to school for credentials to remove us from such direct contact with others. The people we envisioned helping don't always turn out to fit the projections we developed during our special education training. The people we work with do not always provide continuous inspiration, but sometimes provide new vistas of challenge in human relations. And then, of course, there are the parents, the psychologists, and all the other special resource persons, accountability experts, and state, regional, district, and specific program supervisors whose relationship to special education in general, and to us specifically, is couched in vague importance. Unlike "regular" educators, special educators are not only faced with more variety in the students we serve, but usually we are also faced with more variety in the persons to whom we are responsible. The previous chapter looked at the importance of your relationship with yourself and how that relationship affects your daily stress level and work experience. This chapter takes a look at what happens to you physically, emotionally, socially, and intellectually as you relate to the less-than-perfect others in your special education situation. In other words, now we take a look at how interacting with those we serve, those we work for, those we work with, and the various others who have a stake in our jobs, affects our stress or nonstressful experience as individuals "doing" special education.

Sometimes the very persons we set out to help as special educators turn out to be uncooperative and resistant to what we have to offer. Out in the real world we find that the clients and students we serve vary greatly in their potential for rehabilitation and learning. This finding can lead to a challenge to our own well-being and eventually, to stress, especially if our expectations for progress do not fit reality. As Dr. Richard Lamb (1979) found in his study, *Staff Burnout in Work With Long-Term Patients*, when staff members with unrealistic expectations encounter those handicapped persons for whom progress is limited, the result for staff is boredom, frustration, resentment, and ineffectiveness. But not all our frustration and stress as special educators is attributable to interactions with our students and clients. Sometimes interactions with the other imperfect people from within and without the system send stress levels soaring. When we are burned out there exists a tremendous gap between the way we see ourselves actually working with people and the plans we made as aspiring special educators. The problem is intensified by the gap between how outside society sees us and how we actually are.

Working long hours with people with special needs, regardless of the "challenge," is supposed to be something we have no problem doing since these skills are supposed to be covered in our magic coping powers. Many a special educator has reported exasperation after being told by a "regular" education coworker or a parent, "I don't see how you do it! You must really have a talent to take all that you do." What these special educators report wanting to say in return is too confusing and discouraging to report, but usually it's something to the effect that "all that" is taking its toll. But other people don't want to hear about our pain. They want to continue believing we are the one resource who will never say "no," never break down, and always be there to take on what no one else wants to do. This denial of special educator humanity may be necessary for teachers, parents and others who so want to help their children and students with special needs but feel helpless and in need of hope from outside experts. This bestowing of magic skills to special educators is not made with malicious intent and need not injure our ability to find an enjoyable work experience unless we begin to believe we are supposed to be omnipotent.

Maintaining control over your stress level while interrelating with others involves two processes:

1. learning to recover from difficult encounters, and
2. altering your view so that fewer interaction situations are interpreted as threatening or stressful.

Changes in your reactions to the actions and feelings of others are among the most difficult of behavioral changes to make. After all, while the shelves of the local book store are lined with volumes directing you to learning better ways to relate with yourself and to learn to live with your own imperfections, few programs are available today that examine the impact of other people on your comfort and competency levels. To add to the problem, many of us have been rewarded for practicing and maintaining certain destructive behaviors in reaction to others such as long term anger and worry.

STRESS AND OVERREACTIONS TO OTHER PEOPLE BEING THEMSELVES

It's not difficult to see how your daily stress level is affected by your interactions with other people. Nature doesn't know the difference between an encounter with a life threatening tiger and a displeased supervisor (or even a satisfied supervisor if we are threatened by supervisors in general). Thus, most of us are frequently reminded of our body's physiological attempts to deal with our social-behavioral problems with others. We have cold, damp hands before important meetings. Our hands shake when speaking before a group. An overacid stomach makes itself known when, just after lunch, we break up a fight between students. A night of plaguing insomnia sometimes follows a particularly threatening encounter. Or sometimes insomnia plagues us on the night before "the big meeting" just when we'd hoped to have a good night's rest. Our body tries in the only way it knows to help us "win" the struggles we have or expect to have with others. Unfortunately, with two exceptions, the efforts of our body actually interfere with our ability to work effectively with others. An overwhelming stress response will help you react effectively in those rare situations in which the appropriate response to the imperfect other with whom you are interacting is either to join in physical combat or to flee from the other person or persons as fast as possible. In the realistic encounters we have daily as special educators our stress response prevents the calm, well thought out responses required in trying circumstances.

It's So Hard to Get Good Help These Days

The intensive people situations that are the essence of special education are particularly problematic for SPSEs. This is not to say we SPSEs are not adept at working with others or that we do not possess superior managerial and communication skills. The stresses we experience in dealing with others are not the result of a lack of technical skills but rather the result of the four Core Beliefs that motivate our stress-prone behavior in relating to ourselves and our environment. Because we believe that as special educators we are involved in a struggle with time, other people, and events, our basic approach to others is defensive. We expect other people to frustrate us in our battle to accomplish the goals we set for ourselves and our students. We expect to have to work harder than other people and yet we are at the same time angry at others for not suffering the way we do. We are angry with others for refusing or for being unable to meet the ever escalating standards we set for ourselves and our programs. Enmeshed in our "hurry sickness," the unpredictable actions of others and the slow pace of others loom as stressors in each work day. Since we believe "there's not enough time to get everything done," even *before* a student is disruptive or even *before* a parent interrupts a student's progress with a series of out-of-school activities, other people's actions and expressions of needs are often responded to as threats. Since we believe the key to our success is to work harder and faster than other people, cooperation and team efforts add to our stress level rather than to bring the relief such projects are designed to provide.

No discussion of how your stress response is affected by interaction with others would be complete without mentioning the belief that the only ones who really understand what is needed in our jobs are ourselves and how this belief influences the stress potential of special education. Such a belief is, in its very essence, a hostile statement. By nurturing it, we are able to store up weak feelings of worth with illusions of omnipotence left over from childhood. We can try to hold our self-esteem together by seeing ourselves as responsible for everything that goes on around us. We can even secretly pat ourselves on the back for our willingness to maintain above-the-standard "standards" in every area of our work. But the eventual result is a more stressful workstyle and intermittent frustration when we don't receive the feedback or appreciation we need to keep going. When there's just more things to do than even one supremely dedicated person can do, we end up in a heap of exhaustion. Before SPSEs start sounding like completely uncooperative, self-seeking sorts, remember that SPSEs did not learn to fear and distrust other people because they wanted to be megalomaniacs. As children, we learned that the only people we could depend on were ourselves by the warnings of others who were themselves afraid to trust others. They were particularly afraid that we would be too trusting and not put in the necessary effort to take care of ourselves. We were taught that trusting other people would lead to our own destruction and to the destruction of all we were taught to struggle to attain. We learned to fear disapproval from others. We learned to fear evidence of imperfect performances so strongly that we have a difficult time leaving projects in the hands of people who may not fear disapproval and imperfection sufficiently. Other people just might not do things our way and because we are afraid, we insist on things being done the only way we're sure of—our way.

The fourth Core Belief of the SPSE regarding trust of others particularly cripples us in learning to manage stress in relating to others. As a result of this belief SPSEs have strong tendencies toward withholding responsibilities from others and then feeling abused because no one else will do their part. Cammer (1976) in his book, *Freedom From Compulsion* concludes that depressed people manifest two characteristics: people who get depressed are compulsive people who for some reason are not able to function and who also believe that the only person they can trust is themselves. SPSEs want to supervise everything that goes on in the job and then complain bitterly of long hours and an impossible list of daily activities. We expect people to disappoint us. (Otherwise why would we need to always be there supervising?) Our students and their parents pick up our expectation and knowingly or unknowingly fulfill our view of them and other people in the world. The saddest part for SPSEs (who especially need support from others) is that they cannot attract help or inspire independence in our students, both of which would set them free from daily tasks.

At a seminar last summer I was working with a group of educators on the task of reducing the list of daily tasks through consolidation and delegation procedures. A third grade resource teacher reported that a large part of her off period every day was taken up correcting daily handwriting practice sheets so that she had no real break in the morning. At this point, a fifth and sixth grade resource teacher excitedly suggested that her students could correct the papers of the third graders as part of their handwriting exercises. She was sure her students would be more motivated with the opportunity to grade other papers than they were doing their own review sheets. The first teacher's expression froze for a minute and then she went on to explain that such an arrangement couldn't possibly work since she "had to" grade the papers herself everyday; she had to be sure she knew just how each student was progressing.

Anger, Impatience, Aggravation, and Irritation

Overreacting to imperfect others is a characteristic of the SPSE. Meyer Friedman, talking in a Public Broadcasting Service program last fall described the stress-prone individual as a person afflicted with the "a, i, a, i syndrome." The a, i, a, i, syndrome consists of *a*nger, *i*mpatience, *a*ggravation, and *i*rritation—feelings usually thought of as byproducts of interactions with other people. Friedman and Rosenman (1974) identify a pervasive "free-floating hostility" as a major characteristic of the Type A personality. Once SPSEs have set into action behaviors based on our Four

Core Beliefs our interactions with others take on increasingly stressful possibilities. Believing our job to be a struggle with others we begin each project with a stance that makes other, less stressed persons anxious. Then, acting on their anxiety these other people (students or coworkers) begin engaging in whatever they need to do to relieve their own anxiety. Observing these behaviors we conclude that we were right to be defensive from the start because after all, see what other people will do? Sighing deeply, we prepare for battles to come.

The cycle of stress that begins with a stress-prone workstyle and eventually colors the outcomes of most all interactions deserves close attention. Stressful interactions are used as justifications to intensify the original struggle approach. To see how this pattern works, let's say we have a particular male special educator starting out on a day of struggle with students and colleagues. From the day's onset our special educator will be creating within himself heightened blood sugar levels, ACTH levels, and a generally changed internal process as he marches or drives off to war. Because his mind is prepared for confrontation, his body is programmed that way as well. He tightens the muscles across his back and clenches his hands around the wheel, steeling himself. He has changed from a balanced state of alert relaxation (which we can only hope he was experiencing before it was time for work), to an unbalanced state of emergency which he expects, in fact strongly believes, is what he must do if he is to be successful in the day ahead. It may not be immediately obvious how our educator's changed physical condition will affect his interaction with others, but let's watch him carefully as he eases into the traffic. Of course, with his skyrocketing adrenalin level, our educator is probably not merely "easing" into the traffic. He is more likely to be anxiously, and perhaps discourteously, fighting his way into the traffic. He was too wound up for breakfast but now our special educator is hungry and notices a burning sensation in his stomach. In fact, it is while attending to this distraction that he runs over the edge of the curb with his new car. This threatens his self-image and thus our special educator's stress response is intensified as he berates himself and searches the horizon for others to blame. Angry with himself, two stoplights later he yells at the driver ahead who turns around looking bewildered. Realizing he was out of line, our man tells himself he should not have done that and while his self-image takes another blow, so does his endocrine system.

Arriving at school, our special educator is much too tense to reply when someone in the office asks him how he's doing. When an announcement is made to the effect that first period has been cancelled for an assembly, our educator's blood pressure goes up and his muscles tighten further. By the time he gets down to work with his six second period students his tension level is too high to listen or to respond without sounding angry. The students respond by being angry themselves, thus "proving" what an impossible job our special educator has. Our educator's physical response is triggered further, and so it goes throughout the day unless the psychological-physical cycle is broken. The physical response of stress made him less able to interact with others in calm, thoughtful ways. The uneasiness of these interactions further stimulated the original problem response. This analysis of the interactive effects of physiology and beliefs doesn't take into account the additional reality—being constantly prepared for confrontation is not just ineffective, it is also exhausting, boring, and no fun.

THE *OTHERS* WE SERVE

One of the difficulties in working with severely handicapped students is that when an outsider (or even a fairly knowledgeable supervisor) who isn't there every day watches us at work, our students can sometimes make us look pretty bad. One key sign that stress has advanced to serious burnout levels is if you begin to believe that the students or clients you serve are deliberately refusing to progress, or if you begin to think they are trying to make you look bad. You are experiencing another key burnout symptom when the needs of the students you teach, needs you were so anxious to meet at one time, take on new and overwhelming proportions. The needs of students and clients with special requirements can be great. After experiencing long term stress as a result of trying all the stress-prone methods to meet their needs, the result can be a feeling expressed in the following: "Everybody needs somebody sometime, but why does it always have to be me?" (sung to the familiar Dean Martin tune). The tremendous needs of those we serve begin to be perceived as threats; they are difficult to meet and we demand perfection from ourselves. Concern mounts over our abilities to fulfill the needs of others and often we might begin questioning why we ever wanted to do this work in the first place. The ways we have learned to defend ourselves when the pressures of student and client needs take their stress-inducing toll deserve special attention.

Special educators experiencing painful, long term dissatisfaction with themselves in relation to those they serve are candidates for stress. They are likely to become increasingly cynical and negative relating to students and clients. As Christina Maslach and Ayala Pines (1977) reported after surveying day-care staff, "burnout is characterized by an emotional exhaustion in which the professional no longer has any positive feelings, sympathy or respect for clients or patients." Maslach and Pines also reported that "burned out" human service workers are more likely to rely more heavily on the use of labels and that, at the most extreme stages, clients served are viewed as somehow deserving their problems. Another way of talking about how we defend ourselves when we feel overwhelmed is to look at P. G. Zimbardo's (1970) work describing the process of "dehumanizing" others which he explained can happen for one of four reasons. According to Zimbardo we take on the defense of dehumanization when (1) we are involved in a job or social situation that requires emotional distance from the people served because the action of the job requires inflicting pain for the eventual good of persons served, e.g., police issuing traffic citations or nurses giving injections; (2) when others are used for self-gratification such as for pleasure or entertainment; (3) when others are viewed as obstacles or elements in a larger project such as the "marks" of the con artist and the quota numbers spoken of by salespeople; and (4) when separation from others is necessary to be able to perform unpleasant requirements of the job, e.g., when people must incessantly involve themselves in the most unpleasant "cleaning up after" task in institutions and hospitals. *Dehumanization*—a process that produces a decreased awareness of the human attributes of others and a loss of humanity in interpersonal relations—can become the self-defense of the habitually stressed special educator. You are reaching this point when you begin to lose the belief that you have feelings, impulses, thoughts, and purposes in common with the people you serve. Dehumanization is happening when you find yourself referring to students and clients as though they were objects (CPs, MRs, or the Impossibles) and when you evaluate what is happening with them by treating them as extensions of yourself. The second half of that statement means you know you're in trouble when you are handing out praise and the right to feel comfortable only to those particular clients and students who are at the moment making you feel like a good special educator.

Along with using the defense of dehumanization when the problems and needs of those we serve are major sources of stress, we frequently practice developing a sense of detachment from others. The impact of effectively using dehumanization and detachment affects our competence and our quality of experiencing on the job. When we dehumanize and pull back from others, it takes away from our own experiencing of satisfaction. By reducing the pleasure available to us in our people-oriented jobs and by dehumanizing others, we suffer a loss of respect for our own humanity.

Coworkers, Supervisors and Parents

After serving as a special educator for a while, have you ever found yourself starting to believe that you have very little, if anything, in common with your coworkers? Do you tell yourself and others that *those people* don't really understand you and your feelings? Do you join in the gossip you once avoided about how the chief administrator is unfair and incompetent? Do you label parents, referring to them as "the agitators," "the crusaders," or by other pet titles? Alienation from coworkers, fear, trepidation, hostility in supervisory relationships and objectification of parents are all signs of prolonged stress. These are signs that our efforts to be very, very good by our stress-prone workstyles are not working and are in fact resulting in precisely the attitudes and behaviors we had planned to avoid.

One of the most obvious burnout warning signals involving interaction with others is increased irritability. You find yourself more easily upset by the actions of others. Another is when you begin to put off interactions with others either by simply delaying ("Sure, let's do work together on that project. I don't have time to discuss it now, but how about if I call you back next week or the week after?"), or by active avoidance (not answering the phone or finding routes in your work building that keep you from crossing paths with certain others). These responses to prolonged stress can best be explained as resulting from a combination of the particular interaction characteristics of the special educator situation and the workstyle of the SPSE.

Since special education is an intensely people-saturated enterprise, an outsider would likely assume that the last problem a special educator might have would be loneliness. Such is not the case. Most special educators work in psychological isolation. Surrounded by students and clients, we have no one nearby to whom we can openly express our feelings, our thoughts. There's no one to talk to about what we did last night or the activities of our spouses, friends, and children. It's not just that students and clients might not be able to emotionally or intellectually follow our disclosures. Such disclosures simply are not a part of our job description and are usually inappropriate with students and clients. If you've been a direct service special educator throughout your career you may not even realize that in many jobs outside special education, one's arrival at the office is followed by a ten- to fifteen-minute sharing of personal events among adults, a sharing that serves a special orienting function for all concerned. As mentioned earlier, one major characteristic of potentially stressful jobs is that such positions do not allow the worker an easy and immediate outlet for frustration. The job of the direct service special educator fits this pattern. The direct service person faces disheartening, angering, frightening, and even thrilling situations daily, even hourly, and has no one with whom to turn to and share them. And it's not just that sharing sounds like a nice, "good person" thing to do; sharing helps a person manage tension and stress. The one factor that has been shown repeatedly to most determine whether an individual will survive a severe trauma without suffering a debilitating depression or other breakdown is whether that person has some person or persons with whom to share the pain of the experience during the weeks and months afterward. Special educators often are asked to perform day after day in trying circumstances without provision of the support group relationships needed to verify activities and purposes. Of course, what often happens is that we take our frustrations, angers, joys, and fears home and try to share with others who work in fields very different from our own and who are already tired. We may say the same things, but the relief is not the same because, unlike our coworkers, nonspecial educators cannot respond with "I know just what you mean."

The stress potential of interactions with parents and supervisors is highly influenced by your workstyle approach. Certain environmental realities, however, cannot be ignored since the particular characteristics of your supervisor and the parents of your clients and students can make a great deal of difference. Certain managerial styles and personal attributes of supervisors contribute more to the stress potential of the job than do others. These will be described in the chapter on the management of environmental factors that influence special educator stress. For now, let's look at how the SPSE workstyle results in tension problems with supervisors and parents. Meyer Friedman, describing the highly stress-prone person on a Public Broadcasting Service program on stress last fall characterized him or her as someone who has trouble with authority figures and as a person who is oversensitive to criticism, characteristics not conducive to relaxed relationships with parents and supervisors.

Having overt or covert strain with authority figures and being oversensitive to criticism follow logically from the Core Beliefs of the SPSE. When the job is a struggle, when there's never enough time, and when there is a distrust of others, supervisors and parents are going to be perceived according to how they fit into our "battle and survival plan" rather than as people. The words these others say, the expressions on their faces are interpreted according to our beliefs and our fears. Because SPSEs are always afraid they are not accomplishing enough fast enough it's easy to overreact when someone else suggests casually or in a formal evaluation that our performance is not flawless. Criticism is a particularly ominous problem because SPSEs confuse special education performance with self-worth. For SPSEs, criticism from supervisors or parents is a very personally threatening and stressful matter.

Myths That Intensify the Stress Potential with Others

Certain well accepted attitudes and beliefs regarding the nature of other people have a way of increasing the stress potential of doing special education. These attitudes and beliefs inaccurately describe others and serve to inhibit and disturb us in our interactions. Because of our early learning and because of their apparent simplicity, these ideas remain popular and seem to provide reassurance that the environment is easily understood. Thus, much of the stress we experience working in a populated environment results when our day to day experience with others does not mesh with the beliefs we hold dear regarding their natures. Developing a constructive philosophy for remaining stress managed while surrounded by students, clients, parents, supervisors, administrators, coworkers, and others requires a reassessment of the beliefs accepted about other people at an earlier less informed time in life, and before you were able to begin to understand your place in the overall construction of your universe. The following myths need particular review if you are to improve the quality of your experiencing with others.

Myth Number 1

Other People Cause Our Stress. It is probable that no other element of our environment receives more blame for the invasion of stress than does other people. We learn early to say that someone else "made" us angry, that some action of another person "caused" us to be depressed, or that even our overall approach to our job is the result of someone else's (our students', our supervisor's) personality or behavior. And while it can be comforting sometimes to point to others as causing our stress, you know by now how stress responses are initiated and maintained. You know it is impossible for other people to automatically trigger your internal responses. In other words, *only you can continue to upset yourself because others go around being themselves.*

Accepting that your stress level is the responsibility of other people will end up affecting your special education effectiveness in several self-constricting ways. As long as you can be comfortable and unstressed only when students, parents, and supervisors are behaving in certain, prescribed ways, you will end up spending time and energy trying to control the behavior of these *dangerous-to-your-well-being* others. Reasonable management of the behavior of those you serve and the pleasing of your supervisor are realistic aspects of your job. But because SPSEs have learned to react strongly and to be personally affected when other people are behaving in ways we would not choose, we spend more time, worry and energy than necessary trying to over control the behavior of others. We do this both by knocking ourselves out with planning and struggle and sometimes by using emotional blackmail techniques we dislike in others. Because we work overtime trying to control others we feel particularly justified in upsetting ourselves when people go right on being themselves in spite of all our sacrifices of time and energy. Remember it is part of SPSE style to believe everything *should be* in our control. When a supervisor's management style doesn't exactly fit what we'd prefer, we overreact by complaining, refusing to accept policies, and generally stressing ourselves. When our students and clients do not learn at the rate we've decided they should learn and when their behavior is not as cooperative as we demand, we send our stress level soaring, rehearsing such stress-inducing statements as "They should be working faster. It's terrible because they refuse to behave." Because we believe our stress level is determined by others, whether we have a pleasant or unpleasant, stressful or unstressful day as special educators, we leave to chance. Our stress level is determined by needs and behaviors of people that we cannot control.

Stress-Prone Special Educators who believe their stress level is decided by the behavior of others are less likely to try new activities. To do so would mean risking new student and client behaviors that might then "cause" us to become tense and frustrated. SPSEs can be quickly disappointed in others and have a hard time turning learning over to clients and students because when their behavior stretches beyond certain acceptable limits, we "must" feel badly ourselves. It's easier to over-supervise than it is to risk the possibility that others might behave in undesirable ways while we're not watching. But then, of course, even with our over-supervision, clients, students and supervisors (children and spouses) do behave in ways other than we would choose for them. This occurs because people happen to be different from each other and happen to be each responding in a unique way to the environment as each perceives it to exist. Because all persons with whom you work are trapped inside their own perceptions of reality and are responding to those separately constructed realities in the best ways they have learned, one of the most reliable ways of stressing yourself is to live by the belief that your internal feelings are the result of how other people feel and behave.

There are no more vulnerable patsies in the world than SPSEs who become upset every time someone else behaves in a less than desirable fashion. Our students and clients learn we can be easily "had," our supervisors learn to avoid confronting us with reality, and our children and spouses learn to reverse our emotional blackmail techniques and beat us at our own game. Reverse emotional blackmail works like this: First, you point out your stress symptoms (tension, fatigue, loss of enthusiasm) to a student or client explaining that your pain is the result of his or her behavior. The angry or dejected other person eventually learns to play your game by reporting that *his* or *her* anger, dejection, and misbehavior are stress symptoms caused by your demands and your tension, fatigue and lack of enthusiasm. Both people are trying to give away responsibility for their feelings, but, in the case of reverse emotional blackmail, those first blamed are wise to how the game works. Some special educators are not open to learning an in-depth, effective stress management program because emotional blackmail is their chief means of controlling the behavior of clients and students. These special educators are often not aware of the effectiveness of other procedures.

To free yourself from the false idea that your internal pleasant and unpleasant responses are caused by the actions of others you will need to give up trying to control others by pointing out to them just how they have upset you. This does not mean accepting the undesirable behavior of others without attempting change. Of course, you continue reasonable projects of positive behavior change. As a stress-managed special educator, however, behavior management programs are established and maintained without investing such efforts with personal self-worth value. Refusing to blame others for your internal stress level also does not mean turning on yourself in an unsympathetic fashion, "blaming" yourself for allowing others to control your internal responses. Such a conclusion would result in further accelerating stress as you upset yourself because you are human and were upset. Caught in this trap the special educator is likely to rehearse statements such as, "Since I am responsible for my own stress level, I should not be stressing myself like this. Therefore, it is awful that I am upsetting myself." You can calmly accept personal responsibility for your internal experiencing without expecting perfection of yourself. In doing this, you can decide on and maintain your chosen comfort level in the midst of divergent actions and feelings of the many others with whom you interact as a special educator.

Myth Number 2

Other People Should Be and Behave a Certain Way. This myth results in much stress for those of us who believe there is one certain way that administrators *should* administrate, that students and clients *should* act, and that parents *should* behave. Because of this belief, when these people feel and behave differently, we upset ourselves. I'm not suggesting that we have no values or preferences regarding how other people feel and behave. Of course, we would *prefer* that other people did things as we would desire them to do. The problem is that other people, even those closest to us or over whom we have greatest control, are themselves, and continuously or intermittently behave and feel in ways that are *different* from the ways we would choose. Whether or not the actions of others stimulate and raise our stress level depends on our ability to maintain responsibility for internal feelings. We need to learn that it is not "normal" to upset ourselves when students misbehave, or when a colleague is negligent in his or her duties, or when anyone is "out of line."

Before going further, be reminded of the difference between *normal,* natural, and typical behaviors. Typical behaviors are those happening most frequently within the cultural environment. They are often termed normal. These typical or normal behaviors could be quite unnatural. We have accepted headaches as natural and normal consequences of difficult situations when, in fact, headaches are not normal or natural, but merely typical. Similarly, many of us have accepted our overreactions to the behaviors of others as normal and natural, and as the only way to react in the circumstances.

If this were the case, if a special educator had to, because of natural responses, become angry when a student misbehaved, or had to become distraught when parents refused to help their child, we would be back to the situation in which the only stress management program that would make any headway would be the one that reached out and changed all the students, parents, supervisors, colleagues, and clients in special education so that they would not behave in (according to you) undesirable ways anymore. Since this is not going to happen, we are again left with the responsibility of changing the way we respond in the situations of special education. To accomplish this we need to refer back to the model of responding described previously. As special educators responding to the behavior of others we stress ourselves by experiencing reality pain (caused by the inconvenience of not being able to control the feelings and behaviors of others) and compound this pain into the more long lasting and severe distresses of omnipotent demand pain and exaggeration pain. The sequence of cognitive events through which we stress ourselves in relating to unique and imperfect others is similar to the sequence we rehearse to upset ourselves about our own less-than-desirable traits and behaviors.

As an example, let's look at a situation in which a particular child has just broken a piece of art equipment after being cautioned four times to be careful. Identified below are the internal sentences (self-talk) of a special educator headed for an elevated stress level and the sentences of a special educator practicing stress managed responses.

The Special Educator Accelerating Stress

Reality pain statements

She did it. She dropped the varnish jar after all my warnings.

Omnipotent demand statements

She should not have done that.

She should have listened.

She should have been more careful.

She should not even be in this class.

She should show more respect for my instructions.

She should show more respect for the supplies.

Kids today should show more respect for things that cost money.

She should not be allowed to get away with this.

She should keep her hands cleaner so things wouldn't be so hard to hold.

And a few for our imperfect selves and imperfect situations . . .

I should have watched her more closely.

I should have told her to wash her hands first.

I should have stirred the varnish myself.

I shouldn't try to do something else while she is doing her art.

I shouldn't bother to warn her since she doesn't listen.

I should be able to run my class without things like this happening.

I shouldn't even try to work with children.

That varnish jar shouldn't be shaped like it is (or was).

This classroom (table, desk) should be larger so there would be more work room.

Art class should not be so short.

This agency should provide more supplies so that I don't *have to* upset myself when this happens.

Exaggeration pain statements

This child is terrible.

This behavior is unforgivable.

This is awful.

She is intolerable.

She has ruined everything.

I can't stand for this to happen.

She is unbearable.

Her behavior is unfair and I can't stand it.

Now I must fall apart.

This is disastrous.

The Special Educator Remaining Calm

Reality pain statement

She did it. She dropped the varnish jar after all my warnings.

Preference statements

I would have liked it better if she hadn't dropped it.

I wish this hadn't happened.

I would rather she had heeded my warning.

I would prefer that things didn't "go wrong" during activities like this.

Antiexaggeration statements

This is inconvenient and unpleasant.

Cleaning this up is going to take some time.

This is unfortunate.

Her dropping the jar of varnish means altering my present plans.

Her behavior is less accurate than I had hoped for.

Changing internal thinking habits away from the style of the SPSE is not as simple as deciding to change. Just as you learned to respond to yourself and your own ever surfacing imperfections when you were a child, you also learned how to respond to others during your early years. This means you developed your present reaction style during a time when your experience was too limited to provide you with a workable picture of the world, the other people in it, and how you fit in relation to other people. As you will recall from earlier discussions, because of our limited experience when we are very young children, we developed erroneous ideas regarding perfection in ourselves and our personal power to control events. Looking out from our childhood idiosyncratic point of view, we also overestimated the abilities of others to meet perfectly our expectations and we overestimated our power to control others.

The physiological, emotional, intellectual and social differences experienced and displayed by the two special educators described in the example above will not be the result of the size of the mess made by the broken jar or even by the threatening or nonthreatening quality of the girl's reaction to what she had done. The girl's action did not have the power to reach inside each educator and to turn on stress responses. The well rationalized hostility of the stress-prone special educator is easy to understand when you realize that SPSEs are people who are totally at the mercy of others for the right to stay comfortable and relaxed. As long as other people must behave in certain ways for us to be relaxed, we will always be tense. Even when others are cooperating, we will wonder how long it's going to last. One of the biggest steps in developing an effective stress management program for yourself will occur when you take responsibility on a continuous basis for the way you feel inside regardless of the behaviors of others.

If Only People Would Do Things the Right Way. Wouldn't remaining comfortable and nonstressed be a whole lot easier if other people would just cooperate and do things the way they *should* be done? Other people can often seem so unwilling to cooperate with us, to even try to do things "right." Maintaining the idea that there is a right way to do things (and we know what it is) represents a major obstacle to our efforts in learning a way to work with others while maintaining responsibility for our own stress level. By hanging on to the proposition that there is a right way of doing things, we justify our self-destructive stressed behavior by insisting we are only "trying to help," that we are "only upset because other people are doing wrong," and that we are behaving *responsibly* by upsetting ourselves.

To chip away at this myth, consider the following explanation which casts doubt on the "one, great, right way of doing things" idea. There are approximately 250,000,000 people in the United States. Being an SPSE in good standing I pride myself in being quite sure I know the *right way* to do whatever there is to be done. Having a background in developmental psychology I also know that most of what I know about the how and why of things I learned in my growing up years. Isn't it quite a miracle that out of 250,000,000 United States citizens *my* parents were the two individuals who knew the *right way* to do things? Perhaps of even greater significance is the fact that of my parents' three children I alone was the one who was able to put together from the offerings of both of my parents, just the correct combination of values and ideas so that I am now able to observe the behavior of others and compare their behavior to the standard of what is right. Effective living and working with others requires an awareness of the impossibility of the "one right way of doing things" idea.

Nonstress-Prone Special Educators know that a big difference exists between what is right for people in any absolute sense and what is right for a particular individual. Nonstress-Prone Special Educators believe that other people, regardless of how bizarre their behavior might appear, are doing the very best they know how to avoid pain and find comfort with themselves. Therefore, the parents who refuse to care for their child, the student striking out to hurt someone else, and even the supervisor who ignores the needs of direct service personnel, each feels as right in their behaviors as we do in ours. As Richardson and Woolfolk (1978) stated in *Stress, Sanity and Survival*, "the behavior of others usually seems as justified to them as your behavior does to you" (p. 33).

The important benefits of ridding ourselves of this myth are not moral in nature, though there is some argument in that direction. This book is concerned with helping you manage the discomforts of special educator stress and it so happens that giving up the role of watchdog for the whole world and that giving up the myth of perfect rightness will aid you in maintaining the center of your feelings within yourself. No longer demanding that other people see things your way or do things your way, you do not "have to" upset yourself every time you are confronted with the reality that they do not. This will leave you more energy to deal with whatever issues are at hand. You will be better able to deal effectively with unconcerned parents, misbehaving children, and insensitive supervisors when your *should statements* are under control.

Myth Number 3

People Are Alike and Therefore Understandable. How could we special educators, the very proponents of individualization, fall prey to such a myth? It happens every time we are surprised that a child, colleague, or other person behaves in ways that we would not have or think that we would not have in the given situation. Evidences of this myth in action include particularly the disguised Should Statement, "I can't believe he did that!" What we are often saying in this situation is "I can't believe he did that because I wouldn't have in the same situation and shouldn't everyone behave the way I would?" The "people are alike" myth follows closely from the "one right way of doing things" myth. Both are products of our formative years when we had no reason to suppose that there was any way but our way of doing things and no reason to surmise that other people might not be the same as ourselves.

Developing a stress-managed style of interacting with others must include the capacity to accept the "difference factors" not only among our students and clients but with the parents, teachers, and supervisors we contact as well. Accepting the difference factors involves recognizing that we will never fully understand anyone else. Locked in our own unique set of experiences we can not expect others, even the others closest to us, to have the same motivations, goals, and reactions we have. As teenagers, many of us clung together in tight groups of young people who were as much like us as possible in order to avoid being faced with the uniqueness of others. We even denied the reality of existing differences between ourselves and our friends when such differences were pointed out by parents and others. Much of our time with friends was spent reviewing how alike we all were and how strange and impossible everyone was who wasn't in our group. This issue relates to stress experienced by the special educator in that SPSEs will experience accelerated stress when we rehearse the pattern of spending our time in difficult interactions lamenting all the unfathomable ways in which others are too stubbornly strange to accept rather than attending to what we intend to do in the situation. Let's examine the internal sentences of a special educator caught in the "all people are alike and therefore understandable" myth. She has just had a less than positive parent conference in which both parents refused to consider the educator's suggestion for promoting their handicapped child to more time in a regular classroom. The father said, "What difference does it make, she'll never be able to learn what the other children learn anyway."

Reality pain statements

> The conference did not have the expected results.
> I did not acquire the support for changing the student's schedule and will now have to regroup and decide on a new plan.

Should pain statements

> I can't believe that they cannot see how much better off she would be with this promotion. (They should be able to see how much better off she would be with this promotion.)
> I can't believe *anyone* would refuse their child any opportunity that might advance his or her progress. (They should not refuse any opportunity that might advance their child's progress.)
> I can't believe anyone would treat all my hard work so lightly. (They should show more appreciation for what I've done by agreeing to my suggestion.)
> I can't believe I need to start all over on the Individualized Education Program (IEP) for this student. (I should not have to do this over, rather these parents should be more like me.)

Exaggeration pain statements

> This is awful.
> This is terrible.
> Their behavior is intolerable and unforgiveable.

To maintain an internally controlled stress-managed work style in this interaction the special educator would be rehearsing preference or "I would like it if . . ." statements in place of the should statements made in the form of "I can't believe" statements. In this situation, preference statements such as the following would be helpful, "I would like it if the child's parents had agreed to the plan I felt was best." "I wish they were able to see the advantages I can see for making the changes." "I sometimes wish parents didn't lose confidence in their handicapped children." Preference statements regarding the behavior of others are the cognitive structures that allow the special educator to coexist in "grace" with all the unique beings encountered in our work. Preference statements provide a way of admitting that, while we would prefer that other people were like us and therefore understandable, not one person actually is and there is no way we can ever fully understand even one other individual.

A psychologist-teacher shared an analogy with me related to accepting others as unique and it has helped me many times to manage my stress level with others and to return the responsibility for my feelings to myself. The occasion was the group supervision session for a psychotherapy techniques practicum during my first semester of graduate school. The analogy was presented after I had excitedly given a summary of the interaction I had had with my first individual psychotherapy client. With much animation I shared with the group the craziness of my "case." The client was a woman who sought counseling to help her manage her two sons. I had listened, exuding unconditional understanding, as she elaborated on the misbehaviors of her two boys. They "talked back" to her constantly. They cursed at her and refused to tell her good-bye when they left the house or to tell her where they were going. They often lied about where they were going, a fact she discovered by following them from time to time. She gave them money expecting them to account for how they spent it, but they refused to do so. Every night she cooked a well-balanced meal for the family, but rarely were the boys at the table when it was served which meant she "had to" leave food sitting out on the warmer until late in the evening at which time the food would be so dried out she "had to" fix them another meal. Her list of atrocities easily filled my first anxious hour as a psychotherapist, a situation for which I was admittedly grateful. I was about to stage an inquiry into the early childhood social history of the two sons when my abused client let it slip that the two boys in question were 26 and 28 years old. At once I switched from searching for a diagnosis for the sons to finding an appropriate category for the mother. As I relayed these events to my supervisory group I closed my story by stating with obvious amazement, "And the part that makes the whole thing so hopeless is that this woman believes she is absolutely right in every way!"

As delicately as he could the psychologist-teacher suggested that I might consider referring this client to another person in the class. When your supervisor suggests that you refer your first client to someone else the response is not exactly designed to boost confidence in your future as a psychologist. Struggling nobly to regain my composure (I wasn't even a little stress managed then) I asked him to explain the reasoning behind his suggestion. What follows is a paraphrasing of what he said and the analogy I promised.

"I am suggesting that you may not be the therapist to provide services for the woman you are describing because you have decided quite finally that you are right and which means she has to be wrong, and which means very little is likely to be accomplished." (At this point I interjected something to

the effect that indeed I felt more right in the situation. He continued . . .)
"Think about it this way a moment . . . fantasize that you and the others of
your friends here are moving along through a stream of water. This stream
represents a flow of activities which we could call special education, or
therapy, or life. As you swim competently along through the water with
your coworkers you come upon a fish off by itself. This fish is behaving in
the craziest ways. Instead of moving with the flow, this fish is practically
standing on end, thrashing around its little fins, stirring up the sandy
bottom by twisting its tail back and forth. Such energy this fish is putting
out with the only apparent result being to blur its vision and hurt the fragile
edges of its fins! As you swim by with your coworkers, you note to each
other how odd this fish is. What a strange, unintelligent, and energy
inefficient way for a fish to carry on. You remark at the foolishness of such
behavior and take comfort in talking about how the 'outsider' fish would be
so much happier if it would stop all that incomprehensible thrashing and
splashing about and follow the example of you and your friends. In spite of
your reasoning and superior example you have little effect on the outsider.
Your words and shining example have little effect because what you don't
see is that coming down from the surface of the water is a tiny nylon thread
with a hook on it. The hook is inside the 'crazy' fish and it hurts. You will
never understand the gyrations of that fish because the same hook isn't
inside you. Clients, you see, the people you serve, all have their own hooks
inside them. No matter how you study and practice understanding you'll
never completely understand another person's behavior because you'll never
feel his pain. You will never know how logical his crazy behavior actually
is."

So my first client, my "crazy" mother was (is) a woman who had
different hooks than I had. She was different from me. Because I knew
about me and how I would react in her situation didn't mean I knew about
her. People are not alike. Trapped in our own perceptions we often cannot
understand them. This lack of perfect understanding does not mean we
cannot be helpful. In fact, by accepting the unmanageable uniqueness of
others you will be better able to respond to their unique needs. You will
have fewer damaging stress responses when you can give up the expectation
that other people are like (or supposed to be like) yourself. Also, special
education is more fun when you are open to learning how people are
different. Having more fun in special education is the whole point of a stress
management program.

Myth Number 4

Respect from Others Must Be Separated from Affection. A
consistent factor apparent in research dividing stress-prone and nonstress-

prone working people is the difference found in the priority individuals place on gaining respect and gaining affection from others. Specifically, on the assessment used by Friedman and Rosenman (1974) to separate Type As from Type Bs respondents are asked this question, "Do you strive for the admiration and respect of your friends and working associates or for the affection?" Stress-prone persons, as you have likely guessed, place greater priority on respect. The task for SPSEs learning to manage stress while interacting with others is not to avoid the desire for respect as though respect were a totally negative force. Management of clients and students is going to be much more comfortable if they respect our consistency and respect our efforts to act in the best interests of project goals. However, respect for our requests or respect demonstrated through willingness to cooperate is best developed in conjunction with affection. It is not developed in an atmosphere of fear and power devoid of affection. The task of SPSEs working to be otherwise, is to integrate respect and affection. There are stress problems for the special educator who proudly states, "I don't care if people like me. What's important is that people respect me." Respect can be lonely. Respect separate from affection often means standing apart, carefully not letting others know you. It so happens that talking, that letting other people know you is an important element of a stress-managed workstyle. Many supervisors avoid "real" interactions with the special educators they supervise saying that through such encounters they would lose respect. In extreme cases, special educators have been known to feel vaguely uncomfortable and overexposed when encountering students, clients, or parents in settings other than professional situations (such as in the grocery store, or the park, or at a sports event). The separation of respect and affection is easily understandable in light of the beliefs motivating SPSEs. We were taught not to trust ourselves or others and to base our strength on our achievements. People are not drawn together in an affectionate way by the distance of distrust or displays of achievement, but by immeasurable qualities of unique humanness that we were not taught to value.

Stress-Prone Special Educators separate respect and affection because we were taught that it has to be that way. We were taught that if we let other people know we had all the fears and feelings everyone else had, we would lose the respect we had worked so hard to *earn*. Affection is difficult for the individual with a severe stress problem. Not understanding how to value something that is not "earned," quantifiable, or achieved, the most stress-prone among us can be frightened into a workstyle that includes little real sharing with others. What is ironic about our stress-prone struggle for respect is that our struggle is motivated by a desire to be liked. We struggle so that others will see how we've tried. While other people may look with approval on all we've done, such admiration is not equal to being liked. Indeed our shining achievement may only serve to threaten others who are then less comfortable with us. In a group of studies some years ago, subjects were asked to rate the likableness of a taped commentator after listening to a short speech. Some listeners were asked to rate the commentator on likableness (desire to hear him again) after he gave a flawless performance. Others were asked to rate him after a performance during which he spilled a cup of coffee over himself and his notes. The less-than-perfect commentator was the overwhelming favorite.

Affection fills a pocket which can't be filled with respect. One suggestion Dr. Selye gives his patients who are working to reduce stress-prone behavior is for them to acquire a house pet, something to cuddle, to appreciate for existing and for nothing else. Such a suggestion may sound simplistic but there are many SPSEs who have, through the years, eliminated pets, friends, and casual conversation from their daily activities since these things take too much time and don't get one anywhere. With all our energy going into respect-gathering activities we trick ourselves into believing we don't need anything but admiration from others.

As special educators we need the other people in our agency. We need to have a place with them. Being admired by them is nice, but we need a place of affection as well. This doesn't mean we must have everyone in the gang like us. That just loops us right back into unreasonable demands for approval. What we need is to have people in our special education workplace with whom we look forward to sharing. We need to have people with whom we can share our frustrations and our triumphs with our work and with our homelife activities. We need to know others, including our supervisor, well enough to care about them up close as well as at a distance. Because the working situation in special education often encourages isolation, to accomplish the development of an affectionate support group requires more than giving up the myth of the separation of affection and respect. It requires making time to be with your colleagues.

Maintaining the myth that respect and affection must be separate increases the stress potential of your special education job. If your supervisor maintains this approach it will be more difficult for you to follow through on the suggestions in the change procedures section of this chapter related to managing stress when relating to your supervisor. But then your supervisor's workstyle won't be controlling your stress level. You have realized that, while it would be nice if your supervisor were to relax a little, there's no law that says he or she should.

Myth Number 5

Personal Energy Is Totally an Individual Effort. Maintaining personal energy throughout your special education day will be a great deal easier once you recognize the rejuvenating power of group energy. SPSEs, because we have been warned against trusting others, are less likely to take advantage of another stress-reducing technique which comes more easily to the N-SPSE. Rewarded for so long for doing everything ourselves we are likely to miss out on the *synergy* to be gained from becoming more than a leader in the group with which we work. Synergy is a term coined to denote the combined energy of a group of individuals which is greater than the sum of the energies of separate group members. The violinist has more energy to play surrounded by a playing orchestra, an educator has more energy to teach when feeling a part of a team effort. Viewing personal energy as totally an individual effort can result in our perceiving the people we serve as only "drainers" of energy instead of "replenishers" and even "multipliers" of our energy.

Moving away from the myth that "personal energy is a totally individual effort" can be both exciting and frightening. Remember we have been warned about what happens to irresponsible people who give up individual leadership for a group enterprise. You can begin by learning to be aware when your personal energy quotient is low and then bringing your group together to discuss ways to nourish the group energy system. Arrange as many student and client activities as possible in which you are a participant rather than a referee, a judge, or an observer. Participants have higher energy. Before beginning new activities, engage combined leadership from the individuals or group to be involved. To continually "run things" can be exhausting while to be a part of things is rejuvenating.

Myth Number 6

Perfect Harmony among People Is the Natural State of Affairs. Dr. Albert Ellis in his works on Rational Emotive Therapy made note of how the irrational idea that happiness consists of the absence of problems results in a great deal of human distress. Another potentially stressful idea particularly affecting our reactions as special educators is the myth that a state of perfect harmony among people, a state without disagreements or anger, is the natural and "right" state of affairs. Adhering to this myth, we upset ourselves anytime this harmony is threatened, and that must be frequently. As special educators who hang onto this idea, we are particularly susceptible to stress attacks whenever students or clients do any number of deliberate and nondeliberate things that indicate dislike for us or each other, or when the harmony of agency staff is disrupted in the unpredictable course of human interactions. The myth of natural perfect harmony is maintained by the individual through frequent rehearsal of *should statements* such as, "People should be able to always get along," "People should never dislike each other," "People should agree," or "People should understand each other." Frequent stress signals, threats to our well-being, will be the order of each working day as long as you can only be comfortable when perfect harmony exists among others.

Letting go of the perfect harmony myth does not mean automatically encouraging disharmony. With the exception of certain unhappy persons who are convinced they can not win in the system, harmony is the state of affairs preferred by us, our clients and students, parents, and supervisors alike. If you are not in a spiral of *should statement-* and *exaggeration statement-*induced stress you will be better able to encourage the harmony you seek, better able to resolve student differences, and better able to find grounds for negotiation with parents and supervisors.

MANAGING STRESS WHILE INTERACTING WITH CLIENTS AND STUDENTS

For the direct service special educator nothing is more real than all the hours spent watching, touching, teaching, smiling, and listening with students and clients. Special educator skills in serving, surviving, even enjoying the hours and days of direct service have long been attributed to some mysterious suitablility in our personality that enables us to survive in places where others would not. To some extent perhaps this assumption has a bit of validity. There is that special attraction; there is some reason why we chose service to people with special needs. We have the desire, but not the magic coping skill. It's when the hours mount up and the pace of improvement is slow that stress is likely to occur.

Effective management of stress in interactions with clients and students involves adopting an approach of intellectual curiosity about each person we serve, not just a curiosity regarding the needs of each person, but also a curiosity regarding what each person has to teach us. In what ways will *we* grow through learning with each client and student. A posture of intellectual curiosity is again one of those things the N-SPSE does without training, because intellectual curiosity about others is enjoyable, and because it fits with the N-SPSE's expectations that other people are complex and interesting. For those of us still fledglings in the nonstress-prone approach, still questioning human nature, our strongest ally in managing stress while interacting with students and clients will be the program we have worked out to manage our interactions with ourselves. As much as super-helper types sometimes resist admitting it, when we are uncomfortable with ourselves we end up locked into uncomfortable relationships with others. When we are too frustrated with ourselves to be curious about ourselves, we have little room for allowing other people to be themselves.

Four elements of your workstyle approach in relating with yourself will particularly affect your ability to manage stress while surrounded by imperfect others. These include: (1) your practicing ability to separate your right to be comfortable and relaxed from your continuous performances and from your ability to maintain approval; (2) your demonstration of responsibility for your own stress level in working activities; (3) your obvious avoidance of black and white, right and wrong thinking about yourself in the interactions of your job; and, (4) your attending to the quality each situation has to offer you as well as attending to quantifiable variables.

In accomplishing these changes in cognitive habits relating to yourself, you will have made progress toward reconceptualizing your special education career toward a less stress-prone approach with others. Remember, it's not other people or their behavior that cause your stress. Only you can do that. SPSEs can directly change a stress-prone style when interacting with students or clients by altering those thinking habits we rehearse about students or clients that follow from the Four Core Beliefs of the SPSE.

Struggle

When did the enjoyment of the people in special education turn into a struggle? Surely back in school you didn't do all that studying to sacrifice your life in the infantry of special education? It is possible, of course, that you did. You may have had professors and cooperating supervisors who envisioned themselves as locked in the battle of special education and who spent long conversations warning you about the atrocities and futilities of the war. But, assuming you didn't, and assuming your upbringing did not include the teaching that "you're not really working if you're not suffering plenty," you must have picked up the struggle approach to those you serve after joining the special education game. Stress-Prone Special Educator's statements regarding students and clients indicate a struggle approach, statements such as, "I'll try to make him, but he'll fight me all the way," or "We'll battle through reading, then if I'm still moving by noon there's the whole lunchroom scene to try and live through." Reasons frequently cited by special educators for deserting the "people in special education are fun and exciting" camp in favor of the "special education is a constant and dangerous struggle with people" camp include the following:

- Years of being unable to accomplish personal performance goals and contingently taking away the right to like myself.
- Days of viewing students and clients as extensions of myself so that when their performance lagged, my right to like myself was removed.
- Settling impossible performance goals (or having them set by others) and then when the impossible was not reached, contingently taking away the right to like myself.
- Refusing to accept disapproval from anyone without taking away the right to like myself.
- Experiencing less-than-perfect cooperation from clients and students and then withdrawing behind a wall of distrust.
- Working for a supervisor who saw me as an extension of himself or herself and thus based their right to relax on my performance or success in getting students or clients to perform. (This one, by the way, has been known to lead to counterspy tactics and outright altering of documents.)
- Working with students or clients of whom I was physically afraid.
- Going to my job while there is big trouble in the home situation.
- Working for a supervisor who did not believe I did good work or that I was capable of ever doing good work. (Everyday becomes a new trial.)
- Being isolated from other adults on my job.

These, of course, are not all the causes for embarking on a struggle approach with students or clients. You likely have a few of your own. Specific steps for reversing the trend back toward enjoyment of the game are provided in the procedures for change section. For now, consider how it might feel to be paid for playing all day at a game you really enjoy practicing in order to do better and better. Consider how it might feel to be one of your own students or clients.

Time

The SPSE's obsession with time poses a particular difficulty in learning a non-overreaction approach to others. To those of us who never have enough time to get things done the unique characteristics and problems of other people are often interpreted as obstacles. We don't have time for students or clients to be in a difficult mood. We don't have time to hear *why* the homework isn't done. We don't have time to decelerate a fight. We don't have time for someone to reinstate an enuresis problem. We feel we don't have all the time that other people do, but everyday these other people keep interrupting our pace. We SPSEs overreact to interruptions, not because we don't like people, but because we have deadlines, objectives, schedules, standards, and promises to keep. We react to the behavior of others in terms of our deadlines, objectives, schedules, standards, and promises, which means *should statement pain* and *exaggeration statement pain* are frequent companions. The special educator in direct work with others who holds onto the belief (fear) that not enough time exists will be in a state of more or less constant tension. The tension will be characterized by either an overreaction to other people's behaviors (delays in the action) or by a tense waiting for something to go wrong (for someone to dare to be unpredictable).

Some of the factors known to intensify the special educator's absorption in the time problem include:

- planning too much to do each day.
- planning too much for each student or client to accomplish.
- trying to do more than one thing at a time.
- knocking oneself out trying to convince a supervisor of one's superiority (acceptability).
- working for a supervisor who is not aware of the realities of your situation and who demands more and more.
- refusing to plan some "off time" in each day for yourself and for students and clients.
- making your right to feel relaxed in the evening (on the weekend) contingent on accomplishing a certain amount each day (week).
- nursing an SPSE's need to do more than everyone else does, and
- working for a supervisor who believes if you're not "climbing the walls" you're not working.

The time-orientation problem is of particular significance in our work as special educators since the people we serve can so easily see when we "don't have time" for them. They see the way our eyes dart from our desk to our watch when we talk with them. They notice how quickly we walk them to the door after a session. They learn how to use our fear of wasting time against us by causing disturbances which they know we'll handle expediently rather than effectively. Many students learn we'd rather move through material efficiently than make sure the material is mastered. These are the students who dawdle and refuse to work knowing when they are far enough behind we will agree to let them skip all the practice sessions and catch up as best they can. But most of the students and clients do not see our "hurry sickness" as something of which to take advantage. Instead they see the discomfort in our eyes and hear the tightness in our voices and resist the pressure by engaging in all sorts of behavior designed to force us to pay attention to them as people instead of as machines. Our "hurry sickness" ends up producing power struggle relationships with students and clients, and that means the stress potential of our job goes up.

Success

Because SPSEs believe that whatever success has been achieved is a result of our willingness to engage in stress-prone behaviors, we have a tendency to encourage these behaviors in students and clients. Convinced ourselves that no success is possible unless one's soul has been sacrificed, we pressure others to do more and more in less and less time. ("That's great. Now, tomorrow you can do four instead of just two.") We warn others about being too trusting of classmates on group assignments. ("Sure everyone has a separate part, but you'd better be able to run the show by yourself in case John doesn't learn his part.") So anxious are we for certain handicapped persons to achieve what we think they "should," we push them before they're ready and may engender a complete reversal of progress.

One special education counselor related this example. She had been working with a young man who had spent his childhood in a state school for the retarded and had, with the counselor's help just moved out into a semi-supervised group shelter. After two weeks on his own, the young man reported great success at the group home. His counselor was so excited about his progress in independent living that she began talking excitedly about finding him a job. Knowing of several openings, the counselor began making phone calls while the young man was still in her office. An interview was set up for the next day. The counselor didn't notice anything strange in his behavior when he left her office, but the next day she received a call from his group shelter supervisor reporting that her client had not come home the previous night. He did not show up for the scheduled interview. Two days later he was picked up by the police and returned temporarily to the state school. On reviewing what happened the counselor was able to see, "I just was so excited. I wanted him to succeed. It made me feel like a good counselor. I didn't let him enjoy the progress he had made before I started pushing for more."

SPSEs can get pushy. That's the problem. In our pushiness we overwhelm and frighten the very people we are so anxious to help. Most of the time our pushiness is based on the famous standby statement, "I know you can do it." Convinced as we are that our students and clients "can do it" we forget that what matters is what *they* think. We will have problems with students and clients when they feel we are basing our relationship with them on their success or even on their willingness to engage in stress-prone behaviors.

Some of the conditions known to encourage pushiness include:

- basing your self-concept on seeing yourself as the hardest working person on the team.
- rewarding students and clients only when they "do a little extra."

- working for a supervisor who only wants to hear that the triumphs in your program are stacking higher and higher.
- overidentification with students or clients.

Trust

Students and clients know when they aren't trusted and their attitudes and behaviors are changed by that knowledge. Enough has been written and said about the self-fulfilling prophecy. We do cause to happen what we expect to happen, whether it's academic progress or interpersonal difficulties. Trust problems with students and clients are characterized by a constant state of tension and overcontrol on the part of the special educator. Some conditions encouraging this stance include:

- working for a supervisor who expects there to be no "ripples."
- hearing prophecies about particular students that portend doom.
- working with students or clients with handicaps about which you have insufficient knowledge.
- working with students or clients of whom you are physically afraid.
- working for a supervisor who does not trust you.
- overreacting to the unpredictability of students and clients.

When you do not trust your students and clients to be cooperative you are left with the exhausting task of supervising every move. The well-rationalized, free-floating hostility that characterizes the SPSE will be a frequent companion. It is frustrating to *know* that no one else can be depended on in the way you depend on yourself. Doing special education with a low trust approach means giving up all the lovely benefits of synergy described earlier. Not trusting students and clients leaves you running around the orchestra pit playing each instrument instead of standing calmly up front letting the energy of all the combined music flow into you and through you.

COWORKERS, SUPERVISORS, AND INTERESTED OTHERS

Among police officers a major contributor to burnout is a factor identified as the *John Wayne syndrome*. A police officer experiencing the John Wayne syndrome alienates himself or herself from others in an effort to avoid fellow officers' disapproval. Officers caught in this syndrome believe that their intermittent feelings of distress are evidences of personal inadequacies, examples of their own problems of overreacting to situations everyone else is handling with ease. Keeping to themselves, these officers' difficulties are compounded by the loss of therapeutic relationships with coworkers. Without sharing relationships with fellow special educators we special educators do our share of John Wayne imitations. In fact, in agencies or schools in which relationships between coworkers are minimal, each special educator tends to view his or her role as independent from others. Potential stress resulting from lack of team effort is a common theme in human service agencies.

Managing personal stress and "being" with coworkers, supervisors, and interested others involves altering our approach to others within the four essential areas discussed in the previous section: (1) struggle vs. enjoyment of the game, (2) no time vs. enough time, (3) success vs. growth, and (4) trust vs. distrust. With coworkers and supervisors we may not see immediately the need for changing our approach since most of us in a hurry have been taught to put improvement of these relationships in the "if we have time" category. Research on the effects of stress has demonstrated that these relationships need to be placed in the priority category for each of us. As Christina Maslach (1978) found in her studies of long term stress, "Our findings show that burnout rates are lower for those professionals who actively express, analyze, and share their personal feelings with their colleagues" (p. 251). We need sharing relationships with coworkers in order to take care of ourselves. Sharing relationships require a nonstruggle approach, time, and openness to growth, and trust.

Supervisors have a special relationship with us. They are our main disapproval and approval person and usually our source of resource management and teaching power. Bettie Burres Young (1979) surveyed teachers to find out something many of us have known through firsthand experience. She reported, "Incompatible relationships between supervisors and teachers has been identified as a major source of anxiety" (p. 10). Some of this anxiety is reality based, that is, sometimes you are stuck with a particularly unreasonable supervisor. But more often a good portion of the anxiety felt by special educators in relation to supervisors is a result of not being comfortable with and not really knowing their supervisors. When you do not know your supervisor well, you will be experiencing a great deal of wasted stressful energy *guessing* about the supervisor's behavior—about why something was done the way it was and wondering if it will be done the same way in the future, about what the supervisor's behavior *really* means, and about what his or her plans for you are. When you feel your supervisor doesn't know you well enough, you'll be unnecessarily stressing yourself guessing what he or she thinks of your performance and wondering if why you do things the way you do them is understood. You need to take time to know your supervisor because that relationship matters in your overall workstyle approach. Developing a sharing supervisory relationship will cut down on the unpredictability of your job. If there is anything a special educator can appreciate it is predictability with at least some people in what can often be an overwhelmingly fast changing environment.

In Conclusion

Working with others without experiencing undue stress means developing a workable, pleasant, growth-oriented philosophy of "being" with others. The worn-out, stress-inducing childhood philosophy of trying to remain unstressed by getting everyone else to not upset us fails. That philosophy is based on the impossible task of achieving security and certainty in an uncertain, ambiguous and unmanageable world. We cannot maintain perfect control over ourselves; how can we expect to reach such a position with others? The answer for survival must lie in learning to manage our reactions to the behavior of others. After all, when you stop surprising yourself, you've stopped listening to yourself and when other people stop surprising you, you're sleeping through the show.

Altering Your Environment

1. Structure your daily work schedule so as to include some time alone.

It would be nice if you could set aside as much as 15 minutes, but 5 minutes at least twice during the day will suffice. During this time separate from others, find a comfortable place to sit or lie down, practice breathing deeply and slowly with your eyes closed. As you feel your body relax, also feel the center of responsibility for your stress level locate itself within you. Away from the needs and demands of others you are free to review your own alignment of priorities. You are free to collect your energies before re-entering the world. You need your time alone to manage your stress level with others.

2. Arrange your environment to include opportunities to talk with coworkers.

This procedure is a real challenge for those of us accustomed to squeezing product-oriented activities into every non-direct service moment of the day. Fifteen minutes of recalling old times in the coffee room doesn't conclude with a tangible product. Thus, convincing ourselves that anything has been accomplished can be a problem. But something has been accomplished. Your internal responses are affected. Your availability of personal energy has been changed. Of course, it matters with whom you do the sharing. By now you know whom to seek out and whom to avoid.

3. Develop a personal, face to face comfortable relationship with your supervisor.

This is not to suggest bringing brownies to your supervisor or practicing the manipulative acts of insincere flattery. The procedure suggested is for you to approach your supervisor openly and to declare your desire to have a good relationship as a way of improving your stress management abilities on your job. Supervisors appreciate open relationships, but because of the many pulls on their time or insecurities about what you want, supervisors sometimes don't get around to taking the necessary steps. In most education and mental health agency settings, the biggest complaint about supervisors is not that a negative relationship exists, but rather that no relationship exists. This is somewhat understandable given the isolation of many special education jobs and the tendency to avoid persons who have the power of judgment over us. In many agencies special educators know and use intricate pathways through the building to go from any spot to any other without encountering their supervisors. Avoidance of supervisors results in the *boogey man* syndrome. The boogey man syndrome occurs when we do not have sufficient direct contact with persons who have power over us to recognize their human qualities. Existing more in our imagination than in reality these persons take on exaggerated size and ferociousness. The longer the boogey man (or woman) is avoided, the more questions there are about his or her nature. The syndrome builds upon itself. To reduce the stress of guessing how your supervisor feels about certain things and to reduce the stress of wondering uneasily what your supervisor thinks of your work, you need to have a relationship you feel secure enough about to sit down and talk over what's on your mind.

4. Request to attend or have made available training programs providing information and skills for working with clients or students of whom you are physically afraid or who have handicaps about which you do not have sufficient knowledge.

Since the stress response is a call for the body to prepare for physical combat, it's understandable that when you are working with people of whom you are physically afraid, you are going to be experiencing a high frequency of stress responses. Gaining increased skills and developing plans for coping with danger are important stress reducing elements. If the threat of physical danger cannot be reduced to reasonable levels in your situation, management of your personal health may require changing your work situation so that it no longer includes persons viewed by you as dangerous. This can be accomplished by removing certain clients or students from your responsibility, obtaining sufficient personnel to reduce the danger level, or, if nothing else works, removing yourself from the situation.

One group of professionals who must frequently confront these alternatives is the "graveyard" shift of mental health workers at state facilities for the mentally ill. Because most patients are sleeping from 11 P.M.

to 7 A.M., staffing is usually short. One worker will be responsible for many patients. If the worker gets in trouble there are few workers available to help. All the orientation speeches aside, the job can be dangerous. Some people can stay with it for years and others cannot. There is no need to worry that if you opt out of a dangerous situation there will be no one to serve the people you were serving. Other people with stronger skills in the needed areas, stronger bodies, or less concern for physical pain are available.

The more knowledge you have about the handicaps and strengths of your students and clients the better chance you will have to remain unstressed while working with them. There is much to be said for the comfort of knowing what you're doing and why you're doing it. No training program prepares the special educator to deal with all the particular handicapping conditions included in the special education territory. Sometimes the John Wayne syndrome interferes with requesting additional training since to admit a lack of knowledge in the field might open one up to more critical scrutiny in that area. But more often, needed requests are not made. With so many things to do just to stay current, additional training is viewed as a luxury (or an inconvenience). To improve the quality of our "being" experience while serving persons with handicapping conditions, we need to attend to our comfort level. We need to develop a background of understanding of the special needs and possibilities for each person we serve.

5. Include in each period of time you spend "special educating" some time with each individual or group in which achievement is not relevant.

One way to ease the behavior of stress-prone persons is to separate them from the opportunity to achieve. One way to ease your stress during your special education day is to take a time out *with* clients or students. A few minutes each hour can be spent without structure to just "be" together, and to share nonprogress-related items of interest. These breaks in the action interfere with the SPSE's (and the stress-prone student's) habit of charging breathlessly through the day. Pausing occasionally enables the special educator to reflect, to ponder, and to review priorities for those we serve. Plus, allowing those we serve to "be" for a while without producing gives us refreshing insights into the uniqueness of students and clients.

6. Set up your special education environment so that the behavior of students and clients is controlled by environmental systems rather than by your expressions of distress.

In other words, when a student or client breaks one of the important rules in your special education situation, what happens? Is the principal mode of dealing with the infraction to chastise and point out how unhappy or stressed this act has made you? Or do you have a contingency system that involves altering the consequences within the situation? Evidence from applied behavior management research has demonstrated the ineffectiveness of the rule-by-expressed-distress arrangement. But for our purposes, the procedure is being criticized because of the way we feel when doling out displeasure and because of how it feels to hold our breath until someone does something displeasing. The following example of how a control system based on emotions was exchanged for a system based on logical contingencies was shared at a recent conference. A speech therapist working with young children had made part of her room into a fun area with a foam mat on the floor and a dozen odd shaped and brightly colored pillows. Several over-sized stuffed animals were part of the set. As long as her young clients attended to their exercises, their session was conducted in the fun corner. When attention wandered or efforts lagged, it was back to the hard chairs with the therapist behind her desk. Before devising this contingency system this special educator confessed she had spent much of her time chastising and warning children to pay attention. She didn't feel positive about it and neither did they. Using environmental contingencies rather than expressions of personal distress to manage the behavior of others is an important step in taking responsibility for your own stress level. It is also an important step toward shedding the myth that other people cause your stress symptoms.

7. When, in spite of your best efforts, you are stressing yourself over the undesired behaviors of others, do something to improve your work environment.

There's something to be said for the technique of the bored housewife who rearranges the furniture when the walls start closing in. When the unique ways in which other people are different from you start getting to you, change your schedule around. Clean out your files. Take down old pictures and wall ornaments and spring for some new ones. Find a new poster with a picture that touches your heart and a quotation that expresses your priorities. Take time to clear off the stack of unfinished correspondence on your desk. Using your stressful times to improve your environment improves your quality of experiencing for several reasons. The activity distracts you. You will think less about how unforgivable it is that other people aren't behaving as they should and the general unfairness of the situation. Instead your thoughts, at least part of the time, will necessarily be focused on making concrete decisions about what changes to make and just how to arrange new materials. The environmental improvement activity serves to bolster positive feelings as you feel better and better about how cleverly you have altered your surroundings. Actually initiating a concrete activity of environmental improvement serves the function of returning the control of your stress response to you. As the feelings of discontent begin to dissipate through your own decision to act, there is no way to deny who is responsible for altering your internal surroundings as well as your external ones.

8. Review your daily schedule to make sure your goals are realistic.

It may not seem logical to include this procedure in suggestions for managing stress when interacting with others, but planning more than you can realistically accomplish each day sets you up to overreact when other people persist in being human. When you have overloaded yourself, dehumanizing others is an easy step. People become obstacles in your path and the activities of people become means to an end. When we have overloaded our schedule, we do not overreact to others because we don't like them but because we have made our own precarious right to feel comfortable contingent on the accomplishment of tasks that may not be accomplished if other people do not conform to expectations. Overloading one's schedule might not be a problem for an accountant who interacts only with paper during a work day, but for special educators, with people-oriented jobs, an overloaded schedule means trouble with people.

Note also that SPSEs have tendencies toward over-volunteering, refusing to delegate and oversupervising. We set things up so that we *have to* work harder than anyone else and then complain about our many responsibilities and duties. Feeling righteously overburdened, it's not difficult to understand how SPSEs might develop a hypersensitivity to the actions of others. We already have so much to do, "how dare anyone give us any more trouble?"

9. If you work for a supervisor who does not believe you are working unless you are engaging in a frantic stress-prone struggle, learn to fake stress-prone behavior.

Some years ago a movie came out titled *How To Succeed in Business Without Really Trying* in which a young man "worked" his way quickly up the corporate ladder by putting on a show of harried, frenzied striving behavior. One technique he used was to arrive at work 15 minutes ahead of the rest of the office staff wearing the same clothes he had worn the day before. He would set stained paper coffee cups around on his desk, sprinkle crumpled sheets of paper on the floor and fill several ashtrays with smoked cigarettes. He would then drop his head on his arms at his desk and pretend to be asleep. When his boss arrived, he was quite impressed that his young employee had stayed at work all night. So impressed was the boss with the young man's willingness to sacrifice his health and social life for his job that our hero was soon awarded positions of great power.

Often I have been asked what to do in the following situation: "I'm not an extremely stress-prone person, but my supervisor is. How do I keep from picking up her behavior when she is pushing me to be as upset as she is all the time?" It is for this situation that the *faking it* suggestion is made. You know when you're accomplishing what you need to accomplish and if you have your priorities and goals in order. Here are some suggestions if your supervisor doesn't trust that you are trying without more evidence of suffering.

- Carry two or three phone message slips stuffed halfway into your pocket at all times.
- During conversations with your supervisor, dart your eyes toward the telephone from time to time.
- Suspend your breath while talking with your supervisor.
- Speed up your walking pace while passing his or her door.
- Upon leaving at the end of the day, walk as though the world is on your shoulders.
- Always carry a stack of papers home with you.
- Anytime anyone in the office asks how things are going, moan through a few sentences of how impossibly busy you are and how it's not getting any better.
- Put up lists of impressive activities and schedules around your office.

Altering Your Cognitions

1. Practice making preference statements rather than should statements regarding the less than desired behavior of others.

You won't be able to upset yourself as much repeating "I would like it if . . ." sentences as you would to insist that other people are refusing to behave as they "are supposed to." Preference statements are easier to follow with nonexaggerating "it's unfortunate" statements than are demands that emphasize how unbearable it is to be faced with the behavior in question. You will be calmer using preference statements since you won't be responsible for passing judgment on the behaviors of others with whom you come in contact. Giving up the task of judgment over others means you still have available all the energy judges must use up in defending their positions. The special educator making the statement, "He should have contacted me before the schedule change was made," will feel responsible for proving the rightness of the demand—pointing to policy, precedent, or fair play. The special educator who rehearses the statement, "I would have preferred he had contacted me before the schedule change was made," is able to proceed with the matter in a more relaxed way. The concept of preferences over should statements is often a difficult one for special educators. So often the stressed person in the preceding example will keep insisting, "But he *should* have. It wasn't fair. He *should* have treated me the way I treat him. He *should* have contacted me first." So strongly we cling to this form of interacting. Of course, it would have been preferable if he had behaved according to policy and according to precedent. It would have been nice if he had not stepped out of accepted channels. But whether or not he should have is a matter beyond our judgment. In our development of an effective program of stress management we are concerned with how our mode of thinking affects our quality of experiencing. We are not serving as an authority on the rightness or wrongness of the behavior of others.

Deciding whether or not you do something about the less-than-desired behavior of others is a separate matter from passing judgment on the *should* quality of the behavior. Because you exchange demands for preferences does not mean that you accept passively everything that comes your way. Actively changing the behavior of others, or at least attempting to change the behavior of others, can be beneficial in some situations. Such efforts are likely to be less personally stressful and more effective if you are able to maintain the clarity available when you are calmly alert rather than upset. Guidelines for deciding when it is in the best interests of your stress management program to attempt to change the undesired behavior of others are provided in the next suggested procedure for change.

2. Decide when you will do something to change the behavior of others and when you will not. When you are without the power to change the undesired behavior of others or when you are not going to make the effort to change the other person's behavior, stop putting energy into fighting whatever is not changing.

This guideline is a less lyrical restatement of an older one: "Lord, give me the strength to change the things I can, the courage to accept the things I can't change, and the wisdom to know the difference." So much of the stress experienced by special educators is stimulated by mentally reviewing the undesirable behaviors of others we either do not choose to change or are unable to change. It's considered responsible to worry about the parents we can't change or the legislators in far away places whose votes affect our programs. The problem is that worrying or stewing only raises our own stress level and reduces available energy. It dilutes our effectiveness and enjoyment of special education. Not that I'm suggesting you make no effort to improve situations by affecting parents, legislators, and others when you can. I am only suggesting you work toward "the wisdom to know the difference."

Giving up a style of continuous protest because other people keep behaving in less than desirable ways is particularly difficult for SPSEs.

Remember we have a fascination with perfection and consider it our duty to stress ourselves when confronted with evidences of anything less. The idea of "letting" other people continue to behave as they do without protest even when we cannot change them has an immoral ring. There is some argument that our protests are important; because others know we are upset, things may eventually change. Some merit can be acknowledged here *if* our protests are being heard by persons able to make the changes we desire. But who usually hears our protests? Not the persons we're hoping to change but our coworkers, our spouses, our friends. If protests can eventually make a difference then the behaviors of others are maybe in the range of "the things I can change." However, most of our protests are voiced with stress levels zooming over dinner tables and during breaks in the day that were originally designed to be relaxing.

Developing a stress managed cognitive style involves learning a system to determine the difference between behaviors of others you can change and behaviors you cannot. Stress-prone special educators have trouble with this differentiation because we find an ambiguous reality harder to accept than the grandiose prospect that we can change anything and anyone with perseverance. For SPSEs having trouble deciding whether to spend energy trying to change others or accepting things the way they are, the following four questions have been devised. Anytime you are stressing yourself over the behavior of others, ask yourself:

1. Do I have the power to change this undesired behavior?
2. Do I want to change this behavior?
3. Is it worth the effort required to change this behavior?
4. Am I actually going to make the effort to change this behavior?

If the answer to the first question is "no," cognitive rehearsal of acceptance statements is in order, e.g., "I would like it if she behaved differently. It is unfortunate and unpleasant that she behaved differently than I would choose." If, however, the answer is "yes," the next three questions are important. The second question is necessary because much of the time we complain but we really don't care enough about the situation to do anything except complain. This is often the case when we are rehearsing *should statements* about trivial matters such as the way other people spend their money, the arrangement of someone else's work area, or the activities of the agency board or a professional organization. When we stop our protest about these behaviors long enough to ask, "Do I want to change this behavior?", we realize it doesn't actually make all that much difference to us if these behaviors are changed or not. If the answer to question 2 is "yes," then we move to the third question.

Not all behaviors that you have the power to change and that you have the desire to change will be worth the effort required to make the change. For example, you may not like the behavior of a team member who provides specialist input in staff meetings. Let's suppose this man is always late to meetings and then when answering questions he tends to talk around the answer for five minutes before getting to the point. You know that as a team leader you probably have the power to initiate some change in his behavior. His behavior is irritating enough that you do want to change it. But you also know that this man is terribly sensitive to criticism (whether he should be or not) and tends to react to it by withdrawing his input in meetings. He is excellent in his job and his contributions are needed. While you stand a good chance of changing this man's behavior, the consequences just may not be worth the effort. The answer to "Is it worth the effort to change this behavior?" is often "no" when the behavior in question is a habit or mannerism of a student or client that does not seriously interfere with progress nor does it seem to bother anyone else.

Probably there are no better examples of attempts at behavior change that are not worth the wasted efforts than those behavior changes attempted through *nagging*. Not only is nagging an ineffective procedure for changing behavior, but it sets a negative tone for interactions between people. Generally speaking, nagging is not a behavior change procedure but a more or less continuous statement of protest stressing the protester and recipient alike.

From a self-constructive perspective, when others behave in ways you would prefer they didn't, you will need to decide if efforts at changing these behaviors will be worth the cost—the time, disruption, and risk. Sometimes even when you have decided that "yes" you have the power to change the behavior, and "yes" you want to, and "yes" changing the behavior would be worth the effort, the answer to the final question, "Am I going to make the effort to change this behavior?" is "no." Again this is hard for SPSEs to admit since we think we *should* be able to do everything or *should* at least want to do everything possible to improve every situation. And, after all, aren't special educators *supposed* to be able to change everything and fix anything? But, sometimes we simply choose to let the behaviors of others slide by just because other things are going on. The secret to managing your internal stress at this point is to let go of the demand that the behavior change. The preference will still be there, but preferences don't do to our stress level what demands do.

3. Cultivate the cognitive habit of intellectual curiosity about others.

This is best done by viewing other people and their behavior as interesting, rather than boring, shocking, disgusting, ridiculous, stupid, beyond comprehension, absurd, difficult, strange, or weird. Even when the temptation is great to stress yourself by rehearsing protests regarding the ways in which people are different from you, you can further your own inner calm by making out-loud statements to others about how "interesting" people (students, parents, supervisors) are. Along with reminding yourself and others how interesting people are, you can cultivate curiosity about people by seeking actively to know more about each person with whom you are in contact. As a stress-managed special educator you are aware that other people are different from you not because they are defiant or ignorant but because they are operating from a different set of experiences than the set of experiences directing your behavior. To manage your stress level you are better off putting your energy into learning more about those other sets of experience than draining yourself in protests and comparisons. This doesn't mean you necessarily must ask others question after question. All that you need for learning are your own powers of observation. Cultivation of intellectual curiosity about others is not suggested as a means of improving your moral character. The suggestion is made to better enable you to live and work with others while maintaining a positive sense of self and management of your internal self. The most powerful procedure for breaking down prejudices between people has proven consistently to be one in which groups on both sides of an issue work and live together. Under these conditions, human commonalities are discovered and the stress experienced is reduced for both groups. To reduce personal stress in working with others we must nurture the desire to discover more about them.

4. Avoid "hooking into" the progress of certain students or clients as evidence of your own worthwhileness.

Using the progress of those we serve as proof of our worthwhileness as special educators is a foolproof method of increasing the stress potential of the job. When we *have to* have students or clients performing at a certain level to feel okay about ourselves, any evidence of less-than-expected progress is interpreted as a threat to our well-being. Since prolonged stress is most unpleasant, we can easily be seduced into pressure tactics and other acrobatics to convince students and clients to perform. What's particularly interesting with SPSEs is that we often choose the most difficult students or clients as our "challenges," as the ones whose progress will determine our worthwhileness. We pick the one with whom no one else has been successful; we fight for a crack at the impossible. And often our efforts are admirable. The stress problems come in when those students and clients become extensions of ourselves, when we lose the freedom and energy to work comfortably with them because we can no longer afford for them to interact with the program in a way that is right for them. Because you decide not to base your worthwhileness on the progress of your clients and students does not mean you will give up trying to do an effective job. Of course you will desire to be as effective as possible. The belief that the only time you will try is when someone (yourself) is threatening you with punishment if you do not is a belief left over from childhood.

5. Whenever you are stressing yourself over the less-than-desirable behavior of others remind yourself in a caring, gentle way that you have the power to control your own stress level.

The adjectives *caring* and *gentle* are important elements of this procedure. The self-directed reminder that only you can upset yourself can be made in a hostile, self-accusing manner that only intensifies personal stress. In other words, you can stress yourself by being stressed and rehearsing self-statements such as, "I should be able to handle this without getting upset. I am terrible because I am upsetting myself over this. I should not be angry. I can't stand it because I angered myself over their behavior."

Reminders of self-responsibility for your stress level need to be made gently and with care. Dean Shapiro, in a process he describes as *reprogramming*, has several suggestions that can be effective in returning yourself to calm self-control. The method of self-reminding that follows was adapted from Shapiro's more complete behavior change process. To complete this procedure take a few minutes out and carefully follow the stepwise instruction.

1. Determine exactly what it is you are upsetting yourself about.
2. Repeat to yourself several times the following statement filling in the blanks with the appropriate, identified stressor.

   "I (name) am upsetting myself by demanding that (particular person) not (behave in a certain way)."
3. Once step 2 is firmly in mind repeat the following statement to yourself until you feel the center of responsibility returning to yourself. Again, fill in the blanks with the appropriate phrases.

   "I can love myself even though (certain person) continues to (behave in a certain way)."

This procedure is particularly beneficial when you are upsetting yourself over the acting out behavior of a student or a client or upsetting yourself over the lack of expected progress. A comforting, gentle reminder of your own ability to manage your internal affairs might be stated, "I can love myself even though Victor has re-injured himself by turning over his desk," or "I can love myself even though my supervisor has not provided the supplies I need to complete this project," or "I can love myself even though Mary

Ellen has completely ignored instructions all day choosing instead to live in a world of her own design." Once again comfortable with yourself, you will be better able to ponder the best way to handle the less-than-hoped-for behavior of others.

6. Practice the skill of compartmentalization.

Dr. Jerry Lewis (1978), reporting his findings on families able to withstand extremely stressful situations, noted that one characteristic of families best surviving stress was that individual family members were able to put their troubles out of their mind, whenever they were not actually in the difficult situation. Lewis's work involved studying families in which one of the children was suffering from a terminal illness. It's not difficult to imagine the potentially disrupting thoughts about the welfare and behavior of others that would haunt each family member in this situation. Nor is it difficult to see how families whose members were able to suspend their worries and rehearsal of problems would have more constructive energy available to deal with the actual crisis. To best survive the sometimes bumpy interactions with students, clients, coworkers, and others, special educators need to be able to put out of mind disturbing interactions once the immediate situation is past.

More will be said in the next chapter regarding stress-inducing qualities of worry/fretting over environmental situations we cannot control. Situations that are in the past are definitely beyond our control in that we cannot "undo" them. We can, of course, plan strategies for next time, but a definite distinction exists between the calm-inducing effects of *constructive planning* for next time and the stress-multiplying effects of *fretting* over next time. Note the difference between the internal sentences of these two special educators experiencing an unpleasant situation and planning for next time.

Special Educator Stressing Self

He shouldn't have done that.
I hate it because he did that.
This is a terrible situation.
I should have handled it better.
I should know how to handle it better.
I should not ever let this happen again.
I am a terribly inadequate educator because I didn't handle that situation well.
It is awful because next time may not be any better.

Special Educator Planning for Change

I wish he hadn't done that.
His doing that was inconvenient.

I wish I had handled that situation better.
Later, I'm going to figure out how I can handle it differently next time.
It will be more pleasant if I can handle the situation differently next time

Consideration of possibilities for change logically follow from the preference statements of the second special educator. The energy is still positive in relating to the situation. Because the calmer special educator is not caught in how terrible and impossible the person was, he or she will be better able to focus on the present. Since most special educators move from person to person throughout the work day, an important element of managing daily stress is practicing Scarlett O'Hara's "I'll worry about it tomorrow" trick. Once the interaction is passed, actively focus your attention on the new interaction at hand. Do not worry that you will go too far and end up an irresponsible person. Practicing compartmentalization does not mean you do not care about the interaction you're putting on hold; it just means you're choosing to not fret about it during a time when you cannot do anything about it. Preference statements that can help in learning to practice the Scarlett O'Hara technique include:

- While I wish my students had reacted differently, there's nothing I can do about it now.
- While I felt silly at the time it happened, only I can continue feeling negative by actively rehearsing what happened.
- While I wish that hadn't happened, it can only ruin the next hour if I choose to keep demanding to change the past.

Altering Your Physical and Behavioral Approaches

1. Cultivate the *pause*.
   A most pleasant way to alter your pace when interacting with others (while improving your ability to interact in nonstress-inducing ways) is to use the *pause*. To incorporate the *pause* in your interactions when other people are speaking to you, let them completely finish what they have to say . . . and then . . . wait . . . a few . . . full seconds . . . before you respond. Leave an identifiable quiet space between whatever someone says to you and your returning words. Cultivating the pause will have several positive effects on your stress level. First of all, making room for a quiet moment between points of excitement will have a calming effect on you physically as well as behaviorally. Not expecting to respond the instant a breath of silence affords the chance, you will be more likely to actually listen to what the other person is trying to communicate and will improve the congruence of your response. The expression on your face while listening will change as the tenseness required for speedy responses drops away. The hurry

behaviors of nodding impatiently, interrupting, and finishing other people's sentences become unnecessary. You will find that your body remains calmer while listening. The hurry tendencies of walking away while someone is speaking, handling books and other objects while someone is speaking, looking anxiously from object to object (particularly watches and clocks), and picking up items to hold between you and the speaker (such as paper, books, and cigarettes) are all exchanged for quiet. When the pause is integrated into your interaction style other people will respond more positively to you since they will at least have the impression that you are listening to them.

The quick-to-respond style of the SPSEs is an understandable element of our interpersonal structure. We have learned that doing things with speed is the best way to be a good special educator. Listening takes time. To do a better job of special educating, hurrying SPSEs use the time while people are talking to formulate our responses. This way we can give more people more answers in less time. The problem is that when others talk to you most of the time they do not want answers (even when asking questions) as much as they want you to listen to them. The interaction problem for SPSEs is part of the same issue of learning to value *doing* over *being* in every situation. Anxious to fulfill the doing in each situation, we miss the point of many interactions. The constructive philosophy of working that constitutes a stress-managed style must include a nonstress-inducing style of being with other people. This style will involve listening—not just to be good guys and good special educators—but to relate in relaxed ways with others.

2. Practice breathing with a focus on pace and movement.

This procedure is best called the "cool air in, warm air out" technique. When involved in a potentially stressful situation one pleasant, easy method of returning management of your physical and mental processes to yourself is to take a few moments out and to begin breathing deliberately . . . and . . . slowly. As you draw air in, slowly and fully, say to yourself in patient, quieting syllables, "cool air in." As you let the used air return to the atmosphere, slowly and completely emptying out your lungs, say to yourself, in patient, quieting syllables, "warm air out." This quieting response can be accomplished while you are conversing, even arguing and fighting with others. Of course, how long you can practice this response depends on the specific situation. If you are moving across the room to separate two or more crying, arguing children you may have only two quiet, deep breaths before you need to speak. But in the time of those two breaths you will have better prepared yourself to deal effectively with the situation and to respond without personal distress. The fact that you have paused in the interaction, refocused your attention, and reversed the excitable internal trend will slow your response and enable you to stay separate from involvement in already building power struggles among others.

3. When a particular student, client, or other is being or behaving in ways different from those you would choose and when the behavior of a particular student, client, or other is particularly tempting you to stress yourself, go out of your way to do something to please that student, client, or other person.

Now, this one sounds like something out of a citizenship club manual for young people. It's important to note that this suggestion is not being made out of desire to improve relations with others or even to make other people feel better. These will be merely pleasant side effects of managing your personal stress by refocusing your attention and actions during stress responses involving others. As strange as it may seem (and as impossible as it may sound), doing something positive for someone who is "driving you crazy" and totally "undeserving" has an uncanny way of healing the stress cycle. One resource teacher who completed a five-day stress seminar a year or so ago has written to report that the single factor most responsible for changing her pattern of stress cycles in the classroom is a combination of the "cool air in—warm air out" and "making the unexpected pleasant effort" procedures. When she recognizes herself caught in a stress cycle, she moves to a separate area of her room, breathes quietly until a sense of calm returns, and then moves to compliment, to smile at, or to touch warmly the accused "source" of her stress response. These actions change something inside for this educator which, of course, is the point of stress management.

4. Do something physical.

Your stress response is a preparation for combat, whether the identified, original cause is that you have been accosted by a powerful, upset student or that you have been informed your supervisor is calling an impromptu staff meeting after hours. Combat is not usually an appropriate or even legal response to whatever it is that other people are doing that is less than desired. Alternate physical activities can be helpful in working off built-up supplies of adrenalin, blood sugar, and a desire to do something active. If possible, brisk walking is recommended even if you only step outside and circle the building several times. If walking is not feasible, find some more confined task which requires sweeping, pulling, painting, pushing, sorting, or redoing. When working with young children or amenable older people, all will be helped by involvement in a short round of bending, reaching and jumping exercises. As you complete your physical effort, practice the "cool air in—warm air out" procedure.

NOTES

Cammer, Leonard. *Freedom from compulsion.* New York: Pocket Books, 1976.

Friedman, Meyer & Rosenman, Ray H. *Type A behavior and your heart.* New York: Alfred Knopf, 1974.

Hayden, Hiram. Humanism in 1984. *The American Scholar*, 1955-56.

Lamb, Richard. Staff Burnout in Work With Long-Term Patients. *Hospital and Community Psychiatry*, 1979, *30*, (6), 396-398.

Lewis, Jerry. Presentation to the American Institute for the Advancement of Human Behavior, Houston, Texas, October, 1978.

Maslach, Christina. Burned Out. *Human Behavior*, September, 1978, pp. 16-21.

Maslach, Christina & Pines, Ayala. The Burnout Syndrome in the Day Care Setting. *Child Care Quarterly*, 1977, *6*, (2), pp. 100-113.

Rosenman, Ray H., Friedman, Meyer, Wurm, Moses, Kositchek, Robert, Hahn, Wilfrid, & Werthessen, Nicholas T. A Predictive Study of Coronary Heart Disease. *The Western Collaborative Group Study.*

Shapiro, Dean. Presentation to the American Institute for the Advancement of Human Behavior, Houston, Texas, October, 1978.

Woolfolk, Robert L. & Richardson, Frank C. *Stress, sanity and survival.* New York: Sovereign Books, 1978.

Youngs, Bettie Burres. What Can You Do About Teacher Stress? *National Education Association Reporter*, October 1979, *18*, (6), pp. 10-11.

Zimbardo, P.G. The human choice: Individuation, reason, and order versus de-individuation, impulse and chaos. In W. J. Arnold & D. Levine (Eds.), *Nebraska Symposium on Motivation 1969.* Lincoln, Neb.: University of Nebraska Press, 1970.

Chapter 6

The Unpredictable, Always Exceptional World of the Special Educator

6

Regardless of how dedicated and clever we are in planning and arranging our special education environment, we still find ourselves intermittently confronted with less than desirable situations over which we have little control. Frank Devine (1978) included a testimony in his report on the causes of burnout compiled for *Hospital and Community Psychiatry* that states the case well. One staff person interviewed for the report described the burnout problem direct service personnel face by saying,

> I think the major cause of burnout is that most of the time we really can't do anything about most of the problems we encounter. Unlike the physician who can prescribe an antibiotic for pneumonia or set a borken leg, with fairly predictable results, we often find ourselves helpless because of situations completely beyond our control . . . we are like mechanics who are presented with an engine that is not functioning well but who have nothing more than a list of the parts and tools necessary to do the job. (p. 77)

The reality of special education includes unexpected and expected difficulties, ongoing problems and less-than-perfect situations. To manage your personal stress while you function as a part of the special education reality you will need to find a way to relate comfortably with your environment, including its ever-changing and unpredictable elements.

When considering the internal and external effects and outcomes of a traumatic or other special education situation, it's more important to know what kind of special educator is involved in the situation than to know what kind of situation is occurring. The specifics of the problems you encounter in your job are not as important as are the ways in which you handle those problems. Therefore, learning to relate comfortably with your special education environment will mean: (1) altering your stress-prone approach to imperfect reality and, (2) appropriately altering imperfect reality when possible. While the next chapter will describe ten external problem situations, this chapter will focus on internal special educator skills that affect your relationship with the external environment.

THE RELATIONSHIP BETWEEN YOUR PERSONAL ENERGY AND YOUR ENVIRONMENT

The chief factor adding to the stress potential of special education environments is that we, as special educators, have not learned how to maintain positive, healthy emotions within the everyday working reality of our profession. Following the easy action-reaction model, we, like most everyone else, have learned how to maintain good, healthy emotions only as long as our surroundings are predictable and pleasant. Unlike many other professionals, it is taken for granted that special educators enter their chosen field already knowing (by way of magic or birth) an important management skill that otherwise must be learned. This management skill is the skill of producing positive, healthy emotions within ourselves amidst changing and difficult circumstances. Development of this skill enables special educators to go beyond the narrower idea of *coping* with the reality of special education toward a program of job enjoyment. To enjoy your job all the time, not just when everything is going well or it's Friday afternoon, you will need to examine your characteristic ways of relating with your environment.

The SPSE's Power Struggle with the Environment

We SPSEs were brought up to believe that if we worked hard enough, were good long enough, and made all the right decisions, we could struggle our way into an environment without problems, inconveniences, and dissatisfactions. Ignoring all environmental realities and personal limitations, we believed we had a guarantee of a utopia someday brought about through our own efforts, but only if we were willing to struggle, struggle, struggle against difficult surroundings. Eventually (perhaps after we made it out of school, or received our Master's and a new job, or when a particular child moved, or when the agency moved to a new building, and so on) we believed that an environment without problems, inconveniences and dissatisfactions was not only possible, but our deserved payoff for all of our suffering. Because we believed this, we SPSEs are much more easily stressed by external reality than are N-SPSEs. SPSEs believe we should be able to control everything that happens around us. As children expecting to "conquer" our environment and viewing ourselves as very powerful, we believed that if we encountered something in our environment we did not like, we could just change it. SPSEs expect our environment to conform in certain ways and when it doesn't, we expect to feel tension. Recently, researchers, psychiatrists, psychologists, and others commenting on the present state of national affairs have noted a change in the expectations the general public maintains regarding the hassles that come with living in our environment. Dr. Friedman (1979) from the University of Chicago was quoted as saying in a *Wall Street Journal* article last fall that Americans' present expectations of life are different from the expectations of past generations. He stated, "We seem to ask that life provide absolute immunity to any error or to any risk . . . we feel that conveniences are meant for us and we're depressed without them" (p. 1).

The stress prone among us are more likely to suffer in our everyday special education efforts because of our unreasonable expectations. We suffer because of our belief that when expectations are not met, we are supposed to upset ourselves, we are always supposed to fight back. This usually translates into stimulating and maintaining a stress response whether or not any outward assertion is made on the environment.

The "approach to the special education environment" problem for SPSEs is largely one of expectations. The problem with the crises in our special education job is that we do not expect them and we do expect to struggle. When choosing your first profession or making a change later, some idealization of the selected field is part of the choice process. More idealization is often necessary if preparation for your chosen field requires much time, effort and risk. Imagining how wonderful everything is going to be once we're finally out in the field helped us through long hours of study and helped us to accept living at poverty levels while we were in training. Some idealization is desirable and helpful. But if your expectations while in training do not match the special education situation in which you are now working, habitual dissatisfaction (and constant rearrangement of your environment) can result. It would be nice if you could have known what to expect as a special educator. Studies done on the matter indicate that new employees who are given realistic preparatory information when offered the job or immediately after they accept it are more likely to stay with the organization. Of course, providing realistic preparatory information is not as easy as it might sound. Nor was it possible for you to know what to expect from your specific job until you were actually in it for a while.

The Angry SPSE

Anger, hurt, and fear are emotions so tightly knit together that it is generally accepted when you are experiencing one you are, to some degree, also experiencing the other two. As you recall, the stress response always begins with a message to your brain that your well-being is threatened. This experience of threat is very close to the experience of anger though the outward expression of the stressed person may not reveal anger. As SPSEs relate to our imperfect environment, the anger element within our stress response is easily apparent. Believing we should be able to control everything, when we encounter evidence that we are unable to do so we are quick to make the demand that things should be different. We are quick to follow with demands of how things should be different. A generous supply of exaggeration statements reflects how unfair, unbearable and terrible the nonconforming situation is. The result, of course, is anger. Altering this response to the imperfect environment is difficult. Many have been taught that upsetting ourselves when less-than-perfect situations occur is an admirable expression of assertiveness, rightness, and personal strength. With this view in mind, consider who suffers when you or someone else fumes through a staff meeting or spends suppertime reviewing the injustices and unforgivable events of the day.

Selye has described clearly what happens to those of us who, expecting a problem from our environment, are always poised for combat just in case our environment doesn't cooperate. He emphasized that no organism can be maintained continuously in a state of alarm, and pointed out that the individual's energy to adapt to real or imagined crisis is finite. There is no more adaptation energy available for those of us who invent or have more crises during the day than there is for those N-SPSEs who experience fewer crises. As a result we run out of adaptation energy sooner and then nurse our headaches and our exhaustion. Again, the health of our mind determines the health of our body. Selye described three choices each of us has when faced with an unpleasant environmental situation. The first choice we have is to relate in a *syntoxic* way with the environment, that is, in an accepting, cooperative style. The other two choices we have are either to fight the environment or to run from the environment. These last two obviously involve stress and are the typical styles of the SPSE. Although trained to struggle with the environment when things do not go well, we usually do not actually fight or run. We prepare for these actions internally and we express our desires for battle with our anger. In discussing the three styles to interact with unpleasant environmental circumstances, Selye emphasized that the first choice, the development of syntoxic relationships with the environment, is an underrated, viable response choice. He also noted that death can result from choosing the wrong reaction.

Relief from anger for SPSEs comes with greater acceptance of the imperfect, ambiguous, largely unmanageable and unpredictable special education environment. Greater acceptance involves exchanging *should demand statements* regarding the environment for *preference statements* and exchanging *exaggeration statements* for *anti-exaggeration statements*. Woolfolk and Richardson (1978) identify as two causes of frequent anger: (1) having extensive personal boundaries, and (2) having a low tolerance for frustration and discomfort. Another way of stating these characteristics is to say that those of us with frequent anger responses have internal cognitive habits that include responding frequently to environmental situations with the *should demand statements*, "I should be able to control this" (extensive personal boundaries) and "I shouldn't have to put us with this" (low tolerance for frustration and discomfort). These, like other *should statements*, can be exchanged for *preference statements* to reduce anger and to maintain control of your internal quality of experiencing.

SPECIAL PROBLEMS WITH THE FIGHT OR RUN RESPONSE

Three particular thinking habits of the fight or run, always prepared for combat style of relating with the environment are problems that deserve mention. These three are: (1) overgeneralization, (2) dichotomous thinking, and (3) magnification. A discussion of these will help you to recognize when your stress response is interfering with your ability to relate positively with the environment. Each of these thinking habit problems serves to distort your environmental relationship and to increase the stress potential of your environment.

Overgeneralization is what happens when you upset yourself by insisting that a unique situation is "just one more example" of a larger problem rather than a unique and separate event. Labeling is a product of overgeneralization whether you are labeling an individual "autistic" or labeling a situation as "another worthless meeting." Commonly heard overgeneralizations refer to groups of people with one characteristic in common as "those people" or "them," implying cohesion and similarities that may or may not exist. Overgeneralization is a cognitive habit sometimes used by special educators to emphasize the difficulties of problem situations. Statements such as the following are used: "This *exact* thing has happened every year," or, "I've had supervisors just like her before," or, "No one from that school will want to participate."

Overgeneralization has much in common with *dichotomous thinking* since dichotomous thinking requires overgeneralization in order to be effective. Dichotomous thinking is also a method of denying the uniqueness of the situation; it establishes only two categories of recognizable experience. Using dichotomous thinking, situations are viewed as either all good or all bad and once the negative label has been established the environment is given no opportunity to improve. Using this procedure to deny the ambiguous mixture of desirable and undesirable events in the everyday environment, the following statements are sometimes used: "There goes the program!" or, "It's going to be one of those days," or, "What did you expect? It's Monday, isn't it?" Both overgeneralization and dichotomous thinking are patterns frequently used by those struggling with our environment. They are nonproductive attempts to control and understand complex events by simplifying the events. Both are cognitive habits that reduce our effectiveness. They impair our judgments and reduce our personal energy; it's more tiring to battle generalities and polarizations than it is to deal with reality.

Magnification is a thinking habit that uses *exaggeration statements* to emphasize the difficulty of situations. Using magnification we simply exaggerate the effects of less-than-perfect situations out of a fear that we cannot respond competently and comfortably. Most of us have encountered the situation in which several educators and specialists working with a student or client disagree about the student's or client's identified problems. What threatens one specialist's sense of well-being simply doesn't threaten someone else. For the person who feels unable to respond competently and comfortably, the "problem" behavior is likely to be viewed as more damaging and more frequent. An eight-year-old waits for father to come home to administer punishment and, in his mind, Daddy grows to a horrifying height of nine feet. Through exaggeration, difficult environmental situations are magnified similarly from the status of inconveniences, unpleasantries, and unfortunate occurrences to traumas, shocks, dramatic injustices, and crippling events.

Recognizing when you are rehearsing the habits of overgeneralization, dichotomous thinking, and magnification will help you to reshape your relationship with the special education environment. When you recognize that you are increasing the stress potential of your job by distorting reality and reinforcing unproductive, upsetting ideas, you are ready to consider alternatives. Alternative ways are those that recognize the uniqueness of each event and the unpredictability of causes and outcomes. Regardless of the extent and intent of the event, its impact on you is determined by your own internal reaction.

SYNTOXIC WORKSTYLES

Play is the Work of Children
Work is the Play of Adults

The Chinese symbol for crisis has two elements; one represents danger and the other represents opportunity. To manage personal stress while doing special education requires that you view the crises in your work situation as signals that something new is happening. You need to see the situation from a new angle. We know the old stress-prone techniques of fight or flight in the face of crises will keep you in a combat stance. Even learning extensive coping techniques will only provide temporary relief from stress. Rather, it will be necessary to develop a philosophy of working that includes constructive ways to relate to the crises in your work environment.

Working as Learning

Crises are not merely obstacles to perfection but can be important learning experiences. Remember, the truthfulness of the statements that make up your workstyle philosophy is not as important as their usefulness. When you view crises as learning experiences as well as problems you will be experiencing something different inside—where stress lives. The easiest way to incorporate the *crises as learning experiences* element in your workstyle philosophy is to exchange *should statements* made in response to undesired situations with *preference statements including a phrase emphasizing the learning to be gained in each situation*. For example, let's take a situation in which a special educator has just received notice that she will have four additional students for a week due to an illness of another staff member. Note the two ways she can respond to her unpredictable environment.

Should statements only

> This shouldn't have happened.
> She should have assigned them to someone else who doesn't have any special duties.
> This shouldn't have happened at this time in the semester!
> I should be able to do something about this!
> I shouldn't let this bother me.
> I should be able to handle four more students.

Preference statements plus learning phrase

> I wish this hadn't happened, but there must be something to be learned from this.
> I wish she had assigned them to someone else who doesn't have any special duties, but maybe I'm the one who has something to learn from these four students.
> I would prefer that this didn't bother me. I wonder what I'm supposed to learn from this situation.

It is not relevant which set of statements is "right"—which reflects the environment in a way that would be agreed upon by a majority of people. What matters stress-wise is how much internal threat is engendered by each approach. What matters is what occurs inside the individual when he or she chooses combat readiness cognitive habits. Obviously your internal comfort while you are developing a syntoxic relationship with your environment will not be all that separates the new, less stress-prone you from the old stress-prone you. When you are rehearsing *preference statements* in combination with learning phrases, your appearance will be more serene, your movements less exaggerated, your patience extended, your judgment improved, and your chances of enjoying your job, every day and every hour, greatly enhanced.

Your Workplace as a Center for Personal Growth

To open your workplace as a center for personal growth requires a review of your motivations for working in the first place. Surveys indicate that people work for three reasons: (1) sustenance, (2) power and status, and (3) personality enhancement. Stress-prone special educators are likely to insist they are working for sustenance, just to keep food on the table, which makes little sense when you consider the pay scale in the profession. In reality SPSEs are working partially for power and status, although this may appear strange given the structure of the field. We are not working for power and status in the sense of striving to have our picture on the cover of *Fortune* or to climb a ladder of corporate success. Our efforts toward power and status fall into the role of struggling for perfection within our own environment. We try so hard to be a *good* special educator that we lose the ability to maintain our energy and to enjoy the job. We struggle to protect what little power and status we have through our combat stance and our hurry sickness. We work to maintain the status of being worthwhile.

To maintain a constructive philosophy of work, your job must become part of your overall personal development. For you, your job must become a matter of personality enhancement; sustenance, power and status accompanying your efforts become pleasant side effects. Only when you decide to work because of the learning and development available for you will you be able to approach your job with calm and enthusiasm. Young children, before they learn that school is a frightening self-worth proving ground, approach each new workday with excitement and energy. As adults, we have accepted that the workday is approached with dread, that only a crazy person begins each day with an open mind and looks forward to new learning. Because dreading the workplace is the typical approach, many stress management programs focus only on making structural improvements in that dreaded work environment. Making external changes can bring you to a neutral point at which you merely are able to "stand" your job. This stance results in a day-to-day state of *marginal wellness*—a state in which nothing is quite debilitating enough to cause a complete breakdown *now*. In this state of marginal wellness, stress symptoms that include fatigue, headaches, backaches, irritability, and even depression are accepted as part of the reason we are being paid. Accepting your work as an important aspect of your personal growth means moving beyond marginal wellness to full wellness or quantum (unlimited) energy. (See Table 6-1.)

Effective stress management means moving beyond behaviors and attitudes that are typical or even generally admired. Often those typical and admired behaviors and attitudes are stress-producing procedures, leftover lessons from childhood that no longer make good physical or psychological sense for adults. The choice to approach your work environment as a battlefield or a center for personality enrichment, of course, can only be made by you.

Altering Your Environment

NOTE: The next chapter is devoted to identification and alteration of specific potentially stressful elements within your special education environment. Guidelines in this section focus on altering the environment to better approach your job as an opportunity for personal enhancement.

1. Arrange your work environment to be comfortable for you and your workstyle rather than according to instructions from the latest training manual.

In particular this means arrange your desk space and the space in which you interact with students or clients. You can look forward to spending the day "growing" in surroundings suited to your style of learning. Of course, the learning needs of students or clients are not to be denied, but their needs need not be the only consideration.

2. Design your workspace to reflect your "personality enrichment" approach to special education and your job in particular.

Table 6-1 The Special Educator's Work Experiences

Breaking Point Work Experience	Typical Work Experience	Stress-Managed Work Experience
Burnout	*Marginal Wellness*	*Full Wellness*
1. no energy	1. barely enough energy	1. quantum energy (unlimited supply)
2. physical breakdown	2. physical maintenance without painful symptoms	2. sense of good physical health
3. work is not accomplished	3. work is accomplished with stress	3. work is accomplished with enthusiasm

This is done most easily by speckling or covering your walls and cabinet door spaces with freelance bulletin boards and posters reflecting you—your thoughts and your feelings. Have one large bulletin board titled "My Best Teachers" on which photographs of clients or students are placed. Each time you see this bulletin board you can be reminded of your motivation for being a special educator. Reserve one bulletin board or wall space for cartoons, sayings or articles discovered in your reading that reflect pet ideas of yours. Encourage contributions from others for any of your *open expression* spaces.

A number of special educators completing stress management seminars have added personality enhancement touches to their workspace by bringing jungles of plants, stereos and tape systems, stationary bicycles and jogging shorts, and by bringing cameras to work. Accept work as growth. It need not be the suffering you must endure in order to have the right to relax and feel worthwhile after it's over. Linking real life to the work experience is easy and fun. Sometimes SPSE types have trouble with this concept; we believe we're not supposed to actually enjoy work. After all, we're being paid to struggle, not to breathe, renew ourselves, and grow!

3. Make a special poster for your workspace that lists the nine freedoms Friedman encourages persons in his post-heart attack stress management clinics to accept.

The nine freedoms that Friedman hopes his clinic patients can accept are:

1. The freedom to give and receive love.
2. The freedom to restore and enrich one's personality.
3. The freedom to mature.
4. The freedom to overcome one's hurtful habits.
5. The freedom to enthuse in the life activities and events of others.
6. The freedom to recall one's own life in the past.
7. The freedom to indulge in 360° perception.
8. The freedom to listen.
9. The freedom to enjoy tranquillity.

Altering Your Cognitions

1. When encountering less-than-perfect environmental elements within your special education situation, practice using *preference statements* in place of *should statements* and *antiexaggeration statements* in place of *exaggeration statements*. Use the same basic restructuring process described in the previous chapter as a cognitive method to deal with the less-than-perfect people encountered in special education.

2. In your mental preparation for each day, practice strict adherence to the *only one day at a time* principle.

A person involved in the "race of life" rather than the "game of life" will find this guideline difficult. After all, the really competitive racer-worker is always thinking ahead. Otherwise we are sure we will be left hopelessly behind. This guideline is not intended to eradicate all long term planning, but rather to encourage you to use your daily energy on the tasks and experiences that are really available to you. Plan your day around the present knowing that the energy to deal with and learn from future situations will be there when those days arrive. Your clients and students can only deal with today. Many a special educator has been unable to relax and learn with the people they serve because they nag themselves about their client's or student's pasts and futures.

Your stress management program must also be a 24-hour a day affair. You will not be able to simply read this book, try a few things and expect to alter your work approach on a permanent basis. The stress-prone approach is a well learned, well supported style of working. To develop an N-SPSE's approach will require a daily review of your relationship with yourself, others and your environment.

3. As you consider your relationship with your environment, review why, out of all the professions that are available and that continue to be available each day, you *chose* to *choose* special education.

Reviewing your priorities as a special educator can help you to direct your energy within your workspace. Personal energy for adaptation to crises is limited. Use your adaptative energy on movements that really matter. As special educators struggling with our environment we are likely to "waste" adaptation energy on projects that matter very little to us, such as making the best possible time on the freeway, having all our paper work done by five o'clock, or convincing fellow workers to change their modes of operation to our way of doing things.

4. Accept with grace the requirements of certain tasks.

Much personal energy is wasted when we engage in the costly behaviors involved in resisting what must be done to reach whatever goals we set for ourselves. For example, say that you decide you want to attend a particular meeting that requires inconvenient travel plans and doing a great deal of extra work ahead of time. A good way to waste personal enthusiasm is to spend your time after your decision lamenting how horrible and unfair it is that the elements of travel and time will make it more difficult to reach your goal. As SPSEs believing we should be able to control everything, we waste our energy fighting the requirements of tasks we think are unfair or difficult rather than spending our energy in positive action. Often I have encountered a special educator wanting to work in a more specialized area but resisting the work involved to obtain the necessary additional credentials. The special educator in this dilemma will first relate to me how unfair the whole credential system is and then ask me what he or she ought to do. Much to the distress of the inquirer, I have no magic. Certain goals usually require effort. The question you have to ask yourself is, Do I want to reach a certain goal and am I willing to do what must be done? If the answers are yes, your best stress-managed approach is to move forward rather than lamenting the requirements. In other words, once you have decided to move in a certain direction, stop talking about the way you *should* be able to move and how *terrible* it is that the requirements of the tasks are different than you would choose. Freely express your preferences and avoid magnification of the situation.

5. Organize a Worry List and set aside a Worry Time.

Worry is one way SPSEs attempt to gain control over an unmanageable environment. If we cannot in reality control something we at least have the decency to worry about it! Worrying means we are responsible special educators and worrying makes us feel like we are doing something about the situation. But worrying is a stressing procedure; worry messages are constant rehearsals of threatening messages. Worry is a way of stressing ourselves without the occurrence of any external events. Worry can be changed to planning. Planning can be distinguished from worrying: When you are planning you will usually need paper and pen, you will have a positive direction after the time spent in planning and you will feel more energized and relaxed. After time spent worrying, you will feel directionless and fatigued.

To change worry habits develop the practice of using a Worry List. Carry with you a note pad on which to note carefully the things you *need* to worry about. Write down any item worthy of worry. Do not worry about these items at the time you recognize them as Worry List candidates, rather save them until your Worry Time. Set aside a period of at least 15 minutes a day to be devoted to worrying about the items on your list. During your Worry Time devote yourself to thoroughly worrying about each item. No eating or drinking is allowed during this time as these would distract you from your "duty."

Keep your Worry Lists from month to month to enable you to review how effective your worrying has been in altering the course of events.

Altering Your Physical and Behavioral Approaches

1. Practice slowing your pace and moving gracefully within your workplace.

It's no wonder that SPSEs have twice as many accidents as do N-SPSEs. Always in a hurry, we can't keep up with our arms and legs and knock things over and bump into furniture. Practice graceful movement as you walk down halls and interact physically with others. Sometimes a background of soft music can help.

2. When changing your environment or making repairs, take time to gather proper tools and expert helpers.

Our hurry sickness emphasizes getting the job done quickly rather than doing the job well. We end up in painful and often messy struggles with heavy bulletin boards, malfunctioning audio-visual equipment, and new specialized appliances with missing instructions. Return to yourself the right to take time to prepare the way when you work with elements of your external environment. Machines do not have to be our enemies. There are people and tools available to help use machines properly.

3. Bring your favorite items from home for lunch or snacks.

Of course many people dread the workplace when even the pleasure of eating is taken away. Do not take for granted that "just whatever" is okay for lunch. Take what you want or take the time to get what you want. When we have the attitude that work is suffering, we may not make the effort to have pleasure breaks during the day. We would rather hold our breath until we're out of prison at five o'clock. A later chapter discusses the importance of taking care of your physical condition as part of stress management. This guideline is presented as a beginning. Eating is an important direct interaction with your surroundings. Make this interaction pleasurable at the workplace.

NOTES

Devine, Frank. A Hospital Psychologist Responds to an Analysis of Staff Burnout. *Hospital and Community Psychiatry*, October 1978, *29*, (1), p. 77.

Friedman (article) *Wall Street Journal*, Fall, 1979, p. 1.

Selye, Hans. *Stress in health and disease*. Boston, Mass.: Butterworth Publishers, 1976.

Woolfolk, Robert L. & Richardson, Frank C. *Stress, sanity and survival*. New York: Sovereign Books, 1978.

Chapter 7

Ten Potentially Stressful Situations

7

This chapter describes ten situations known to increase dramatically the stress potential of the special educator's environment and provides specifics for change in each problem area. Identifying potential sources of stress and procedures for change can be helpful as this information will enable you to be more aware of how your environment can affect your comfort, energy, and functioning. But note also that altering your environment can often cause as much stress as it eliminates. Change is almost always stressful even when the outcomes are positive. And remember that even the ten situations to be described do not exist separately from one's stress-prone or nonstress-prone internal cognitive approach. As you read each situation, relate these elements to your own environment. Your interpretation of the stress potential of your own job will depend largely on how you are thinking and feeling during the time you read the chapter. You will judge the stress potential of your job and its potential for change using as criteria both the ten situations provided and your perceptions, expectations, and mood at the moment. Thus, while the following chapter is devoted to guidelines for making specific external adjustments to reduce the stress potential of your special education environment, do not be wooed into believing that the existence of potentially stressful situations is the major problem for special educators and do not be tempted to believe that changing these situations is the solution.

As a special educator you are well aware of how a day on which you are determined to create positive environments for yourself can run into undeniable snags well before noon. Arriving at work, first you learn that the legislature has cut funds for next year and that means an increased service load. Next, the behavior modification program you have had working beautifully for two weeks folds, and then a review of your records reminds you once again of the slow pace of change in your profession.

Without question the special education environment has characteristics designed to stress professionals in the field. You are now making changes in your internal approach to your environment. It will be helpful for you to be aware of potentially stress-inducing external variables within your job. Ten areas known to increase the stress potential of the special educator's environment are presented in this chapter. The best way to use this information is to note for yourself whether your work environment does, in fact, include the potentially stress-producing elements described. Many stress-producing factors on the job occur at a level that is not quite severe enough to demand immediate attention. Thus they are allowed to continue unchanged and unnecessarily add to the daily stress potential of the workplace. We know these factors are bothering us but we do not realize the actual stress costs since we can still "get by." The ten areas described in this chapter are presented to increase your awareness of their potential for affecting your stress level. Once aware, you can decide which of these situations you can avoid, which you can change, and to which you choose to adapt through an internal cognitive adjustment.

A word here is in order regarding making changes in your environment. You have more power to change your situation than you think and you have more power than you realize to control the impact of situations you can't control. Most of us, having learned more restrictive methods of making changes, have steered away from effective choice-making and communication with leaders as techniques for improving our environment. Instead, well schooled in stiff-upper-lip/work-is-suffering techniques, we rely on chance and periodic complaining to coworkers as methods of change when we are unhappy with our situation. Randy Kunkel is a training consultant with *Potential*, a Colorado based human resources development firm. He related this descriptive example of the kinds of choices we have when we find ourselves in a painful situation we would like to change. Kunkel (1979) was waiting for an elevator with a friend in the lobby of a Midwestern hotel when a big, rough-looking cowboy came over to wait for the elevator, and stepped on Kunkel's toe as he took position. Caught in this stressful situation, Kunkel described his change technique options as: 1) saying and doing nothing, just bearing the pain; 2) ripping his toe out which could be painful; 3) doing nothing externally but making an internal adjustment to reduce the pain; 4) telling the cowboy about the situation and asking him to please move his foot; or, 5) turning to his friend and complaining quietly about how terrible and unbearable the pain was. You have these same options as you determine change techniques in the painful situations of your work environment.

The first option, saying and doing nothing, bearing the pain, is chosen frequently by those of us especially dedicated to trying to be perfect. After all, we expect ourselves to be able to handle anything and everything.

Usually this option is damaging not just to ourselves but to those we serve and our coworkers as well. People who suffer in silence find other ways of expressing their pain. By suffering in silence, supervisors and others who might be able to effect change do not even know that a painful situation exists. Too often we assume supervisors and others know what our problems are and how much pain we have when, in fact, they do not know.

The second option for our man with the trapped foot was to rip his foot away but change nothing. This is what happens when a person changes from job to job or project to project without examining personal needs. With this option, there is a painful recovery period and after a while the next job or project is found to include the same problems as the escaped situation.

The third option, making an internal adjustment, was what the previous chapter was all about. The fourth option, telling someone who can make changes about the stressful situation and the pain experienced, is what this chapter is all about. The last option, turning and complaining to someone who cannot make needed changes, is not actually a change technique at all. This frequently chosen path accomplishes little except to encourage the doer to rehearse stressful ideas. This option provides a great deal of negative energy during coffee breaks, lunchtimes, and on the home front. How many times have you spent hours intended for relaxation telling your spouse or a friend (neither of whom can do anything) just how things ought to be changed at the agency? You have more powerful ways to control your environment.

NOTE: Because of the nature of this chapter, techniques for change will be provided in the context of problem situation descriptions rather than at the end of the chapter.

POTENTIALLY STRESSFUL JOB SOURCE NUMBER 1

Having More to Do Than You Can Do Well

Note the last part of that phrase, "than you can do well." We achievers usually learn early in life that the more we can accomplish, the more worthwhile we are. With this assumption to guide us it's not difficult to end up with more responsibilities than we can do well. As you look for ways to add enthusiasm and a game theory approach to your job situation, you will need to examine how your energy is being spent during each work day. To approach your job with energy and enthusiasm you need to feel reasonably confident that you can afford to be involved in each activity of the day ahead without a constant nagging sense of "falling behind" in the great race of special education. The special educator with more to do than can be done well skims through the day with a familiar sense of free floating hostility. After all, we see other people who are not frayed at the ends. Why do we have to take on all the responsibility? It isn't fair that we have to work harder than other people! (Of course, we actually believe we should work harder than other people and are uncomfortable when we are not doing so.) A reminder is needed here. A hectic pace, a busy schedule, and long hours do not automatically cause you stress. Your stress level within these conditions will be determined by how you relate as a thinking, feeling person to environmental factors. Some persons actually experience intensely stressful episodes because they have too few responsibilities to keep them occupied. I have yet, however, to encounter a special educator with this problem. More often what I find is special educators going through day after day with a sense of being overwhelmed.

When you are involved in doing more than you can do well, your self-esteem will suffer as you watch yourself performing at "getting by" levels. Available energy decreases partly because of the number of tasks you have to accomplish and partly because of the lost powers of nourishment and energy renewal that could come from an appropriate number of tasks done well. The first lost source of energy renewal when you have more to do than you can do well occurs when you relegate to low priority participation in special, time consuming, recreational, creative, and people-involvement projects that you used to enjoy. Although such activities are not essential to daily functioning, they did provide energy. As you become overburdened, these projects are merely squeezed in between everything else that "needs" your attention. Sometimes when such activities are not absolute job or family requirements, they are squeezed out of the schedule altogether.

In addition to the loss of energy occurring as a result of eliminating special projects, when you are overscheduled the everyday *unscheduled* bits of physical, social, and intellectual nourishment—the family chats, the evening walks, the lingering over the newspaper—all of which once picked you up from time to time during the day are eliminated as "time wasters."

Of course, giving up your energy providing activities—both the special ones that are unique energy re-chargers and the less structured, spontaneous ones—isn't accomplished in one day. The process is gradual. A little bit is taken off your "getting ready" time on weekday mornings to enable you to accomplish an extra task on the way to work. Your Saturday activities change so that the entire day is spent catching up on the errands and small jobs that you once did on weekdays before they became overloaded with meetings and work extras. Under pressure of "so much to do" you learn how to close conversations quickly and how to talk your spouse, friends, and family into carrying on without your involvement. After a few years of surviving the situation in which you have more to do than you can do well, others will accept your justification for giving up involvement and relaxation and stop asking for your participation.

Just as the process of rejecting your special energy-providing activities is a gradual one, so is the process of adding more and more to your own daily agenda. Reversing this potentially stressful situation can be a difficult process for two reasons, one related to others and a second stemming from certain misguided, stress-prone personal needs. First, other people—colleagues, supervisors, family members, and friends are not likely to welcome your unburdening yourself of responsibilities since this will mean returning those responsibilities to others. Even the suggestion of re-evaluating who should continue with responsibilities previously and happily shouldered by you may be rejected. It could be that for a long time you have accepted duties with either the statement, "It's not any trouble, really," when it was, or by convincing yourself that since "somebody has to do it, it might as well be me." If you fit these patterns, others will likely be quite surprised that you feel overwhelmed or even uncomfortably busy. If you intend to reduce the stress within your work environment and to increase the satisfaction you find therein, some *honest* talks and renegotiations with others are in order.

The second reason reducing your "to do" list may be difficult involves looking inward at possible underlying reasons for allowing or even striving to work yourself into such a fix. Early we are taught that:

1. people who take on the tasks of others deserve special treatment and consideration; and,
2. people who are very, very busy are more valuable people.

Such ideas result from a cultural confusion between our value as people and our productivity, a particularly confusing concept for product oriented, time-conscious SPSEs. (The ways in which this confusion contributes directly to the individual's ability to remain enthusiastic and relaxed on the job will be delineated further in discussion of Potentially Stressful Job Source Number 2.) Adhering carefully to the idea that people who take on the tasks of others deserve special treatment and the idea that people who are very, very busy are more valuable people, we SPSEs pay no attention to the costs in terms of stress that result from these unsatisfactory ways of trying to merit consideration and attention from ourselves and from others. Note also that while taking on more and more tasks may win us brief approval, it does not lead to the significant and satisfying relationships with others we are seeking. In fact, the SPSE's belief that the only person who can be depended on is old number one can be given at least partial credit for the "having more to do than can be done well" predicament. While we might take on all these tasks in order to be responsible and to win favor, being overwhelmed with burdens actually has the effect of keeping other people—family, coworkers, clients, and friends—at a distance. (Speaking of underlying reasons for staying too busy, think about that last statement!) After all, who has *time* for idle conversation? Or to really know how others are getting along in their lives? Who has time to slow down and enjoy simple events?

As you may have surmised by now, dealing with the problem of having more to do than you can do well requires a more complex approach than simply "deciding" to change. Several of the guidelines presented later in this section will be useful in helping you alter this potential stress intensifier. It would be simplistic to suggest at this point that you review your daily "must do" list and break free of well learned overburdening habits. SPSEs are much too good at coming up with reasons why we are the only people in the world who can do the things on our lists and why each item must be accomplished at all. We are much too afraid of losing esteem based on our sense of extraordinary accomplishment. We are afraid to take back our right to like ourselves without our busy schedules. Those fears make it difficult to accomplish a simplification of our working lives.

Therefore, it is suggested that, at this point, you review the chapter on the eventual physical results of the stress-prone workstyle and stay open to applying guidelines toward simplifying your working life. A poster suggestion for your work area to be used as a reminder of your stress management program is provided in Exhibit 7-1.

Exhibit 7-1 Laws of Social Dissatisfaction

Social Dissatisfaction Law #1:	The less you do, the less people will be satisfied and the more they will be angry and frustrated with you.
Social Dissatisfaction Law #2:	The more you do the more you will be expected to do. Thus you will wind up being able to do less than you are asked to do and more people will be angry and frustrated with you.

POTENTIALLY STRESSFUL JOB SOURCE NUMBER 2

Lack of Fun on the Job

What is this, "lack of fun on the job?" Work is not supposed to be fun, is it? Aren't we paid a salary to do our job because work isn't fun? Of course, it isn't all laughter and relaxation but the lack of some infusion of fun activity in the day can lead to a stress born out of boredom and the strain of pressing in a single direction without revitalization. Comic relief serves an important purpose in tense drama and while your job may not qualify as tense drama, comic relief is still needed if you are to keep your energy at a high level. The fun interspersed in each work hour may not be in obvious comic form. Your students, clients, and coworkers will usually be more than willing to provide comic relief. In fact, an excellent sign that stress is getting the best of you is when the previously pleasant comic relief gestures provided by clients and students become only irritating. Improving the quality of your job when it lacks frequent moments of fun is a very personal endeavor since humor is interpretive in nature. It should be noted, however, that as SPSEs discovering this difficulty you will need a two-pronged approach. First, determine the avenues for fun you used to use but have eliminated in your efforts to forge ahead. These will likely include coworkers with a good sense of humor whose presence could be cultivated, spells of coffeebreak interaction that always bring a laugh, and listening to clients and students with real life "funnies" to share. Second, determine direct ways to increase the smile potential of your work environment such as cartoons, funny sayings, photographs and moments highlighting funny occasions. Learn to tell jokes and riddles as a way to help others have fun. This will have the nicest stress-reducing effect on you. Do whatever brings stress-reducing fun to your job. Now, the firmly entrenched SPSEs among us may balk at this idea since we are convinced that nothing significant is being accomplished by a smiling, relaxed, and laughing person. But you are beyond such a stress-inducing notion by this time, right?

POTENTIALLY STRESSFUL JOB SOURCE NUMBER 3

Lack of Structure and Poor Management

You can effectively increase the stress and burnout potential of your job by failing to establish a reasonable, organized structure and by not abiding by a corresponding management system. Also, your supervisor or agency director can go a long way toward creating potential job stress by not providing the agency with sufficient, reliable structure and sound management. Each of us has a management system by which we operate.

It's just that some systems are effective while others guarantee a series of "lost item crises," deadlines missed, and eventually lowered competence and enthusiasm in the work setting.

But wait.

Aren't programs on stress reduction supposed to be about relaxing, about letting go of the need to have everything in its place?

In a way, yes. Time consuming, compulsive needs for organization and order can result in continuous and damaging stress reactions. Imagine how uptight a special educator stays when he or she must at all times have regularity, cleanliness, timeliness, and order! Working under these self-imposed conditions can best be compared to having responsibility for a hopeless war effort in which every day a new losing battle must be launched. Special educators lost in compulsive organizing behavior rarely have room to find the job itself enjoyable and are more likely to have a "work is struggle, work is suffering" orientation since so much effort must be spent counteracting the less-than-perfect organization.

Using compulsive organization and management as a way to deal with anxiety results in an increased stress potential on the job, but to neglect using any reasonable organization and management system also ends up increasing the likelihood of stressful conditions. The idea for stress control is to develop and use an overall management system that will *better* enable you to relax into the *essence* of your job. Rather than crippling you with an endless and stifling structure, implementing a few basic management techniques will set you free, leave more time for the parts of your job you especially like, and allow time away from the job to be less cluttered with details and problems that pile up from your day.

Personal difficulties with structure and management frequently result from being so overwhelmed with tasks requiring immediate attention that organizing an overall system is given second priority day after day, week after week, and eventually year after year. SPSEs are so busy with brushfires we never have time for second priorities, which means we end up with more brushfires—and so the cycle continues. This predicament brings to mind the cartoon of the woman, obviously a wife and mother, who is standing at the back door of the family station wagon, surrounded by piles and stacks of blankets, tents, assorted camping gear and beach supplies. As her husband approaches she is saying, "Okay, I can do one of two things. I can either *organize* for this trip or I can *go* on this trip, but I cannot do both!" Caught in a similar dilemma and looking for immediate results, SPSEs go on a lot of unorganized trips.

For now, to establish a reasonable organization and management program, consider structuring your *time* and *space*.

Structuring, of course, means planning. And planning requires paper and pen. Review the difference between worrying about something and planning. Planning is distinguished from "worrying about" and "trying to improve" in three ways: (1) some writing is nearly always required, (2) you will feel better afterwards, and (3) you will end up with a definite plan of action. Every effective management program begins with setting aside a definite segment of each *week* for major planning and a shorter period of each day for daily planning.

When considering management of your time within a stress reduction framework, watch out for the SPSE tendency to underestimate the time required for tasks and travels. Also, work to avoid the SPSE tendency to plan a schedule of activities that will work only if nothing goes wrong during the day. Accept the N-SPSE realization that when operating in an unmanageable, unpredictable, people-filled environment, things will go awry every day. We can learn to arrange our schedules with room for contingencies. Schedule all tasks, even phone calls and minor reports, for a specific time during the day. Learn to use scheduling as a freeing mechanism; you can feel more relaxed when you do not need to carry so many "things to do and remember" around in your head. Several excellent books are available on this specific aspect of environmental management.

Organization and management of your *space* means structuring your special education environment to best facilitate completion of paperwork and routine tasks. Using desk tops as "pile" areas invite the *I know it's here somewhere* stresses. Do have a labelled place for important items (even if you are the only user). Teach students, clients, and coworkers where completed work, returned work, and other correspondence are to be placed. Provide an "in" box for others bringing you items throughout the day. At home, design specific, labelled areas for special education work, correspondence, and materials used frequently.

POTENTIALLY STRESSFUL JOB SOURCE NUMBER 4

Getting Behind

Once behind in your tasks, the rate at which you are likely to fall still further behind and to experience stress accelerates. The principle is the same as the one that applied when many of us less-than-compulsive college sophomores missed a class session. Once a class had been missed, we felt a bit more anxious about going the next time. We didn't know for sure what was covered or whether or not the professor noticed we were absent at the previous class. As our anxiety went up, so did our desire to avoid the situation entirely. Our likelihood of missing a second time increased. After a second miss, the anxiety again increased as we felt sure we were hopelessly behind and the professor must surely have noticed us missing. The desire to avoid was then even stronger. If we bent to the desire, we were likely to miss additional classes, become confused about when exams were to be given and what material was to be covered. We eventually adapted to the continuing anxiety by assuming an uncomfortable, haphazard approach to the class. Once this situation was established, we were constantly on guard. In our confusion we never knew what "surprises" might come our way. We learned to rehearse a set of excuses in case our behavior was challenged.

It's impossible to completely separate the contribution of *getting behind* from the stressing effects of *having more to do than you can do well* and *lack of structure and poor management*. However, falling behind is important enough to receive separate treatment because so many persons have reported this difficulty to be a source of potential stress. In any program designed to increase levels of available energy, the amount of energy lost to *worry*, particularly worry about all that needs to be done, is a factor to be considered.

It would be easy enough to suggest that you just "not let yourself fall behind" anymore now that you are aware of this habit's propensity for adding to your stress potential. Such a suggestion would be obviously naive. In your work situation, probably the best you can hope for is to recognize when you are behind and structure catch-up programs for yourself. This means putting aside several hours (or whatever time it takes) and setting yourself exclusively to the task of catching up. During this time, no new tasks are begun no matter how tempting may appear the chance "to accomplish something." The focus must be on clearing things up, straightening what needs to be straightened, and evaluating and planning for upcoming activities.

As part of your new stress management approach to special education, give up the idea of limiting yourself to being in the workplace and working only during the specific hours for which you are being paid. Sticking rigidly (and proudly) to this schedule with a statement like, "They are paying me to work till five and that's all they are going to get," are products of the *work is suffering* philosophy. The attitude of maintaining rigid hours only contributes to your stress. If the time comes when you need to catch up, staying after the appointed quitting hour would be a process to help yourself function in a more relaxed way in the upcoming days and weeks. Many times we hurriedly turn our backs on confusion and overdue work on Friday afternoon because our "work time" is up and it seems so important to make the weekend as long as possible. Often, if we had stayed even an extra half hour, the entire weekend would have been more relaxing.

The cumulative effects of getting behind are usually visible all around us and observable in our behavior traits—rushing to and from activities, forgetting items and events, misplacing items, and eventually, becoming irritable and visibly distressed. These evidences do not even take into account the considerable, internal, physical penalties. With regard to burnout, it's rather easy to see how the college student class-skipping analogy fits. In both situations enthusiasm wanes and, unless you're careful in the special education environment, it's not uncommon to take a defensive stance and start finding fault with your job and maybe the whole field of special education.

POTENTIALLY STRESSFUL JOB SOURCE NUMBER 5

Having a Poor Relationship with Your Supervisor

In some cases this may mean having *no* relationship with your supervisor. Isolation is a problem for many educators. Another frequent problem is when the special educator doesn't like his or her supervisor. In either of these cases, developing a positive supervisory relationship will be more difficult. However it is still important; increased stress potential on the job results when this relationship is nonexistent or negative.

Each special education situation varies depending on its organizational structure, but in most cases your supervisor has a great deal of control over aspects of your job that affect your potential enjoyment of the working process. Your supervisors may be less visible than those in business settings but their power is usually still there should they decide to make it felt in your situation. Also, your supervisor will likely be the person you need to contact when you want to make changes in your program. Your supervisor is usually the key in determining your access to needed resources. You may need the cooperation of your supervisor to make changes you would like to reduce stress on your job. Like it or not, it's easier for a supervisor to listen openly to your view of the situation and to new ideas when a pleasant, honest association has been established previously.

Because of the complementary nature of this relationship, each of us needs to develop a positive orientation rather than a punishing orientation toward supervisory interactions. Sometimes it sounds like this suggestion involves "brown nosing" manipulation. Such is not the case. You will increase your chance for a positive relationship if you are open and genuine in expressing your desire for a good relationship. There is no need for hypocrisy or thinly-veiled flattery and gifts. Most supervisors welcome an open approach since having a positive relationship with those they supervise will decrease the stress potential of *their* job. You can achieve positive results by simply walking up to your supervisor and announcing, "I would like to have a positive, open relationship with you since I have learned that not having an open relationship increases the stress potential of my job."

Last summer during a week long program for a cluster of school districts in east Texas, six resource reading specialists began the week by announcing that the whole reason they were attending the seminar was because they had been assigned to a supervisor who was notoriously unreasonable and unlikable. During the discussion of the importance of developing a positive relationship with one's supervisor we had time to role play methods to approach supervisors and to maintain openness. The notorious reading specialist supervisor just happened to be attending another in-service seminar in another part of the same building and just happened to encounter the Stress Management participants each day after training seminars. This provided the resource reading specialists with opportunities they needed to practice their new ideas. On Friday, the supervisor tracked me down during lunch and, with an expression between bewilderment and pleasure, said, "I don't have the faintest idea what you are doing in that class of yours, but every one of my six resource specialists has come to me and made the identical statement about her relationship with me next year. I don't know what's happening but it feels better. I know none of them like me and that I have a reputation as a tyrant. But with their attitudes I feel like there's hope for next year."

Along with the practical reasons for working on your relationship with your supervisor, there is an even more basic reason—your own level of enthusiasm and enjoyment. When you are fearful or resentful or even detached from your supervisor, you will not easily be able to relax and grow personally and professionally in your job. You need to know your supervisor and his or her goals and priorities so that you have a way of judging how you are doing in relation to plans and expectations.

Without sufficient data about your supervisor you are likely to stress yourself frequently using valuable energy in guessing games regarding how your supervisor would respond if you asked for a particular schedule adjustment, a change in your environment, or for an application for an advanced position. Uncomfortable about how he or she will react, you wonder whether or not you ought to even make a request. Then, instead of directing your attention to the supervisor (where it belongs) you talk to other people, trying to collect opinions and ideas. Meanwhile the appropriate time for notifying your supervisor may have passed by. To be comfortable in your job you will need to maintain a relationship with your supervisor that is open enough and comfortable enough to allow you to walk into your supervisor's office and express what's on your mind.

POTENTIALLY STRESSFUL JOB SOURCE NUMBER 6

Lack of Recognition

Having no one to acknowledge work done or work well done has been found to potentially contribute to higher stress levels on the job. One high school teacher recently reported these feelings after spending four days accompanying a group of students to a statewide Pan American Conference: "By the fourth day I was so exhausted and frustrated. I missed being at home. I missed getting enough sleep. I was tired of teenagers. The air conditioner in my room hadn't worked for two days and my bed was comparable to sleeping on plowed ground. But—if just one student had said 'Thank you,' if just one set of parents had called to say they appreciated my efforts, if just one person had noticed at all that I was working so that the club would have a successful trip—I would have picked up and felt much better. With just a few 'thank-you's' I could have lasted four more days. But no one said anything. It was like I was just expected to do what I was doing. It really hurt."

Recognition for your efforts on the job may be largely out of your control as far as your supervisor and even your clients and students are concerned. The recognition received after having to ask for it doesn't feel as refreshing as that which is given spontaneously. The best we can hope for then may be that your supervisor will participate in training where he or she, too, will learn that a strong pre-condition for stress and burnout is 'lack of recognition.' While gaining more recognition for the work you do may be largely out of your power, there is a reason beyond increasing your awareness for discussing the problem. Probably little else besides a major life crisis can so quickly lead to burnout as does associating with or trying to serve people who are suffering from burnout. The same conditions that result in burnout for special educators facilitate burnout in clients and students. You have a part in determining whether or not the debilitating condition known as *lack of recognition* is a factor with those you serve. In fact, if you recognize them (or their parents) for recognizing you, you are likely to increase your own recognition quotient.

Also, there's no law against recognizing yourself; there is no law against announcing your appreciation of your own efforts. There are many of us in the field who believe that special educators are very special people.

POTENTIALLY STRESSFUL JOB SOURCE NUMBER 7

Using Comparison Tactics To Determine Your Effectiveness

One easy way to encourage stress in a child is to point out how poorly he or she is doing compared to another child or to other children who are neatly organized along a "normal" curve. As a grownup involved in a profession, you are not likely to have anyone easily available to accelerate your stress level with such tactics. However, if you learned your early lessons well, you are likely to do these same things to yourself. An internal policy of continually comparing how you and other individuals fare or how you do things compared to others will effectively raise your tension level. This source of job stress is not really an aspect of the workspace environment, but rather a result of a stress-prone approach to relating with the environment. Each person has a unique set of experiences from which he or she operates. Trying to judge yourself and others with a common ruler will only lead to frustration and dissatisfaction. Even if your comparisons repeatedly show you to be ahead of the others, the overall result will still be tension. You will fear losing your right to a sense of well-being if ever you should lose your superior position. Comparison tactics distance you from other people. Alienation from coworkers represents one of the most painful symptoms of burnout. In the alienation phase of burnout, remarks like the following are often heard.

I just don't have anything in common with other special educators.
No one where I work ever even thought about the things I think about.
I don't like anyone here.
No one at my job could understand me.

Since these thoughts and feelings often accompany comparison tactics, these procedures negatively affect relationships. The symptoms of burnout are likely to accelerate in this situation since the loss of social nourishment adds to an already uncomfortable problem. Once alienated, we put out messages telling other people to stay away. Then, not having the closeness with others needed to discover human commonalities, we are likely to rely further on comparison tactics to rate the worthwhileness of ourselves and others. And the painful cycle continues. Techniques for breaking this cycle were described in Chapters 4 and 5.

POTENTIALLY STRESSFUL JOB SOURCE NUMBER 8

Having a Stress-Prone Special Educator for a Supervisor

From time to time in seminars with special educators, a participant will come up to me at the conclusion with this situation. He or she reports, "I believe I have learned to approach my work in a more comfortable, energy producing way but my boss in one of those super-stressed people you described and she is driving me crazy. I'm afraid she won't be satisfied until I'm as stress-prone as she is. What can I do?" Having an SPSE for a supervisor does add to the stress potential of your job since he or she will be likely to reinforce whatever hurry sickness and struggle behaviors you possess and to ignore or discourage behaviors indicating a less stress-prone approach.

What can you do? First recognize that your supervisor is not stress prone in hopes of upsetting progress and unity but because hurry sickness and struggle are the only approaches he or she believes will work in the circumstances. Being caught in stress-prone behavior is painful and your supervisor is dealing with that pain in the best way he or she knows how. Whether or not you want to or have the power to influence your supervisor to consider a healthier approach depends on your specific situation and relationship. Even if you cannot change your supervisor's approach it is often helpful to discuss your different styles of working with him or her as a way of reassuring your supervisor that even though you aren't climbing the walls or rebounding from crisis to crisis, you are working and you have as a personal goal doing a good job. If your stress-managed workstyle is totally unacceptable to your supervisor, learn to "fake it." Walk with efficient, clicking steps when you pass your supervisor's door. At all times have two or four phone call message slips peeking from your pocket. When your supervisor talks with you in your office, train your eyes to dart from the speaker's face to the phone and to stacks of incomplete work. Nod impatiently when spoken to and arrive late to meetings, dropping books and writing notes as you find a seat.

You can change outside behaviors. Yet do maintain the internal calm that comes with knowing that you can accomplish your work without constantly being on your own back and with knowing there is enough time for everything that is important.

POTENTIALLY STRESSFUL JOB SOURCE NUMBER 9

Lack of Direction and Predictability

Another frequent plea expressed by special educators at the conclusion of a seminar has to do with the often polymorphous direction and unpredictability of doing special education. Usually the predicament is stated this way: "I arrive at work all stress managed, organized, and feeling energetic. A few minutes after arrival I'm confronted with a totally unexpected event, a mere behavior problem, or a set of unhappy parents. And there go all my positive intentions." Working as a direct service person in special education means choosing a profession built on the principle of unpredictability. The people we serve are "special" which means they do not fall into the limits of predictability necessary for "regular" education. Thus, counteracting the inherent unpredictability of your job will mean first accepting the conditions of the profession. This means giving up your surprise whenever the unplanned happens. You take the punch out of unpredictability when you expect the unexpected (which, please note, is vastly different from the sometimes touted practice of expecting the worst in order to avoid disappointment).

In addition to changing your expectations to include the unpredictable, make sure your daily schedule includes room to deal with these matters (see Potentially Stressful Job Source Number 1). Your job description needs to include a direct statement that a part of your time and energy is to be spent resolving unpredictable events.

If you lack direction on your job or if your supervisor fails to provide a reasonable pretense of the direction of the organization for which you work, the stress potential of your job will be increased. You need to know where you are going and what are the most important goals in your work if you are going to be able to plan adequately and make decisions for yourself and for clients and students. When disparity occurs between an organization's goals and those of persons authorized to fulfill goals, a major stress-producing situation is underway. Assuming you generally support the goals of your organization and your supervisor, you need to know specifically what those goals are if you are going to be able to make decisions consistent with them. Say, for example, you are trying to decide whether to recommend an intensive summer school tutoring program or a summer camping adventure for a mentally retarded client who is rather burned out on school. It makes a difference whether the most important goal of the agency is to advance clients academically in relation to their chronological peers. If the most important goal is to encourage the all-around growth of clients with less regard for maintaining academic progress as compared to chronological peers, you need to know that, too. You would probably also need information on the direction of the child's parents as well. Without being provided sufficient organizational direction, special educators spend a lot of time guessing and a lot of time wondering how higher ups will respond to decisions made. A more stressful condition than having no direction provided by your special education supervisor occurs when you have a supervisor who keeps switching directions on you. One day the purpose of the agency is to serve as many different clients and students as possible and the next day you are in trouble because the purpose of the agency is to provide long term and follow-up services for a smaller number of severely handicapped clients. In this situation you never have a firm sense of where the organization is headed. Nor do you know when your efforts are in line with or antithetical to what the organization hopes to accomplish.

To cut down on the stress-inducing problems that lack of direction can inspire, first make sure you are aware of your own goals so that you may comfortably fit your behavior with your priorities. Always operate with a written job description agreed upon by you and your supervisor that reflects your goals and the goals of the organization. This job description needs to be reviewed at least annually. To help you define the direction of the organization, ask for clarification as to the major goals of the agency. Often these can be printed or calligraphed and framed in the front office space of your agency so that those you serve as well as the employees will know by what criteria organizational planning and decisions are made.

Of course, the essence is the journey rather than the destination. But, at least knowing where you're heading can save a lot of wrong turns and confusion. (And besides, if you don't know where you are going, how are you going to know when you are on the right road?)

POTENTIALLY STRESSFUL JOB SOURCE NUMBER 10

Lack of Control over Your Situation

To describe the efforts of this situation it will help to recall Dr. Richter's (1957) experiment with the two rats dropped into vats of water and allowed to drown. The first rat, dropped without discouragement into the water and who presumably felt some hope of controlling the situation, swam for over six hours before giving up and sinking below the surface. The second rat, who was held tightly and was completely unable to move until all struggling had ceased and then dropped into the vat, lasted only a few minutes before sinking and drowning. While it is difficult to describe the function hope serves for drowning rats, quite a number of research projects have demonstrated that humans who are given responsibility and hope of controlling what happens to them in their work situation are more highly motivated and satisfied workers. Some supervisors are well aware of the power of supervisee involvement in the control of the organization while others try to control without input from supervisees.

What can you do if you lack reasonable control over what happens to you in your special education position? In considering the effective options described at the beginning of this chapter, you can either change jobs, work to change your present job, communicate with others able to make a change, or you can make an internal adjustment to the external unpleasantry. A combination of changing the job you have and making an internal adjustment are usually the least complicated stress-managing approaches. Remember you have to tell supervisors and others what you need. Assuming supervisors already know the needs and changes desired by supervisees is a frequent mistake of special educators.

HELPING STUDENTS AND CLIENTS MANAGE STRESS

Our students and clients actively strive to create in others what they feel inside themselves. The stress potential of our work environment is greatly increased when we are serving clients who (1) have more to do than they can do well, (2) lack fun in their work/learning environment, (3) lack structure and management systems, (4) are behind in their programs, (5) have poor relationships with us, (6) do not receive recognition for their efforts, (7) use comparison tactics to determine progress, (8) have educators who are SPSEs, (9) have programs that are unpredictable and lack direction, and (10) lack control over their situation.

You are creating your environment at all times. Knowing what you now know, you can help make your special education work a growth enhancing experience for those you serve.

THE WORK ENVIRONMENT AND JOB SATISFACTION

Much publicity and strife are engendered when educators and others make requests (or demands) for increased salaries, benefits, or improved working conditions. Presumably, granting these requests for external improvements will raise the job satisfaction of recipients. In reality, however, the relationship between the external niceties of the job and job satisfaction is not nearly so simple. Frederick Herzberg (1968), in his studies of the worker's relationship to the job environment, identified the "niceties" or external elements of the job as "hygiene factors." He found that improvement of hygiene factors such as policy and administration, supervision, salary, interpersonal relationships, and working conditions, served to relieve active job *dissatisfaction* but do not result in job *satisfaction.* According to Herzberg hygiene factors meet a person's need to avoid unpleasantness and hardship but only what he identified as "motivation factors" can serve the uniquely human need for psychological growth and job satisfaction. Motivation factors include achievement, recognition, the work itself, responsibility, and advancement. On the basis of this research, changing external factors may bring temporary relief from stress in your special education situation, but satisfaction and growth possibilities will come from the nature of the tasks that you are actually doing.

The relationship you create with your special education environment is a critical element determining your daily stress level. As a way of pulling together the elements of a nonstress-prone work environment, the following description of a desired work-person relationship is provided. The seven descriptive labels presented below were used by Albert Ellis when he described the elements of a healthy love relationship to the Institute for the Advancement of Human Behavior (Houston, 1979). They have been adapted here to describe the healthy relationship between the individual and the job.

Stress-managed special educators in relating to their special education environment are:

1. noncompulsive. Stress-managed special educators like to be good at special education, but do not *have* to be good at doing special education in order to survive.
2. nondependent. Stress-managed special educators see themselves as complete, interesting, and precious people who happen to be doing special education.
3. nonmasochistic. Stress-managed special educators do not have to give up everything for their work. Stress-managed special educators do not use their work as a place for suffering nor do they use suffering in their work as a way to avoid enjoyment at home and work.
4. nonobsessive. Stress-managed special educators do not think about special education all the time.
5. nondepressing. Stress-managed special educators have energy and enthusiasm at the close of the workday and on Monday mornings.
6. nonself-downing. Stress-managed special educators do not use their performances as special educators as a means for judging self-worth. Stress-managed special educators do not judge their performance as special educators against childhood perfectionistic and absolute standards.
7. nonexclusive. Stress-managed special educators enjoy knowing people from other professions. Stress-managed special educators enjoy learning in widely divergent fields.

NOTE

Herzberg, Frederick. One more time: How do you motivate employees? *Harvard Business Review*, pp. 53-62.

Chapter 8

The Special Educator as a Physical Being

8

Let's say you are walking down the hall at work when you meet a coworker friend coming the other way. Your friend will likely inquire, "How are you?" You may respond automatically or you may give a more soul-searched, complete answer. Without being explicit, your friend is asking how you are getting along physically, socially, intellectually, psycho-emotionally, and spiritually. Usually your first response will reflect your physiological state. Unless you demonstrate actual physical discomfort by putting your hand to your head, sneezing, or lifting your sleeve to show a fresh arm cast, the inquirer will likely assume you are "fine." At least in this sort of interaction the presence of physical wellness is recognized as a critical element in determining overall functioning. Recognition of the importance of physical well-being is not always a priority for special educators. In fact, many of us educator-types have ignored our bodies for years in favor of an exclusive appreciation of our brains.

Yet, it is the moment-to-moment condition of our bodies that largely determines the availability of personal energy and our ability to manage externally- and internally-induced stress. The first signs of special educator personal burnout are physiological—usually fatigue, headaches, and various vague muscular discomforts. While our stress-prone themes of rationalization often persuade us to maintain an unrelenting, tense vigilance of struggle in our profession, our bodies will eventually intercede in our behalf, registering protests in the form of tiredness, pain, or disease. Because stress is most basically a physiological response and because there are specific steps that can be taken in the areas of nutrition, exercise, and relaxation to aid in stress management, no book on stress management for special educators would be complete without reference to these basic steps.

This chapter is not intended to provide a comprehensive picture of nutrition, exercise and relaxation as related to health and stress. There is not sufficient space and, in addition, there are a number of excellent books dedicated specifically to each of these aspects. Rather, this chapter is intended to stimulate awareness of your body-mind relationship and to provide you with the essential elements of physical management necessary for promoting personal energy availability and management of stress.

The body-mind interaction is on obvious display anytime you place an animal within easy reach of a natural enemy. Flaring nostrils, unsheathed claws, or a speedy retreat indicate clearly that the visual image of the enemy has induced a series of physical changes. For that matter your own body-mind interaction relationship has been brought to your attention in times of sudden fear. It may have been felt as the warm rush of a blush coming to your face when your self-esteem was in question, or when a racing heartbeat or trembling hands accompanied physical danger. Efforts toward managing habitual stress responses in your special education situation can be made at several levels of the body-mind interaction. Since the stress response is composed of the perception of a threat to your well-being and your body's concomitant reaction, methods for altering responses logically include: (1) procedures to reduce the frequency of perceived threats to well-being, (2) procedures to increase your body's capacity for handling the response, and (3) procedures to manage the response once it has already begun its cycle in your body. To this point we have focused mainly on management of stress by reducing the frequency of perceived threats using two methods. The most critical procedure has focused on changing your interpretive, cognitive responses toward yourself, other people, and your environment. SPSEs characteristically view our imperfect selves, imperfect others, and imperfect workplace environment as more threatening than do N-SPSEs. Secondary procedures have included suggestions for altering the actual environment. In this chapter attention is given to the second level at which you can affect your stress responses—the level of preparing your body to better be able to manage the threat signal when it is received. We will also discuss the third level, managing the body's response once it has occurred. If your body is in good physical condition you will be better able to withstand barrages of stress responses before breaking down. Also, when your body is strong, your "threat threshold" is higher. This means that when your body is feeling well it takes a bigger situation to constitute a threat than it does when you are run down. Most of us are aware of how little it takes to set us off when we are overtired or hungry. Of course, the habits of the SPSE lend themselves to encouragement of low threat thresholds since proper eating and regular exercise require "too much time" and interfere with production. Once stress and tension have taken over and your body is locked into combat posture, procedures at the third level of stress management are helpful. At this level relaxation, movement (exercise), and diversion can be used to relieve the body-mind cycle of stress.

This chapter is designed as an introduction to management of stress at the level of body preparedness and body recovery from distress.

STRESS MANAGEMENT THROUGH BODY PREPAREDNESS

SPSEs are likely to allow themselves to become physically run down and to allow the environment to disintegrate in the name of getting our job done. These two happenings, physical and environmental disintegration, often go together: Fatigue is accepted as normal and there isn't enough energy left over from our overburdened schedule to keep the environment organized. Then the disintegrated environment takes its toll on physical health as we eat whatever is handy and quick. The refrigerator is empty and going to the store is a low priority for such a tired person. We have no energy left for physical exercise because the very sight of our disorganized surroundings makes us question the sanity of walking around the block when so many things right around us need our attention. The very persons most likely in need of stress management help at the level of body preparedness are exactly the persons least likely to take care of themselves.

SPSEs often have an aversion to learning about the specific workings of the body. So much discomforting publicity has come out linking the stress-prone workstyle to breakdown and disease. Stress-prone workers are going to do something about our health habits—someday—as soon as this or that project is completed, as soon as school is out, as soon as our children are out of school, and so on. One easy step SPSEs can take toward becoming more like N-SPSEs is to take a healthy interest in our bodily well-being—to make the care of the body not a minor issue to be discussed over coffee, cokes, and cigarettes, but a priority. You actively create your body's ability to manage stress responses.

Nutrition

You have two opportunities to relate directly with your environment: breathing and eating. Both processes are for the purpose of nourishing the body, providing the basic elements necessary for the development of personal energy. Therefore, it makes sense that how you fulfill your body's food needs makes a difference in your available energy and your ability to manage the stressful events in your work day. There seem to be no magical formulas for nutritional health. Though it might be comfortably easy to be advised of a vitamin pill regimen, which, combined with eating whatever you want, would transform your body into the picture of energy and health. Such is not possible.

The basic recommendations found here will remind you of the simple suggestions found both in grade school health books and sophisticated nutrition research works.

The difficulty with making recommendations for nourishing your body with food is that you already *know* what you optimally need to be eating and what you need to avoid. Newspapers and periodicals are loaded with this information. In fact, month after month magazines with the same basic information are tossed into grocery carts laden with sodas and potato chips. The key for stress management is not in providing you information but in providing an impetus for choosing one food product over another in each eating situation. For this reason this section provides only a short review of actual dietary information and then describes the *nutrition-weight management clinics* conducted as part of intensive stress management programs. The majority of energy and space in this section is devoted to the principles on which the clinics were based because it has been through application of these principles that stress management participants have been able to alter their eating habits and the shape and condition of their bodies. A review of the following recommendations is suggested before considering any change in eating habits.

Basic Dietary Recommendations

1. Eat less fat
   a) From 40% to 30% of our caloric intake (for most of us) is fat.
   b) We need to reduce our daily intake of fat by about six teaspoons.
   c) There is one teaspoon of fat in each of the following:
      • 1 teaspoon of butter or meat drippings
      • 1 ounce of cold cuts (or hot dogs)
      • the skin on a chicken has 1 teaspoon extra
      • If you eat fried chicken, add 2 teaspoons per ounce
      • 1 ounce of cooked steak or chop
      • 1 ounce of cheddar or jack cheese

2. Eat less saturated fat
   a) We can do this by using less:
      • Butter, lard, shortening, and margarines
      • Salad dressing
      • Beef, lamb, pork
      • Whole milk, cream, high fat cheese (cheddar, jack)
   b) Use instead more:
      • Oils (safflower, corn, soy, avocado, olive, and peanut)
      • Poultry, fish
      • Non-fat or low-fat milk
      • Low-fat cheeses (cottage, mozzarella, ricotta, parmesan, and jarlsburg)

3. Eat less cholesterol
   a) We need only about 300 milligrams daily
   b) Achieve reduction by reducing your intake of:
   • Animal fats
   • Eggs (only about 3 per week)

4. Eat more starchy foods
   a) Increase carbohydrates to about 55 percent of your calories.
   b) We can do this by using more starchy foods such as:
   • Potatoes and other vegetables
   • Whole grains
   • Legumes
   c) And we can do this by replacing your 6 teaspoons of fat with:
   • 2 slices of whole-grain bread *and*
   • 1 small potato *and*
   • 1 cup dark green vegetable

5. Eat more fiber
   a) Increase use of whole-grain bread
   b) Increase use of fruits and vegetables
   c) Increase intake of beans

   In bread—be sure that the first ingredient listed is *whole, sprouted,* or *malted*. Don't be fooled. Wheat flour is the same as white flour. Probably the best bread has no added flour.

6. East less sugar
   a) Reduce sugar intake from 25% to 15% of your calories
   b) This can be done by reducing to 6 tablespoons of sugar daily (or less)
   c) How? Avoid any food with sugar as one of the first 3 ingredients

7. Eat less salt
   a) Reduce to 1/2 of what you are currently consuming
   b) Avoid foods already salted
   • Also be careful to add only 1/2 teaspoon of salt to food daily

8. The primary health problems today are not the result of vitamin deficiency

The Stress Management Nutrition-Weight Loss Clinics

The nutrition-weight loss clinics, affectionately known as the "F.C. s" (Fat Clinics) began at the suggestion of the faculty of a local school district after a series of stress management presentations. At the conclusion of the stress management series participants were asked which particular area of the program they would like to investigate further and in which area they would like more consultant assistance. The overwhelming choice was nutrition and weight management. The F.C. group title is somewhat misleading because many participants were not overweight. The central purpose of the group was to change SPSE eating habits to N-SPSE eating habits and only indirectly to lose weight. The major purpose of the F.C. was to help participants change their eating behavior from a product-oriented status, "get-it-over-with" experience (resulting in overeating and poor nutrition) to an enjoyable "being" experience that involves appreciation of the process itself. The F.C. program is presented here as an example of a procedure to change a behavioral habit from a stress-prone approach to a nonstress-prone approach.

The F.C. met once a week after school for an hour and a half during which consultation and information was provided. Group members shared experiences with modifications in eating behavior and food choices. Throughout the program the basic behavior change strategy had two results: (1) improvement of the stress managing capacities of participants through improvement of personal health, and (2) reduction of the weight of overweight faculty members as part of their overall health improvement.

It was steadfastly agreed from the beginning that the F.C. would not be a "diet group." In fact, the first principle that group members agreed to follow was to *never again go on a diet.* Each aspect of the F.C. program was based on integrated principles of stress management rather than magical formulas or guilt-inducing, self-hate programs. When the program began it was experimental. We had no idea of the impact it would eventually have on the physical health of the faculty involved and on school morale and the mental health of everyone involved. The implementation results of the F.C. provided a shining example of the body-mind connection as reports of physical, social, intellectual, psycho-emotional, and spiritual improvements were contributed by educators throughout the school.

The F.C. concept is based on acceptance of the following approach. Each participant agreed with the statements of principle as a requisite for group membership. There were six such statements and they are discussed below.

I will never go on another diet.

Diets are tailor-made for self-abusing, unaware SPSEs. If diets worked there would not be any overweight people in the United States. Certainly a plethora of no-effort-instant-magic-formulas is available and if none of these suit the buyer, next month is sure to bring several all-new-super-melt-off regimens. Diets do not work because they are designed by someone outside yourself. By adhering to someone else's plan, you eat what you don't want to eat and do not eat what you really want to eat. The result is that you feel deprived, angry, and anxious to escape the punishing situation as soon as possible. From the first day of the diet, plans are being made for when you go "off" the program. The result? Only a very small percentage of people who lose weight by dieting maintain their weight loss. In fact, in the majority of cases, the dieter gains back the lost weight plus a little more!

Another problem with deprivation dieting is that it results in a lot of overeating. Instead of going "off the diet" and eating moderate amounts of forbidden foods, experienced dieters take advantage of escapes from the torturous routine. They eat large amounts of calorie-laden goodies during "off the diet" periods since tomorrow or Monday they are going to have to go back on the horrible regimen and won't be able to eat anything they enjoy. Dieters are well known for over-eating frequently after "breaking" the diet. After one forbidden treat, they eat everything in sight since the diet had already been "blown anyway." Since F.C. group members agreed to never go on another diet we had no need to hungrily take advantage of times when usually forbidden foods were available. We could be satisfied ordering a banana split and eating only a few bites knowing we could return to the ice cream parlor tomorrow if we desired.

My body knows what it needs and how much it needs.

On the first reading, this statement may seem a bit simplistic. Learning to judge kinds of food and amounts of food according to internal bodily responses is an important step for SPSEs. We are out of touch with what makes us feel energetic and what drags us down. Most stress-prone persons eat too fast and eat too much. Both of these difficulties will be eliminated if the individual is attending to internal signals while eating. The overweight SPSE needs to re-learn to use the whole body in deciding on foods and amounts, not just the eyes. In the old stress-prone, nonaware days we decided whether or not we were full by whether or not anything was left on our plate. Now fullness is judged by pausing and noting internal comfort levels.

I will eat anything I want, but I will eat only what I want.

Success has been possible through the F.C. experience because not one group member ever felt deprived but everyone ate considerably less. Eating anything you want, but only what you want means getting very specific and choosey about *every bite* you eat. The F.C. group members actively learned to avoid the *Mount Everest Syndrome*, that is, eating food because "it was there." Each group member learned to identify specific individual preferences and practiced saying "no" to any foods that were not favorites. Following this principle helped to reduce overall intake. When we ate whatever was handy rather than what we really wanted we ended up eating too much. What we were taking in was not satisfying. Of course, to follow this principle extra effort was required. To make available exactly what was wanted might be difficult since the rest of the family might be eating something else. Sometimes exactly what we wanted was not always easily available. No one is promised magic.

To aid in the process of basing amounts eaten on internal signals, "eating only what I want," F.C. group members practiced a four-step eating decision process. Before putting food on the plate, the F.C. group member asked, "Do I want to put this on my plate? Do I want all of this serving or just part of it?" The next question was, "Do I want to put this on my fork?" Next, was asked, "Do I want to put this in my mouth?" And then, "Do I want to swallow this bite?" Group members have reported various ways this process has helped. One educator buys the same chocolate doughnut he always has during his coffeebreak but he takes one bite while waiting in line to pay and puts the rest of it in the trash! After going through the four-step decision process daily he learned that all he really wanted was one bite, a taste, not the whole doughnut.

I will record everything I eat.

This important part of the process is discouraging for SPSEs who don't have time for paying attention to themselves. Recording food eaten is necessary for SPSEs who do much of their eating while in almost a semi-conscious state. We don't even know what or how much we're eating. Since it's usually too much we actively avoid facing reality. By recording each item, awareness of your body's reactions to foods will be increased. Daily review of foods eaten will be helpful in determining eating patterns. It is also helpful to determine the caloric values of each food eaten. For completing this process a good calorie counter manual is a helpful reference. The purpose of determining caloric values is to see if your average daily intake is exceeding your body's needs and to educate yourself on the comparative calorie "costs" of various foods.

The daily food intake records of F.C. group members were discussed in weekly meetings with an emphasis on discovering *danger times* when eating was likely to be directed by the environment, by anxiety, or by habit rather than internal desires and needs.

I will eat only when I am hungry.

Obviously overweight people eat in response to more stimuli than just hunger. Eating is not an appropriate response to fatigue, tension, loneliness, desire for attention, desire for sensual pleasure, or boredom. Clinic group members reviewed daily food intake records to discover what stimuli they were responding to with the behavior of eating. Tiredness led the list followed by boredom and work frustration. Individuals worked to develop alternative, more appropriate responses to these stimuli.

I will walk 20 minutes a day.

This principle is not included to increase calorie expenditure through exercise. It is included to help F.C. group members with their personal commitments to body awareness and health. By walking each day individuals are able to spend time considering their commitment and sensing their improved body strength and more graceful body size. The inclusion of 20 minutes of walking each day is not optional but an integral part of the program.

F.C. group members through participation in the program experienced many changes in addition to weight loss and improved vitality. Of greatest note was the increased ability of members to recognize and control personal stress levels. Participants reported that once they learned to trust their bodies and to manage food intake through awareness, taking responsibility and personal control were extended to management of the work environment, career planning, family issues, money expenditure decisions, and others. The present space does not allow for a complete recounting of the F.C. program but of importance here is that the key stress management result achieved was the willingness of the participants to accept responsibility for what occurs inside themselves.

EXERCISE

Exercise is essential to vitality and energy. With regular exercise, adults have up to a full quart more red blood flowing in their veins as compared to nonexercising persons. If you enjoy some form of daily exercise, your metabolic rate will be higher all 24 hours. This means you burn up more calories per hour and your oxygen usage is improved. With even mild exercise your muscles are strengthened and tightened. Machinery wears away a little more with each use; your body gains strength each time it is used. And the best part is that exercise doesn't have to be horrible, boring, or painful if you can accept a nonstress-prone approach rather than a competitive and suffering approach most of us have associated with exercise.

Just as you would have to be a nonreading hermit not to know what you need to be eating and what you ought to avoid, you have been informed many times already that lack of exercise constitutes a serious health problem. The lack of exercise problem is often coupled with other stress-prone characteristics since exercise takes time and of course SPSEs never have enough time. In addition SPSEs are usually tired at the conclusion of our well-burdened day and "is it really fair to ask someone who's already exhausted to do anything else requiring energy?" The commitment to a personal exercise program takes a willingness to spend a section of time daily and a willingness to dedicate energy and attention to physical health. Because, as with dieting, most adults have begun and abandoned many exercise routines, the focus of this section will be on procedures which can help SPSEs establish and maintain individually suited exercise programs rather than on extolling the common knowledge advantages of doing so.

Before listing procedures, a word on exercise and personal readiness is in order. If you have done no more than walk from your automobile to buildings and back for years, if you are overweight, or if you have had any serious or chronic medical problems, you should have a complete physical examination before changing your activity patterns in any way.

Many books are available on the physiology of exercise and specific suggestions for program planning. Which program is best for you depends on your age, your fitness, and what you want from your program. The procedures presented in this section are based on the assumption that what you want from exercise is a program to coincide with and support your overall efforts in personal stress management. Winning races, setting records, and running for hours in Adidas packed with petroleum jelly involve goals beyond the scope of simple management of personal stress for most of us. In fact, my usual recommendation, if you haven't been engaged in regular exercise, is to begin your program by *walking 20 minutes each day*. For many special educators there is not even a need to change this routine greatly with time. This is not to say there isn't a place for runners in this world. The evidence regarding running is mixed but mostly positive and difficult to interpret. It's just that not many of us special educator-types fit into the runner category. It's plain silly to continue to do nothing because we don't have what it takes to hit the streets at 5 A.M. in short shorts and headband. There is a place for us on the streets. The following guidelines are provided to help you make a positive exercise program a part of your everyday stress-managed, growth enhancing work and lifestyle.

The Stress Managed Exercise Program

Exercise must be viewed as a normal part of everyday living.

As long as exercise is viewed as something extra or a punishment stuck on to an already busy schedule you will be less likely to experience the reinforcing satisfaction that comes with a lifelong program. Regular exercise must be a habit so well ingrained that forgetting to do your walking would be impossible. To achieve this level of commitment one must incorporate the walking habit into his or her workday and weekend routines. My suggestion to clients and seminar participants is that for the first month you *must* walk everyday whether it is snowing or sweltering, raining or blowing, and whether your only opportunities are sometimes at midnight and sometimes at lunch. The only reason to delay the program is if you are sick enough to be confined to bed. Do not *try* to walk everyday—walk everyday. Do not listen to the dozens of excuses and reasons your clever mind uses as pressure to skip "just one day." You cannot trust your mind in this matter but must go ahead and walk everyday knowing that your body needs the experience and your mind will appreciate it later. Regardless of what rationalizations you come up with for staying in, tell yourself that *only 20 minutes is required* and *I will live through it.*

During the second month of your walking program allow yourself to walk six out of seven days a week, if you choose. Most people go ahead and walk everyday once the increased vitality is experienced. To help include your walking in your daily activities, plan the night before or during your morning planning exercise, when and where you will take your walk. Then you can know if you need to work it in by walking at lunch or by walking around the workplace neighborhood during a break.

Make Exercise Fun

Stress-Prone Special Educators, as you will remember, are experts at suffering. They are the first to volunteer to suffer for the rewards of admiration and success. Fortunately for our health this approach to exercise won't work and can cause us to miss the point altogether. To include exercise as part of your stress management, actively seek to make your "movement time" pleasurable and growth enhancing. Find friends to walk with or save contemplative topics for solitary pondering while you walk alone. Buy yourself a good pair of running shoes or other comfortable sport shoes with arch supports and construction suited to movement. Take your special shoes with you wherever you go so you can slip them on at a moment's notice and take your walk. Do not take your walk in high heels or any shoes intended for style. Doing so will result in discouraging sore feet and a lack of that powerful feeling one senses from the solidarity of running shoes. I have taken many a jibe after being observed circling hotels and convention centers during seminar lunch breaks dressed in a smart wool suit and my glow-in-the-dark orange and lime-green running shoes, but I certainly felt strong inside.

Planning where you want to walk can do a lot to add to the enjoyment of walking. On weekends visit nearby parks and scenic areas. Plan errands usually requiring expensive stop and start driving as walking adventures. For example park your car in a central spot and if the trek can be accomplished within your walking capacity—walk to the bank, the post office, the drug store, and then the shopping mall. Usually these are located close enough together so that at least several stops can be done walking whether in a downtown or suburban shopping area.

Remind yourself that you are walking for the experience and health benefits.

After several months you may be ready to increase your pace or your distance. Most people want to increase distances because once they begin the program many walking activities are found that require 30 minutes to an hour. Increasing for these reasons is fine and will not accelerate the stress potential of your exercise program. But then there are the stubborn stress-prone among us who must increase their rate and distance out of a basic self-dissatisfaction and a discomfort with anything in which progress in terms of numbers is not obvious. Avoid pushing yourself. Maybe it would be better for your heart to be doing a mile in 16 minutes instead of 20, but if you do it only four times a year it is not nearly as beneficial as walking 20 minutes 300 times. And, healthy or not, the majority of people do not stick to punishing projects. Pushing will result in pain and pain will result in your resentment and avoidance of the process altogether. Think of your exercise as being kind to your body, not as challenging or pushing your body. Walking can be pleasurable and involving.

Smile while you are walking.

The most critical element of your stress management program is your approach style. Relax your face and shoulders while walking. Look around you! See what you can see that you hadn't noticed before. Say "Hello" to people. Note the weather and the sky. Feel your body and your mind relating to your environment in special, pleasurable ways.

RELAXATION

"When a person feels like acting but does not allow himself to act, his muscles remain tensed in readiness sometimes for months or years at a time, immobilized into a state of semicontractions even during sleep." (McQuade & Aikman, 1974, p. 82)

All things considered, your efforts at attitude and environmental management are not always enough. Just when you think you have it together, unique challenges and difficult situations arise on a particular day and you find yourself tense, stressed, and feeling negative about the whole situation. When this happens the unhealthy effects of enduring stress will take their toll on your body and your enthusiasm. To return yourself to positive functioning you need to know and be able to use a technique for reducing body tension.

Most people begin each day with a sense of energy, a low stress level and a relaxed approach to the job. (NOTE: an early sign of burnout is a sense of fatigue at the beginning of the day.) However, with the wear and tear of the environment, by mid-day many of us are plagued by a sense of anxiety and a certain tightness expressed often in headaches and irritability. In fact, tension along with its accompanying headaches and frazzled nerves is almost accepted as a normal part of every day. Television commercials for headaches and acid indigestion remedies promise relief and improved coping abilities in various familiar situations. Contrary to media impressions, a person can work and live without regular doses of medication to soothe the ravages of tension. This is accomplished by learning to manage the body tension itself.

So far you have studied ways to counteract stress through altering your overall interpretive approach to yourself, others, and your environment, through altering your environment to reduce known stress-encouraging situations, and through improving your body's ability to withstand stress and maintain energy. Another important skill can be learned and practiced by you which will effectively reduce damaging stress, increase your accessibility to enjoyable job experiences, and thus, move you toward creative growth and away from burnout.

This skill is relaxation training.

Relaxation may seem like a strange process to need to "learn" at all. On the surface it appears logical that each of us ought to be able to relax simply by telling ourselves to do so. But then how many times have you experienced increased tension after being admonished by someone else to "just relax?" Relaxation is not something you can accomplish merely "on call" without training. Effective relaxation is instead a definite skill that must be learned and practiced in much the same way you would learn and practice a new physical feat before you would consider that feat a part of your skills repertoire.

Before moving on to actual skills training some clarification of the relaxation process is in order. Relaxation is not so much something you work at doing. Relaxation is more a process of allowing something to happen—specifically, allowing tightened muscles to elongate, soften, and relax. To maintain muscle tension you must *work* at not allowing this relaxation to take place. During periods of anxiety and tension this work of maintaining muscle tenseness and inflexibility can best be categorized as a general bodily attempt to deal with perceived threats to the self whether the perceived threats are physical, directed toward self-esteem, or only vaguely related to present reality. When your body is tense, you are literally "poised for attack."

Relaxation training will be accomplished in this section by having you follow basic relaxation training directions. The instructions given below are intended as beginning measures and include all basic steps. The major factor determining whether you will be able to use relaxation training to your benefit is whether you will take the time necessary to learn the process. To add relaxation to your skills repertoire, time and some practice will be required. After learning the basic relaxation skill by following these stepwise instructions, you will be able to increase your flexibility. A gymnast, having once accomplished the basic walk on the balance beam, can then add speed and embellishing touches to his or her moves. This will be true for you, too.

Once you are a qualified relaxation specialist you will be able to maintain your skill without continuous daily practice, dropping back to several times a week. If you like, you will be able to complete the relaxation procedure without referring to written instructions. In fact, you will be able to relax yourself, on call, in situations outside of relaxation practice such as while teaching, driving, or speaking to a group. Once you are aware of the difference between the sensation of muscle tension and the sensation of muscle relaxation (which is a large part of training) you will be able to practice differential or specialized relaxation. Differential or specialized relaxation means allowing particular muscle groups to relax while others continue at a working level of tension. For example, you might want to soften certain of your neck and forehead muscles while driving or you might want to relax your back and shoulder muscles while teaching or walking.

One very special benefit of relaxation training demonstrated by research is that when a person regularly practices a relaxation technique, blood pressure is lowered at the time of practice and remains at a lower constant throughout the day and night. Also, practice at any time during the day or night increases your capacity for relaxation during the other 23½ hours. However this improvement is actually accomplished—whether through increased awareness of tenseness or through attitudinal changes achieved during relaxation—it is certainly a most desirable result.

To Allow Yourself To Relax:

1. Either sit or lie down in a comfortable, preferably quiet place. (It doesn't have to be quiet. Relaxation can be accomplished in hotel lobbies, airports, or wherever you are when you *decide* to redirect your attention and allow relaxation.) Shift your arms and legs to comfortable positions with no crossed limbs.

2. Close your eyes. (Also this will not be necessary once you are skilled in calling forth relaxation.)

3. Focus on breathing.

This process is the key. Breathe in . . . deeply and quietly through your nose. Feel the air fill your lungs extending down to fill your diaphram. Let the air out slowly, more slowly than you took the air in. Notice your breathing as you continue to breathe slowly in and even more slowly out. Notice that your breathing changes because you are focusing on it. This is normal and okay. You are supposed to feel more conscious of your breathing. Take in another deep, quiet breath and hold it. This time when you exhale say the number "one" slowly to yourself. Continue breathing *slowly* and *quietly* counting each slowly exhaled breath up to "ten." On reaching ten start over again with "one." Notice the fullness and richness of each breath, how each breath fills every corner of your lungs. Continue focusing only on your breathing.

4. When your attention wanders, do not upset yourself, but rather watch these outside thoughts as they move across your mind as though you were watching a movie. Watching your thoughts this way, your thoughts will travel across your mind without stimulating anxiety or pressure. Let your thoughts pass through your mind separately from you, let them just pass by you, as you continue to focus on your breathing.

5. Notice again how deeply and slowly you are breathing.

6. Notice that new thoughts, thoughts you cannot quite verbalize, are near the surface of your mind. These thoughts are pleasant and integrated with your relaxed state.

7. Focus again on your breathing, how fully and slowly you are breathing.

Each time you exhale quietly and slowly, you say to yourself the next number in your sequence. You notice how good it feels to allow tension to float away from your body. Notice how the tension centers and floats up through the top of your head.

8. Notice the absence of tense internal chatter, of categories and worries and schedules. Notice your fresh internal experience. Notice the rich internal softness.

9. Stay where you are in this quiet relaxed place as long as you like. Enjoy this richness. When you are ready . . . only when you are ready to return . . . open your eyes and slowly stretch your arms and legs. You can return to functioning without losing the inner calm achieved through relaxation.

10. Enjoy.

A NOTE ON THE BODY-MIND

Awareness and care of your body is important in your stress management program. To change your special education workstyle toward an N-SPSE style will require a shift in mind and a shift in body. As you have learned through your understanding of the stress response, the mind and body do not function as separate units. Sometimes this interrelationship is not pointed out in brief research releases or articles reporting on health habits and workstyles. For example, a recent syndicated newspaper article appeared reporting a demonstrated difference between the concentrations of HDLs (High Density Lipoproteins) in the bloodstreams of marathon runners as compared to a group of sedentary men the same age. High concentrations of HDLs have been correlated with low incidences of heart and artery disease. The article reported that the blood samples from the marathon runners did indeed contain higher HDL concentrations than did the blood samples from the sedentary group. Quickly judging these findings it might be said, therefore, that training to compete in marathon running reduces one's risk of heart attack. But look more closely for the complex mind-body connection. Marathon runners are likely to be different from those in the sedentary group in more ways than the running factor. Marathon runners pay closer attention to what they eat and are generally much more body conscious than most sedentary people. Marathon runners are people willing to spend a large portion of time and energy each day running. What struggling SPSE is going to allow that kind of time to devote to body strengthening? Marathon runners' daily goals must to some extent be governed by the requirements of running. Stress-prone individuals have too much to "accomplish" at the workplace to consider other demanding goals. Marathon runners practice mind control techniques to use their bodies fully in order to endure the pain and fatigue of distance running. Most of the rest of us do not practice daily management of our thought activities and are more susceptible to influence by the many external signals we receive to upset ourselves. This analysis is not to say that distance running is not effective in increasing blood levels of HDLs, but rather to alert you to the intricate relationship between self-chosen physical health programs, attitude, and environmental factors.

Marathon runners are likely to be different from sedentary persons in more ways than the fact that one group runs a lot and the other doesn't. The lifestyles and workstyles you maintain encompass your body-mind approach to yourself, others, and your environment. For you, deciding to reduce your food intake or taking a 20 minute walk will change you physically and mentally. No one activity chosen by you can function separately from who you are and who you are becoming both in body and in mind.

NOTE

McQuade, Walter & Aikman, Ann. *Stress.* New York: Dutton Publishing Co., 1974, p. 82.

Chapter 9

Beyond Special
Educator Stress

9

For you to function with enthusiasm and plentiful energy, your work in special education must be accepted as a process to be enjoyed, not as a sentence to be endured. John Holt, author of *Growing Up Absurd* (1956) and other landmark critiques of American education, has most recently been writing about the work and school relationship. While describing this relationship in a recent *Psychology Today* article (1980), Holt makes a poignant distinction between having a job, having a career, and working. He describes having a job as doing something someone else tells you to do strictly to receive the money promised on completion. Having a career means having a series of jobs with each job in the series usually netting a little more money, more favorable job conditions, and, sometimes, more control over specific activities and power over other job holders. For Holt, working is something quite different from having a job or a career. Working is having a "vocation" or a "calling." Working means involvement in activities deemed so worthwhile that the worker would do them without pay. In a society so convinced that self-worth is purchased by suffering in jobs in order to collect goods, Holt's ideas may first appear too idealistic, as only applying to a chosen few individuals. If you accept (even insist) for yourself that you are doing what you are doing everyday because someone else is making you or to have enough to eat and tires for the car, special education will become your personal prison. As long as your role in special education is a "job" or a "career" you will be limited to implementing the stress management techniques of cleverly rearranging elements of your cell and your schedule and adopting elaborate medical and physical routines to reduce the pathological effects of imprisonment. Only by altering your cognitive approach, and only by refusing prison can you affect the inner core habits that are the source of stress.

Your workstyle as a special educator is more than an expression of your relationship with one specific job description, one particular supervisor, or one set of clients or students. Your special educator workstyle is an expression of your attitudes, your orientations and your expectations as a person. Each hour you do special education, you do more than a *job*. You also experience and express your relationship with yourself, other people, and your environment. Prior to research on the physiological accompaniments of strained relationships with self, others, and the world, it was assumed that mental anguish was the only result of such distress and that such distress was to be expected, an acceptable side effect of making a living. Now the evidence is otherwise; now we can show on blood pressure gauges, blood fat content measurements, the actuarial tables of insurance companies, and on dozens of other readouts and charts, that what we used to describe as merely psychological pain involves physical destruction as well. Observation of job holders with stress-prone approaches to their tasks have shown that, along with the internal destruction measured by graphs and scales, these are precisely the people who are also likely to abuse their bodies by overeating, overdrinking, and avoiding exercise. Even if you are willing to accept intangible dissatisfaction and displeasure as typical and therefore normal working conditions, you will still have your health to consider.

Rather than emphasizing environmental adjustments and techniques for dealing with physical tensions, I have chosen in this book to focus on management of the mediational or internal thinking habit component of your stress response. Only through management of these processes will you have gained broad coping skills. By focusing on thinking habit changes, your environment and your physical being, and thus the physical accompaniments of stress, will be affected. Your special education work environment and your physical self are continually designed by your cognitive processes. Both are the creations of your workstyle approach, of your orientations, and your expectations as a special educator. Viewing your environment and your body as your own creations may be overwhelming at first. This view leaves you with a lot of responsibility. But, on the other hand, consider the possibilities such a perspective reveals. An understanding and acceptance of your role in determining your experience puts you in the position of deciding for yourself how special education is going to be for you each day. When you pass through the door frame of your workplace, you will make that decision rather than allowing it to be made by people, furniture, time, and other factors outside of yourself.

Before closing, a word or two needs to be given to answer the many inquiries regarding how to avoid encouraging stress-prone habits in clients and students, how to avoid raising stress-prone children, and how to help coworkers and other adults experiencing the pain of a stress-prone workstyle. Two suggestions are given here both of which require a commitment on your part to a stress-managed workstyle and lifestyle. The first and foremost way you can help anyone else change painful habits is to provide a *model* of a person who values work as an expression of personal growth, a person who behaves as though there is enough time to get everything done that is important, a person who sees the collection of achievements as a pleasant side effect of doing what one enjoys, and a person who trusts himselves and other people to be doing the best they can with their lives. Being such a model, implementing the second suggestion will be easy: reinforce the person you are trying to help for nonstress-prone behaviors, for valuing the quality of experiencing each moment, for trusting their feelings and ideas, for enjoying work activities as well as completing them. Every move of your body, every word spoken will demonstrate to others what you do and do not value in them. As a part of your creation of your environment, you create other people. Some of them you create extensively because you are with them everyday; others you create for moments at a time as you interact with them over counters and by telephone. You are at every moment affecting your internal being and your environment. The only question is how.

NOTE

Holt, John. Growing Up Engaged. *Psychology Today*, 1980, *14*(2), 14-23.

Index

About the Author

BARBARA RICE DESHONG received her Ph.D. in educational psychology from the University of Texas and is now a practicing psychologist and associate director of DeShong Associates, a consulting firm based in Austin, Texas. She has instructed at various colleges throughout the nation and was the coordinator of staff development at Austin State Hospital from 1975 to 1977. Since then she has been a consultant for many governmental and private programs and had numerous articles published in education, managerial, and hospital journals.